# The Fundamentals of
# Corporate Communication

The Chartered Institute of Marketing/Butterworth-Heinemann Marketing Series is the most comprehensive, widely used and important collection of books in marketing and sales currently available worldwide.

As the CIM's official publisher, Butterworth-Heinemann develops, produces and publishes the complete series in association with the CIM. We aim to provide definitive marketing books for students and practitioners that promote excellence in marketing education and practice.

The series titles are written by CIM senior examiners and leading marketing educators for professionals, students and those studying the CIM's Certificate, Advanced Certificate and Postgraduate Diploma courses. Now firmly established, these titles provide practical study support to CIM and other marketing students and to practitioners at all levels.

The Chartered
Institute of Marketing

Formed in 1911, The Chartered Institute of Marketing is now the largest professional marketing management body in the world with over 60,000 members located worldwide. Its primary objectives are focused on the development of awareness and understanding of marketing throughout UK industry and commerce and in the raising of standards of professionalism in the education, training and practice of this key business discipline.

**Books in the series**

*Below-the-line Promotion*, John Wilmshurst

*The CIM Handbook of Export Marketing*, Chris Noonan

*The CIM Handbook of Selling and Sales Strategy*, David Jobber

*The CIM Handbook of Strategic Marketing*, Colin Egan and Michael J. Thomas

*CIM Marketing Dictionary* (fifth edition), Norman A. Hart

*Copywriting*, Moi Ali

*Creating Powerful Brands* (second edition), Leslie de Chernatony and Malcolm McDonald

*The Creative Marketer*, Simon Majaro

*The Customer Service Planner*, Martin Christopher

*Cybermarketing*, Pauline Bickerton, Matthew Bickerton and Upkar Pardesi

*The Effective Advertiser*, Tom Brannan

*Integrated Marketing Communications*, Ian Linton and Kevin Morley

*Key Account Management*, Malcolm McDonald and Beth Rogers

*Market-led Strategic Change* (second edition), Nigel Piercy

*The Marketing Book* (third edition), Michael J. Baker

*Marketing Logistics*, Martin Christopher

*Marketing Research for Managers* (second edition), Sunny Crouch and Matthew Housden

*The Marketing Manual*, Michael J. Baker

*The Marketing Planner*, Malcolm McDonald

*Marketing Planning for Services*, Malcolm McDonald and Adrian Payne

*Marketing Plans* (third edition), Malcolm McDonald

*Marketing Strategy* (second edition), Paul Fifield

*Practice of Advertising* (fourth edition), Norman A. Hart

*Practice of Public Relations* (fourth edition), Sam Black

*Profitable Product Management*, Richard Collier

*Relationship Marketing*, Martin Christopher, Adrian Payne and David Ballantyne

*Relationship Marketing for Competitive Advantage*, Adrian Payne, Martin Christopher, Moira Clark and Helen Peck

*Retail Marketing Plans*, Malcolm McDonald and Christopher Tideman

*Royal Mail Guide to Direct Mail for Small Businesses*, Brian Thomas

*Sales Management*, Chris Noonan

*Trade Marketing Strategies*, Geoffrey Randall

**Forthcoming**

*Relationship Marketing: Strategy and Implementation*, Helen Peck, Adrian Payne, Martin Christopher and Moira Clark

*Services Marketing*, Colin Egan

# The Fundamentals of Corporate Communication

Richard R. Dolphin, MBA

*Published in association with The Chartered Institute of Marketing*

B.C.F.T.C.S.

085596

OXFORD  AUCKLAND  BOSTON  JOHANNESBURG  MELBOURNE  NEW DELHI

Butterworth-Heinemann
Linacre House, Jordan Hill, Oxford OX2 8DP
225 Wildwood Avenue, Woburn, MA 01801-2041
A division of Reed Educational and Professional Publishing Ltd

A member of the Reed Elsevier plc group

First published 1999

**British Library Cataloguing in Publication Data**
A catalogue record for this book is available from the British Library

ISBN 0 7506 4186 X

Composition by Genesis Typesetting, Rochester, Kent
Printed and bound in Great Britain by Biddles Ltd, Guildford and King's Lynn

for my son
Robert John Mercer
without whose original idea it would never have happened

for David Stoker
who gave me the opportunity that made it possible

for
Ying Fan
who gave me unstinting encouragement and support

# Contents

*Foreword*                                                                xi

*Preface*                                                                xiii


**1  Towards an understanding of corporate communications**                 **1**
   Origins of public relations                                            2
   Attempting a definition of corporate communication                     4
   The narrower view of corporate communication                           5
   Key management tool                                                    7
   Role in boundary scanning                                             7
   Differences between corporate communication, corporate affairs and
      public affairs                                                      8
   Numerous job titles                                                    10
   Objects of communication                                              11
   Marketing communications                                              12
   Corporate advertising                                                 13
   The present shape of corporate communications                         15


**2  Audiences – who – and where – are the key publics?**                   **19**
   Many different publics                                                 20
   Reason for communicating with the publics                             20
   Identifying the audiences                                             21
   Is the internal audience an important audience?                        23
   Stakeholders – who and where are they?                                27
   A vast new global audience                                            30
   The financial publics                                                 30
   The media – is it the number one audience?                            32
   Opinion formers                                                       33
   Government and politicians                                            35
   Corporate abstention                                                  36

3   **Corporate identity – the role and value of corporate identity**
    **programmes**                                                            **40**
    Defining corporate identity                                               41
    Revealing the identity                                                    43
    The sense of self                                                         44
    Integrating corporate identity into the communication process            45
    Transmitting the identity                                                 45
    The types of corporate identity                                           47
    The importance of corporate identity                                      48
    The importance of corporate identity from a practitioner's
      perspective                                                             49
    Corporate identity programs                                               49
    How the communication executive creates corporate identity               50
    Definition of corporate image                                            51
    The image maker                                                          54
    Does the communication executive create an image?                        55
    Actuality versus image                                                   56
    Image not matched by actuality                                          58

4   **Strategy**                                                             **61**
    Corporate communication's unique qualities as a management
      discipline                                                             62
    Supporting other management functions                                    63
    Communications inform you about other organizations                      64
    Strategic value of scanning the environment                              65
    Strategic value of communicating with key constituencies                68
    Strategic input to CEOs and key senior executives                        69
    The strategic role of the communication executive                        72
    Strategic objectives of corporation communication                        73
    Formulating the good communications strategy                             74

5   **Using the tools provided by corporate communications**                **79**
    Lobbying                                                                 81
    Sponsorship                                                              83
    Consumer public relations                                                86
    Financial communications                                                92
    Corporate reputation – an intangible resource                            97
    Researching the attitudes of key publics                                101
    The bottom line – how corporate communication adds to economic
      performance                                                           104
    Communications facilitating the management of change                    105
    Communications facilitating culture change                              106
    Communication facilitates a new identity                                107
    The face of the organization                                            112

6  **Crisis communications – truth at all costs?**                                    **117**
   Defining a crisis                                                                 120
   Do organizations prepare to handle crises?                                        124
   The form of crisis communication planning                                         126
   If a delay in communicating is unavoidable                                        130
   The importance of fast reactions                                                  133
   A pivotal role for communications                                                 133
   The best way to handle communications in a crisis                                 133
   The legal side versus the communication people                                    133
   Communicating during a financial crisis                                           135
   Poor crisis communications lead to loss of confidence                             137
   Truth at all costs in a crisis?                                                   138

7  **The background of the communication executive**                                  **145**
   The origins of the communication executive                                        146
   Is there a typical model for a communication executive?                           147
   The personality types suited for corporate communications                         148
   The qualities needed to be a successful communication executive                   149
   The background of a director of corporate communication                           156
   The academic background of a successful practitioner                              158
   Headhunting – a typical approach                                                  158
   Experience of consultancies                                                       159
   The communication executive – the nature of the role                              159
   A new role                                                                        160
   An uncertain role                                                                 161
   An imprecise role                                                                 162
   An increasingly important role                                                    165
   To whom does the communication executive report?                                  166
   The fit in the structure of the organization                                      168
   The status of the role                                                            170
   The management title allocated to the role                                        172
   The director of corporate communications                                         173
   A changing role – a wonderful job!                                                174

8  **A bright future for corporate communication**                                    **179**
   Evaluating communication performance                                              180
   The use of consultants                                                            188
   International or intercultural communications?                                    192
   Issues management                                                                 197
   Funding the communication function                                                201
   The next frontier for corporate communications                                    203

*References*                                                                         208

*Index*                                                                              216

# Foreword

I think I am very lucky. I get paid for doing something I enjoy – wrestling with the issues thrown up by a big company working hard to manage relationships with its stakeholders.

The stakes are high. My own company manages £5 billion of shareholders' money, serves over ten million people a week in our pubs and restaurants and is responsible for the livelihoods of over 80 000 people. We operate from more than 6000 locations, which gives us a stake in a host of local communities as well.

Where do you start to tackle the myriad of demands of a group so diverse?

There are literally hundreds of books and consultancy studies on aspects of corporate communications. Many are self-seeking promotions for the author or the services of an agency. Most suffer the fault of being highly partial. Virtually none attempt to pull everything together and present a coherent picture.

Richard Dolphin has the advantage that he brought an enquiring mind to the study of corporate communications relatively late in life. He brought with him no pre-conceptions.

The outcome is this book. It is truly comprehensive. It is founded in solid academic research but is written with the practitioner in mind. Everyone from the student thinking of a career in the field to the most seasoned professional will gain from reading it.

David Reed
*Director of Corporate Affairs, Whitbread plc*
29 April 1998

# Preface

In the summer of 1996 I found myself as an (albeit rather mature) student, near the completion of the one year taught MBA programme at the University of Durham Business School. I was writing a dissertation on the Role and Function of the Director of Corporate Communications and had embarked on research which took me into the corporate headquarters of companies at the very summit of British industry. In the course of that research two things became abundantly plain to me.

The first was that, to my astonishment, no one, globally, *appeared* to have succeeded before in researching the precise academic field which I was investigating. The second was that there were few books published in this management area which were aimed at the practitioner and those who would be practitioners. Indeed, it proved to be the case, that there were few books aimed at the related field of the upper echelons of public relations. Indeed, both the main university library and the business school library at Durham were woefully weak in this area.

After leaving Durham I continued extensive research in this chosen field in my own time, at my own pace and at my own expense. By the summer of 1997 I had come to the conclusion that writing a comprehensive guide to a management discipline which I concluded was now a major strategic resource was a personal imperative.

In deciding to write this book I had two objectives in mind. First, to write a text which was well grounded in present management and academic thinking. Second, to produce a text which was both understandable and hopefully of value to the interested layman. It was a deliberate policy decision to avoid writing from a purely theoretical standpoint in order to achieve these twin objectives. The reader will judge if I have succeeded in my purpose.

It is evidently the case that corporate communication now has a leading edge role in the strategic process of successful corporations. Philosophically it is abundantly plain that if only people could communicate better with each other most of the world's problems would not arise in the first place. Over and beyond that, as this text will show abundantly, successful organizations in today's competitive market place are those who care about corporate reputation and who seek to communicate with key audiences – whoever and wherever they may be. They are the companies who ensure that the result of those communications works to the mutual benefit of both parties.

Books which start with lengthy salutations to dozens of diverse parties of whom the prospective reader has probably never heard are books which have the potential to get off to a boring start. Accordingly, this is not going to be such a one. But, I do have two sets of thanks to express.

First, I wish to thank the nearly two dozen communication executives (and Lord Marshall, Chairman of British Airways and Inchcape) who gave me their time when I was doing my research (from which this book springs) while I was at Durham. They were all extremely busy people. At least 50 per cent were executives at the pinnacle of their profession; without exception all were not only kindly but gracious – some amazingly so. One or two like Geoff Potter at GlaxoWellcome and Michael Prideaux at B.A.T. Industries indicated that time was simply no object at all. I was overwhelmed by the kindness shown to me by so many people. The whole experience proved to be one of the most fascinating and rewarding of my life. I ended up wishing that I had gone into corporate communications myself as a young man.

Second, I wish to thank my wife Rosemary Dolphin who sustained me with moral support and a whole stream of jugs of coffee and hot meals through the heat of the summer of 1997 whilst I spent four months non-stop putting the book together. Without her support the project – particularly in view of the deprivations that went with it – would not have got off the ground.

My concluding hope is that readers, whether professional communicators or students of communication, will gain not only an appreciation through this text of the powerful force that effective communication can be in modern business; but also an understanding of why it has become a tool which an organization seeking competitive advantage will ignore very much at its peril.

R. R. D.
Foxhunters, West Hatch

# Chapter 1

# Towards an understanding of corporate communications

The corporate communication function resists a single fixed definition. It is a dynamic mixture of problem solving skills and insights. It should be viewed as a process rather than as an entity. But there are three key responsibilities encompassed within a truly effective corporate public affairs function:

- Aiding the management of change
- Helping to define a corporation's role in society
- Assisting the creation of corporate vision and purpose

The need to navigate through complex public environments; to mediate with government, employee and complex stakeholders; to manage the effects of change and to operate ethically whilst projecting an inspiring sense of corporate pride and vision; are amongst the pressing tasks facing communication executives today.

Adapted from Finlay (1994)

## Introduction

No organization exists in a vacuum. Every organization has a place in, and impacts upon, its own environment. Each organization needs to communicate with those key publics whose perceptions and opinions it deems important.

An organization needs to impact upon its environment by communicating integrated, coherent messages and themes to those internal and external audiences with which it desires to have relationships. Communications is thus a process that nourishes those relationships.

Communications is a process that needs to be geared to the needs, ideals and aspirations of all its audiences. It can facilitate an understanding of, and deepening appreciation for, the organization. It is an enabling process; one which should form an essential part of corporate strategy. It is a process that can impact upon performance and upon overall competitive advantage.

Corporate communication is an approach rather than a technique. It has developed into an essential management discipline. It is an approach that sets out to ensure the consistency of the corporate message and the transparency of the organization. It is a function that anticipates issues, events and crises before they occur. Through its messages and themes the organization conveys its desired image and persona.

Thus through communication the organization functions, its character and identity takes on life and form, and it becomes known to its various audiences.

> Some people tell us that Public Relations, Public Affairs and
> Communication in all its commercial forms is about nothing more
> than messages and their perceptions. That's true — if unduly
> simplistic.
>
> Marshall (1997)

There are references in a budget speech to broad money and narrow money. These are terms used in macro economics. There is a broad understanding of what the term corporate communication means – and there is also a narrower definition. We shall try to understand why academics find it so difficult to define what is meant by corporate communications.

Hart (1995) states that the definition of corporate communication should be broad – rather than narrowly focused on message exchange. Goodman (1994) says that as a focus of academic study, corporate communication may be considered in the large context presented here or it can be seen as part of public relations. Given the business environment the more encompassing definition works well in both the applied context of the workplace as well as within the context of academic study. We will first consider the arguments that await resolution before a definition can be agreed.

# Origins of public relations

Corporate Communication may be thought to have emerged from the field of Public Relations. Because public relations, as we know it today, developed in the US largely after national unity was achieved, it did not serve as a major tool of government; in less developed countries it often serves that role (Botan, 1992). However, Nessmann (1995) believes that Hundhausen (Flieger and Ronneberger, 1993) was the first to use the term public relations in its present-day meaning, in 1937 in Europe. He goes on to say that the term public relations is used in German-speaking countries throughout Europe and that, although many US ideas crossed the Atlantic, public relations theory and practice in Europe have developed largely independently of each other.

According to Cline (quoted in Kunczik, 1993) the roots of modern public relations are solidly planted in persuasion theory based on Freud's psychology. Pioneer public relations expert Bernays was a nephew of Freud and took a number of his theories from Austria to America, where he is credited as being an early pioneer of public relations. White and Mazur (1995) remind us that he perceived public relations to be a vocation in which the practitioner advised on social attitudes and actions aimed at winning public support.

## Ancient origins

There is a modernistic view that public relations is an invention of the twentieth century. In real management terms that is almost certainly the case. That being so it is largely an American creation. But the origins of the public relations function are ancient and they date from early Egyptian and Mesopotamian civilizations (Grunig and Hunt, 1984). The public relations function has been called by a variety of different names. It has performed a variety of different tasks in different organizations. Without doubt over the last half century it has developed into an applied social science. Botan (1992) observes that differences in the level of national development are important because they influence not only those upon whom public relations is called to serve but also how it serves them.

Academic literature refers to public relations and communications in changing terminology. Similarly, the emphasis placed on certain nomenclature varies according to the country of origin. In the United Kingdom – but not in the United States (although White and Mazur (1995) report Bernays as saying that public relations had attracted a negative image in the US by the late 1960s) – public relations has become debased. What used to trade under the name of public relations is now known variously as:

- Corporate Affairs
- Corporate Communications
- Public Affairs.

Wilcox et al. (1986) found a vast range of definitions of Public Relations. Harlow identified nearly 500 different definitions half a century ago. Even here there is debate about what is, after all, such a practical area of activity (see Olin's introduction to van Riel, 1995) and there is little agreement concerning that which the practitioner does. Those practising the craft have many different titles; some reflect positions of real significance; some apply to positions of no influence at all. However public relations may be defined, it has developed and grown and has metamorphosed into a wider business and organizational discipline. It has taken on a powerful strategic role in many companies. The head of what was once the public relations department is now the head of the corporate communications function. It is a wider role, it is close to the summit of the organization, and it needs redefining. This is especially so as few writers have had the courage to try to define it (van Riel, 1995).

# Attempting a definition of corporate communication

Some academics believe that corporate communication is the collective name for all communication disciplines (Nessmann, 1995). van Riel (1995) suggests that corporate communication is an all-embracing framework co-ordinating marketing, organizational and management communication – integrating the total business message. He suggests that this helps to define the corporate image and assists in the process of improving an organization's overall competitive advantage. Nessmann proposes that communication specialists from all three areas need to agree on a policy framework for communications within which co-ordination is possible. Perhaps this is a Pan-Continental view of corporate communication.

van Riel (1995) proposes an all-embracing framework – one that sees corporate communication embracing three branches:

- Management communication – by senior managers
- Marketing communication – advertising, sponsorship, sales promotion, direct mail
- Organizational communication – public relations, investor relations, corporate affairs, environmental and internal communication.

Harrison (1995) proposes that:

> corporate communication brings together all communications which
> involve an organization as a corporate entity. Everything, in short,
> that originates from corporate headquarters, is targeted at
> employees, or which reflects the organization as a whole. Therefore,
> it does not include communications such as departmental
> newsletters and public relations activities on behalf of brands or
> subsidiaries. But, she suggests, it does include annual reports,
> corporate identity programs, corporate advertising and the greater
> part of investor relations activity.

## An aid – not a solution

The breadth of the Pan-European definition is the core of the debate with which management scholars wrestle. But Nessmann notes that while corporate communication may be the collective name for all corporate communication disciplines – and whilst this may well be a good idea in practice – as long as the individual disciplines of:

- corporate communications
- corporate identity
- corporate culture
- social communications and
- public relations

have not been defined precisely in theoretical terms (to prevent them overlapping) the collective name Corporate Communications can only be seen as an aid and not a long-term solution.

This may be a broader framework than that envisaged by some scholars – it may widen the definition too far. Some academics might conceivably see Corporate Communications involving Public Relations, Corporate Affairs (also referred to as Government Relations), Marketing Communications, Sponsorship, Issues Management but little else. These are issues open to debate.

Communication as a management tool is used in many areas other than public relations. It is used by the CEO and by line managers. van Riel and Nessmann's interpretation (the Pan-Continental approach) is beyond reproach. Corporate communication as an academic discipline can embrace every communication made by every person within a company in a theoretical context; but it provides a very wide field for scholars to study. Management communication by senior managers may be a significant area of communications practice but it is referred to only in passing in this text.

Senior communication executives in organizations globally are involved in a process of relating with their publics, of seeking to influence the perceptions that those publics have of their organizations, and of developing communication programmes that will put their organizations at a strategic advantage. It is on this narrower field (whilst still accepting the Pan-Continental definition) that this text attempts to focus.

# The narrower view of corporate communication

van Riel (1995) observes that every line of strategy should be the consequence of setting priorities – and for choosing priorities for competitive advantage. As noted, communications should be an integral part of corporate strategy. Communication is concerned with facilitating the achievement of organizational goals (Cutlip et al., 1994) and of contributing to the bottom line. In what way is corporate communication a wider management discipline than public relations? Certainly, it can include a plethora of different forms of internal and external communication including:

- advertising
- brand PR
- community relations
- corporate advertising
- crisis communications
- employee relations
- financial communications
- government relations
- investor relations
- issues management
- labour relations
- lobbying
- management communications
- marketing communications
- media relations
- product PR
- public affairs
- public in general
- sponsorship
- stakeholders
- technical communications
- training and employee development.

Although the term itself may not be new, the idea that corporate communication is now a very important (and some would argue critical) functional area of management is of very recent origin. Academics agree that an understanding of corporate communication becomes more critical by the day, for a week never passes without the importance of effective communication in modern organizations increasing. The essential functionality of good communications can hardly fail to be appreciated by the modern executive; yet, surprisingly, it is by some. It is multifaceted in nature and it has a direct impact on strategy. Therefore, by correlation, it impacts on competitive advantage and on the long-range success of the corporation. Without question good communications are a powerful tool for any company.

In major corporations across the globe corporate communication is now of equal influence and importance as the legal department, the corporate finance department, and the production department. It is what White and Mazur (1995) refer to as a respected function in its own right. So, has public relations now transmogrified into a wider social science altogether?

# Key management tool

Old-style public relations relied on a system that simply does not work any longer – sending out press releases and hoping that someone would write about them (Argenti, 1994). Communication has become a key management tool and it is not an amateur game. It helps to form and shape attitudes on many diverse issues. Corporations exist today in environments in which they are surrounded by diverse audiences with whom they seek to develop relationships and understanding.

## Purpose in communicating

All forms of organizational communication are directed at one target public or another, for communication provides the interface between an organization and its audiences (Sperling, 1983). But why do organizations seek to communicate? Is the purpose to avoid problems? Is it to create an image, or to convey a corporate identity? Is it to get the message across? If the latter, what is the message and does it vary between organizations?

Communication is a facilitating process that enables an organization to evaluate attitudes and to have an understanding of those publics that impact upon the organization. Sophisticated management now understand the strategic importance of communicating with those publics; and of having a constant dialogue with them. Communication is the process that enables organizations to develop relationships with important stakeholders, to identify with them and by which to gain their approval.

# Role in boundary scanning

Communication executives have a role as boundary scanning personnel, so they are in a unique position to understand organizational environments (Lauzen, 1994). In that role they act as an early warning system for their organizations (Dozier, 1990). They need to be aware of the many elements making up the business climate, keeping the environment under constant review, detecting storms heading in the organization's direction and scanning the environment for issues that might impact on the organization.

Corporate communications – unlike most other management disciplines – is capable of providing detached, objective, analytical thinking about the impact and consequences of corporate decisions on potential audiences (Finlay, 1994). However, although the communication implications of decisions need to be considered, management decisions should not be taken for communication reasons alone.

If the communication process is to be judged a success, it will result in the enhancement of the organization's reputation. Successful corporate communication concerns the management of the reputation of the company

(Osborne, 1994). Lord Marshall, Chairman of British Airways plc and Inchcape plc, is quoted (*Air Transport World*, 1996) as saying that it is no good striving to be the best airline in the world unless you are seen to be so – which makes the work of public affairs vital to British Airways. Further, you have to be seen to be so by both your internal as well as your external publics. This might have been a highly pertinent point in the summer of 1997, when BA staff were staging three-day strikes, perhaps BA's internal public did not perceive British Airways as the best airline in the world.

One function of the communication department is assisting the organization with the process of defining and finding its most advantageous role within the context of those key publics with which it seeks to interact (Finlay, 1994). Communication contributes to organizational responses by devising action and communication strategies to manage relationships with key publics and around important issues (Lauzen, 1995). If an organization reviews the relationships it enjoys with its various publics, and if it does so on a continuous basis, it positions itself so that it is able to maintain its place as a successful and dynamic constituent within its environment (Finlay, 1994).

# Differences between corporate communication, corporate affairs and public affairs

As noted academics are engaged in a continuing debate concerning the differences between:

■ public relations
■ corporate communications
■ corporate affairs
■ public affairs.

A small number of companies favour the term 'communications' to describe the external affairs function. This reflects a long-standing, continuing debate within the field as to the appropriate name and focus for external corporate affairs management. Many argue that the focus is – and must be – on governmental institutions and the public policy process. Others stress the role of corporate communications with stakeholders as the essential focus (Post and Griffin, 1997).

In practice Corporate Affairs and Public Affairs are expressions used largely interchangeably. The expression Public Affairs is used more frequently in some industries than others. In heavily regulated sectors public affairs can be a separate department altogether. It may well be that the old specification 'Public Relations Director' is now often used interchangeably with that of 'Public Affairs Director' (Simon, 1986). However, although examples of this may be identified, public affairs and public relations, despite sharing functions and responsibilities, have an essential difference.

Many scholars of management consider that public affairs concerns the management of relationships with government, whereas White and Mazur (1995) note that public affairs is often referred to as government affairs in other countries.

There can be no questioning the necessity for good communications with government at both macro and micro levels. At the most senior level practitioners are involved increasingly in government. In some organizations a separate executive may have responsibility for this audience. It can be a delicate assignment, for example in a European country the public affairs specialist may well be involved with twelve different governments (over twenty if EFTA and the Eastern bloc are taken into account) not to mention diverse regional authorities.

Certainly, government is one of the many audiences with which major organizations have to communicate. This is the case especially where more and more industries find themselves subject to an ever increasing number of regulations. British Airways is only one example of a major corporation that suffers very heavy regulation.

> 'Public Affairs' is a sort of upgraded title to take into account the relationships with government. An intermediate step is 'Corporate Communications.'
> Director, Corporate Affairs, GlaxoWellcome, in conversation with
> the author

In practice 'corporate affairs' or 'public affairs' may be used to describe the work of the whole communications department, and the scope of the public affairs responsibility is growing. Public affairs departments, whatever their name, share a broad responsibility for managing corporate reputation and image. The growth in activities and responsibilities reflects new realities facing businesses across industries (Post and Griffin, 1997).

As noted some academics feel that public affairs is concerned with government affairs while a few senior practitioners consider that, in reality, it is a polite word for political lobbying, which is considered in a later chapter. Not all, however, put a governmental perspective on the affairs connotation. Some simply think that it reflects a perception of external forces/outside issues. The director of group public affairs at GlaxoWellcome commented:

> Public relations is an outmoded term and is now rather disdained. 'Public Affairs' is a sort of upgraded title to take into account the relationships with government. An intermediate step is 'Corporate Communications'.

## Numerous job titles

Communication executives throughout industry are allocated a very wide range of titles and no single one is used much more than any other. Whatever the job title allocated to them, most executives perform similar duties. Perhaps 'public affairs' or 'corporate affairs' is still used frequently, but it can be misleading. While some corporations clearly intend the title to reflect governmental aspects of the task, in some instances it is simply a title.

> One of the most misunderstood and untapped resources of the
> modern manager is that of the public affairs function. Paradoxically,
> it is also becoming one of the most important.
>
> Finlay (1994)

---

## Different titles given to communication executives

| | |
|---|---|
| Communications Manager | Tennent Caledonian Breweries Ltd |
| Director of Corporate Communications | Whitbread plc |
| | Wessex Water plc |
| | J. Sainsbury plc |
| | Asda plc |
| Director of Corporate Affairs | The Boots Company plc |
| | Storehouse plc |
| | W.H. Smith Group plc |
| Director, Corporate Affairs | GlaxoWellcome plc |
| Director of Corporate Relations | British Telecommunications plc |
| Director of External Affairs | South Western Electricity plc |
| Director of Public Affairs | British Airways plc |
| Director of Group Public Affairs | B.A.T. Industries plc |
| Director of Group Public Relations | Vaux Group plc |
| Group Director of Corporate Affairs | Yorkshire Tyne-Tees Television plc |
| Group Publicity Manager | Avon Rubber plc |
| Head of Media Communication | London Transport |
| Head of Corporate Communications | Lloyds/TSB plc |
| Marketing Director | Wm. Morrison Supermarkets plc |
| Public Relations and Marketing Manager | Northumbria Ambulance |
| Public Relations Manager | Avon and Somerset Constabulary |

from a sample taken by the author

# Objects of communication

Corporate Communication is concerned with non-economic indicators such as changing attitudes, altering perceptions and affecting what an audience believes about the organization. Keeping management informed about public reactions to what the organization does is now recognized as a prime communications function, as is identifying problems, needs and issues that may impact on the organization. The communication executive has the responsibility of making certain that public opinion and social responsibility are properly considered when any corporate decisions are formulated. Many academics consider that much of corporate communication is directed towards bolstering corporate image (which van Riel, 1995 considers is the reflection of the identity of the organization in the eyes of it stakeholders). van Riel sees this as the Mirror Function – monitoring developments and anticipating their consequences on audiences.

Organizations communicate with those that they perceive as stakeholders because they desire an enhanced awareness, understanding and appreciation of their identity and of their core beliefs, as well as of their products and their services. Every organization has its own identity and reputation. The primary role of corporate communication is to manage the company's reputation and help build public consent for the organization and for its businesses. In today's globally competitive business environment public consent can no longer be assumed, it must be earned and earned continuously (Osborne, 1994). Activists, in particular, pose a threat to organizational autonomy, and without an understanding of these adversarial groups organizations may well be at their mercy (L. A. Grunig, 1992). The organization desires a favourable attitude towards itself from key publics just as it wants a heightened perception of its purpose and culture. These desired perceptions are focused on helping to secure a sure foundation for the commercial relationship between the company and its constituencies. Perhaps the ultimate purpose of communication is to improve the economic performance of the corporation.

> I am a reputation engineer.
> Director of Group Public Affairs, B.A.T. Industries, in conversation
> with the author

As every organization has a persona and style of its own, perhaps the communication content of each organization has a different focus? Skolnik (1994) reports that Redmond (Washington, USA) based Microsoft devotes no more than 25 per cent of its communication output to telling the story. The other 75 per cent of Microsoft communication focus is, he says, devoted to promoting and selling Microsoft products. Their communication function works closely with marketing even while products are developed – and not just when they are brought to the market.

## Marketing communications

There is a distinction between communications and what many regard as the allied functions of marketing, advertising and selling. Communication essentially providing a service to the organization as a whole (Winner, 1993). That means it serves many of its individual departments. The relationship between communications and other management processes depends largely on the individual organization, its culture and environment.

Some academics might argue that communication is not 'a function of marketing' – as the director of group public relations at Vaux remarked. It might also be hypothesized that it is 'not advertising' – as the head of corporate communications at Lloyds/TSB commented. Perhaps, as the executive at Vaux Group suggested, 'Communication is the senior of the skills.' The acting director of corporate communications at J. Sainsbury differed; her opinion was that 'Marketing and communications are much of a muchness', while the group publicity manager at Avon Rubber commented that 'Communications and marketing must work together.' van Riel (1992) writes of his finding in a survey of European financial institutions that a problem area he identified most frequently was co-ordination between traditional marketing departments and other departments.

As noted, van Riel (1995) perceives three main arteries of corporate communication of which marketing communications is one. Kitchen (1993) notes that while public relations may have significant value in terms of corporate communication activities it is also significant in terms of marketing. Kitchen subdivides marketing communications into five branches:

1. Advertising
2. Sales promotion
3. Personal selling
4. Marketing PR/product publicity
5. Sponsorship.

He believes that it would be inappropriate to view these elements of marketing communications as mutually exclusive. The more correct approach, Kitchen suggests, is to view them as mutually interactive and synergistic. Each area, he considers, needs to be planned and co-ordinated with the other areas to achieve communication objectives; and with these objectives he sees much interaction between corporate and marketing public relations.

> The aim is to keep everything consistent with core values. Abbey National has 150 years of branding and image and it can easily be destroyed. So marketing and communication people have to stay in close contact.
>
> (paraphrased) White and Mazur (1995)

Marketing communication concerns those mechanisms specifically aimed at promoting the corporate brand, its goods and services. Hart (1995) draws attention to a divergence of opinion about the definition of marketing communications, which he suggests may be split into two categories:

1. The non face-to-face promotional activities of advertising, publicity, direct mail, exhibitions and sales promotion.
2. Across the board communications to help move a potential customer from a state of ignorance towards a position of decision and action.

Marketing communication seeks to address both customers and prospective customers and Hart recalls that channels of communication to these audiences include advertising and direct mail. Marketing – of which advertising is an essential part – has as its chief purpose:

- the task of promoting both the company and its products, and
- helping to enable the sale of a company's goods and services.

## A sterile argument

As noted, advertising is a subdivision of marketing, which some regard as a subdivision of communication. However, at least one writer sees the argument about whether marketing is a subset of public relations, or the other way round, as a 'sterile argument' (Harrison, 1995). She believes that taking an informed view on 'which discipline is appropriate to a given set of circumstances' is more to the point.

> I think that communications and advertising are two different ways of getting a message out. Charities need to consider which of those ways is going to be effective. In terms of getting a message out I think that *public relations* is more effective.
>
> Lamplugh (*PR Week*, 1997a)

# Corporate advertising

Corporate advertising transmits messages that have been encoded by the communication or marketing department – these are messages that may affect buying decisions, may be aimed at investors or might even be directed at employees. Corporate advertising attempts to try to sell the company itself and it helps to promote the image of the organization.

The purpose of corporate advertising is to benefit the image of the corporation rather than its products or services. It involves the use of media advertising, for the media helps to shape our lives and even, in some cases, our behaviour. Normally the marketing department funds the cost of product advertising, whilst the corporate communication department bears the cost of corporate advertising. Argenti (1994) reports that 50 per cent of US firms have corporate advertising programmes. There is, he says, usually a correlation between the size of the corporation and the amount of the budget and some sectors are more likely to advertise than others.

Corporate advertising should set out to present a clear identity (and therefore an equally clear image) for the organization. The advertising programme should be a cohesive part of the overall communication strategy, which will in turn will be an essential component of the overall corporate strategy.

> Traditionally marketing a company's products and services has been
> kept separate from the promotion of corporate image and
> reputation. Procter and Gamble (which is an almost unknown name
> to the average consumer) is one example. This lack of recognition is
> in spite of the widespread recognition of products Fairy or Bold;
> both of which have their own very distinctive brand characters. In
> contrast McDonalds is the omnipresent corporate brand that
> over-rides and unites all of its products in the consumer's mind.
>                                     adapted from *Sachs, (PR Week,* 1997b)

Sachs (*PR Week*, 1997b) is not alone in believing that the dynamics between the product brand and the corporate brand are changing and that companies are appreciating the added value of making the relationship between the two work to their mutual advantage.

Twelve months after he was appointed to his position at Whitbread plc, the Director of Corporate Communications commissioned research into the perceptions of his organization to find out what other 'players' in the City thought of his company. Following such an audit a communication executive may find that the perceptions revealed by the research are not those desired by the organization. In which case, the organization may feel the need for a corporate advertising programme to restate to key publics what the organization is really all about: or, perhaps, to effect a change from one image to a totally new one – such as rebranding the Spastics Society as Scope.

> We are a pretty small charity and are totally dependent on
> donations. We have limited resources and thus try to use the most
> cost effective communication tools. Our fundraising activities are
> aimed at raising public awareness. To be effective advertising must be
> linked to precise business objectives; money spent on raising
> awareness through advertising is not money well spent.
>                                     adapted from Simons (1997)

Corporate advertising is often used for image enhancement. The news media is now a powerful part of our society; use of the media for this purpose has increased considerably over the last decade. Following a merger, such as that between Glaxo and Wellcome, there may be a need to communicate with those who see themselves as stakeholders in the organization, just as there is a need to communicate when an organization has undergone enormous change. Corporate advertising can help to generate goodwill by ensuring that various stakeholders know what is going on within the organization. Successful corporate advertising can greatly boost the self confidence of employees, impacting on the internal audience by increasing the feel-good factor.

As noted elsewhere, the financial public has become an audience of supreme importance – for investors own the corporation. Media advertising is used to great effect to promote the organization to financial publics, enhancing the organization in the eyes of investors and analysts alike. It can also encourage interest among potential investors. Media advertising can impact on corporate strategy, underlining the financial situation of an organization, positioning the organization for future success, getting the message across. It achieves this effectively and quickly. Argenti (1994) reports that corporate advertising in the financial area has a statistically positive effect on stock prices – an effect that he suggests can be very exciting for organizations that consider their stocks to be undervalued.

Media advertising can also be used for issue enhancement – responding to special issues raised by those who would make themselves the organization's stakeholders. This type of advertising can be controversial and often ends up as a public debate. The Brewer's Society embarked on just such a campaign as long ago as 1959 when it tried to resolve a public debate between the perceived and differing advantages of bottled versus draught beer.

Customer relations is another branch of marketing communications that helps to support and nourish the marketing function. Its primary purpose is to help create and establish strong ties with the organization's customers through communications. As stakeholders become an audience of ever growing concern to corporations – pressure groups trying to exert their influence on organizations are a particular example – customer relations have assumed an increasingly significant role in corporate communications.

## The present shape of corporate communications

Public relations is still used terminologically as a management discipline but it no longer exists at the top of industry. Management's original perception of communication has metamorphosed; it is no longer an amateur game. Traditionally practised public relations can still be found, but in a decreasing number of smaller and outmoded organizations, perhaps confirming Guth's (1995) view that the size of the corporation appears to influence the role of the communication function within individual organizations.

Communications have become a resource and as such they must be controlled in the same way that any other resource is managed. Communication is now a major and sophisticated speciality and its directors are men and women of signal influence, if not power. White and Mazur (1995) refer to the importance of giving the communicator a central strategic role; assisting the formulation of corporate strategy and promoting the organization's strategic direction to all its key audiences.

So, the first priority of effective communications is to determine the corporate vision and to devise a communication strategy that drives towards that vision. Heath (1994) notes the concern that so many voices emerge from within a company and that they do not express a common desirable theme, but express competing and conflicting themes, themes that lead away from unity of purpose and effort. Thus the communication executive faces a special difficulty – the task is to create a cohesive and well co-ordinated communication strategy.

## Case study

There are many definitions and they vary according to the particular approach taken to organizational, social or marketing theories (Signitzer, 1992). Nevertheless, and in spite of these differing points of view and approaches, most definitions have one thing in common. This commonality is that they consider *public relations* as *communication* (Windahl and Signitzer, 1992). Europe has seen the adoption of some American definitions including some organizationally-oriented approaches (as defined by Grunig and Hunt, 1984). For instance 'public relations is the management function that identifies, establishes and maintains mutually beneficial relationships between an organization and its various publics on whom its sucess or failure depends'. At the present time Long and Hazleton's (1987) definition of public relations as 'a communication function of management through which organizations adapt to, alter or maintain their environment for the purpose of achieving organizational goals' is considered to be the most exacting analytical definition, at least from a theoretical point of view.

Some of these American definitions are not accepted as widely among European academics. Indeed, there are visible differences between what practitioners do – and how they think of – public relations in their own countries.

The definitions of European management scholars and communication executives generally consist of lists of aims and functions. An analysis of these definitions generally identifies these elements:

■ Creating trust, comprehension and sympathy
■ Arousing attention, interests and needs
■ Creating communication and relationships
■ Creating mutual understanding and agreement
■ Articulating, representing and adjusting interests
■ Influencing public opinion

- Resolving conflicts
- Creating consensus

There are fundamental differences between theory and practice regarding the function of public relations. One clear example of this is that many practitioners still take the view that public relations sets out to manipulate public opinion and that it represents an unethical and asymmetrical dimension. Practitioners are not at all sure either regarding the function 'of creating mutual understanding' and some regard it as a rather vague and unprecise concept (MacManus, 1994).

Frequently, corporate communication is thought of as the collective name for all communication disciplines. This may work well in practice but as long as the individual disciplines of corporate communications, corporate identity, corporate culture, social communications and public relations have not been defined in exact theoretical terms (which would prevent them overlapping) thinking of corporate communication as a 'collective name' can only be viewed as an aid and certainly it is not a long term solution. This theoretical difficulty has been the subject of much serious discussion in Europe and indeed the Euroforum conference in Munich in 1993 was entitled 'Integrated Corporate Communications'.

adapted from Nessman (1995)

# Key terms

**BOUNDARY SCANNING**   Term used by academics to describe the process of observing external audiences and environmental factors; evaluating how – and to what extent – they might impact upon an organization, carrying information to them and conveying information back into the organization. A watchdog role. This is also referred to by some as Environmental Scanning.

**CORPORATE AFFAIRS**   Generic term to describe macro (national) and micro (local) governmental matters that may impact upon an organization. This is also referred to as Public Affairs, sometimes referred to sneeringly as Lobbying.

**CORPORATE IMAGE**   How an organization is perceived by its various publics – based on the nature of the corporate identity communicated to them. The perception held of the organization both by those internal and external to it.

**CORPORATE REPUTATION**   The public esteem in which an organization is held by its audiences; the 'name' which (by repute) it has – or does not have – for its performance, service and products. The reputation of – and the regard for – an organization; that is how audiences feel about it.

**CORPORATE VISION**   A term used to describe how and where a corporation sees its commercial future.

**INTEGRATION**   When used in connection with corporate communication refers to the process of ensuring that internal and external messages say the same thing.

**LOBBYING**   The process of trying to influence legislators on behalf of special interest groups.

**MACRO**   *See* Corporate Affairs.

**MARKETING COMMUNICATION**   Those communication processes devoted to assisting the process of marketing and promoting an organization's goods and services.

**MEDIA**   A channel of communication enabling the organization to reach the desired audiences. Important external audience made up of local and national press; trade, technical, professional press; radio, television, that is all those who report corporate happenings to their audiences.

**MICRO**   *See* Corporate Affairs.

**PERSONA**   Used in the context of corporate identity – the perceived character of an organization.

**PERSUASION THEORY**   Academic process, which seeks to persuade people to think or believe in a certain way.

**PLANNED COMMUNICATION**   Process of producing a devised and organized communication programme for the organization.

**PUBLIC AFFAIRS**   *See* Corporate Affairs.

**REGULATORS**   Government appointed bodies that regulate certain aspects of personal or organizational life.

# Chapter 2

# Audiences – who – and where – are the key publics?

You cannot communicate externally without communicating internally – the two are interdependent.

Director of Group Public Relations, Vaux Group plc, in conversation with the author

Corporate reality as we know it today forces organizations to play ever closer attention to their *shadow constituencies*. This new breed of corporate stakeholders is outside a company's traditional scope of influence – but their opinions can shape and impact upon the public's perception of the organization – even if they do not have a direct impact on the bottom line (which they may well have). Shadow constitutencies (which vary all the time) might well include political groups, women's organizations, arts and education advocates, supporters of safety and health interests, and minorities. Companies who decide to ignore these stakeholders are missing a good opportunity to learn things that they might not otherwise find out. Shadow constituencies often have a way of forcing companies to face issues that they need to address (but which they are otherwise reluctant so to do). Communication executives are in the best possible place to build good relationships with all those stakeholders who may impact upon their organization.

adapted from Mau and Dennis (1994)

## Introduction

Corporate Communications has developed into a significant management discipline; although it is not yet regarded as an indispensable tool. Communication skills are needed in many facets of generalist management practice, promoting the organization's messages and themes. Organizational communications provide an interface between the organization and its audiences (also referred to as 'publics' and by the Americans as 'constituencies') promoting knowledge and favourable sentiment towards the organization, evaluating public attitudes and developing relationships.

As a result of effective communications an organization's reputation is enhanced – for communication concerns the management of the reputation of the company. This chapter seeks to identify those publics at which corporate communications are most frequently targeted and to discover whether those publics include opinion formers and stakeholders (both of which groups may be important new shadow constituencies).

## Many different publics

> A New Age of corporate distrust is plaguing institutions. Corporate reputation is under attack. There is a broad, growing recognition among corporate executives that the ability to succeed will depend on the corporation's ability to communicate effectively with its employees, customers, shareholders, suppliers and the public at large.
>
> Graham (1994)

Writing about the diverse audiences with which a major corporation is confronted, L. A. Grunig (1992) argues that public relations should have been restyled 'publics relations', because the present designation is not justified by the emphasis placed on a single public (which is, according to her, the media). Leichty and Springston (1993) go a long way towards supporting this view when they remark that they would not endorse a simple dyadic model of organization–public relationships because organizations have relations with multiple publics and no single relationship can exist in a vacuum.

## Reason for communicating with the publics

Any organization faces a vast number of diverse publics at any one time – women, unions, young people, academics, the media, governments, environmentalists, consumer crusaders, minority groups and assorted lobbyists – all those groups of people with which the organization is – or wants to be – in communication (Harrison, 1995). The range of potential publics for a major organization is enormous. Those relationships must be reviewed continuously so that the organization can keep its place as a dynamic part of its wider environment. One of the tasks of the communicator is to provide a framework in which the organization can comprehend, assess and control the various forces of social and political change which surround it and impact upon it.

Organizations cannot hope to escape their environments – which in turn decide their key constituencies. The Director of Corporate Communications at Whitbread observed that the communicator has to question with whom the corporation needs to have relationships in order to sustain its business. As organizations function in different environments they, therefore, approach their publics from differing standpoints. Diverse groups have varying needs, which require different information – this has to be transmitted in ways appropriate to the audience. The Director of Corporate Communications at Whitbread added to his earlier observation, saying that his company is constantly researching the views and perceptions of all those audiences which it perceives make up its publics.

No successful organization ignores its audiences. Thus a statement of communication policy from an organization demonstrates implicitly that it recognizes that a favourable impression on key constituencies is important. The effectiveness of any organization – and indeed its very survival – may come to depend upon how the corporation establishes and maintains relationships with those publics which are important to it.

## Cross fertilization with key publics

Management scholars accept that communication practitioners exist to create and foster relations between organizations and their publics. These relationships, Harrison (1995) notes, help influence their behaviour towards the organization and increases sympathy for its aims. Lauzen (1995) suggests that practitioners provide cultural cross-fertilization with their publics and that they relay the values of an organization to and from their audiences. Sophisticated management now fully understands the real importance of communicating with key publics and of establishing good relations with them – relationships that are achieved by creating channels of communication to facilitate a two-way flow of information.

Conveying the reputation and image of an organization to key publics is considered by many people to be a prime responsibility for the communication executive. But there is more to communication than just presentation, image and reputation. Part of the central plank of communication strategy is the transmission of an overall picture of the organization.

Whatever the content of the communication programme, it is aimed at those audiences that an organization seeks to impress, or with whom it seeks to have a dialogue. These are the constituencies considered in this chapter.

# Identifying the audiences

Identifying publics provides a special difficulty for scholars of management, for audiences change all the time. Indeed, the range of constituencies is not merely changing – but is growing in number.

The first task of the communication executive is thus to identify the constituencies that are important to the organization. Those audiences identified and targeted by the communication executive are determined by the activities of the organization and by aspects of its activities which may be considered problem areas. The potential scope for communication involves identifying groups, such as opinion formers or stakeholders, which may impact upon the organization. Often groups are members of more than one public simultaneously. Customers of a supermarket may be part of an audience as customers and part of another audience as opinion formers – presenting a double challenge for the practitioner. The director of corporate affairs at Boots plc commented that one of his audiences is 'the entire population of the UK'.

Here is a list of the publics – defined as 'any group of people who share a common interest' Bowman and Ellis (1969), quoting Professor E. J. Robinson – which academic literature suggests might be the most important:

- customers
- educational bodies
- internal publics/employees
- investors/shareholders
- local authorities
- local communities
- media
- opinion formers
- politicians
- suppliers
- trade associations
- trade unions.

## Are important audiences external or internal?

Once upon a time it was assumed that communication was a one-way process – and that the one way inevitably was outwards. van Riel (1992) suggests that most communication objectives are focused externally and he asserts that internal communications get little attention. Successful communication encompasses maintaining harmonious and understanding relationships between the organization and all its numerous publics.

Are key audiences outside the organization? Could employees be a major audience? Members of an organization may well be less than happy if they learn about the future direction of their organization from the media instead of from their own management.

> Many people (and especially corporate leaders) miss the fact that you cannot separate internal communication from external communication. Anything that is published within the organization, whether it is a newsletter or a memorandum, must – by definition –

be considered a public document. Employees take their staff
newspaper home and their wives and families read it. I think that
communication practitioners are beginning to realize the special
advantages that can be gained by connecting internal communication
strategies with external communication strategies.

adapted from Brown (1995)

## Is the internal audience an important audience?

In any organization too large for every employee to be known by name there
might be a communication problem. van Riel (1992) proposes that perhaps the
internal audience is given less attention than more visible external publics.
Wright (1995) refers to findings by both Jackson (1994) and D'Aprix (1984) who
have both criticized communication managers for being more concerned with
media communication than with developing internal communications strategies. But today employees have become a critical audience for communication
activities. This is recognized increasingly by the allocation of resources devoted
to it.

Too often communicating with the internal audience was treated as an
afterthought – a process of issuing bulletins or news releases – and not as a
means of harnessing the creative energies and enthusiasm of staff. However,
although employees may not be ambassadors, they are a valuable resource.
They are a resource which, once empowered, can play a key part in the pursuit
of competitive advantage. In the past communicating internally might have
been an afterthought. Modern managers realize that if personnel do not know
what the CEO is thinking it is hardly likely to be to the long-term advantage of
the organization.

At least 50 per cent of change management is related to internal
communications. Without communications things can revert back to
old belief systems. Securities analysts think that cultural issues are
the most difficult to resolve successfully in the wake of a merger or
acquisition. If employees are not told what is happening how are
they meant to know in which direction the company is heading?

Unknown

Most large corporations today understand the importance of the internal
audience. Without good internal communications there is the potential for
frequent misunderstanding between management and staff – particularly so in
large organizations. The Head of Corporate Communications at Lloyds/TSB
noted that 'it is very important that whatever the organization is trying to get
across gets down to people at the sharp end' – a view endorsed by the public
relations manager at Northumbria Ambulance. She sees employee relations 'as
the Cinderella part; but as important as external.' That importance was well

summed up by director of group public affairs at tobacco and financial services group B.A.T. Industries. He said that 'If you could find a company which has its act together internally, everything externally falls into place'; an opinion which underlines the point that the first step towards successful external communications is to get internal communications right.

> Organizations need to communicate complicated health and benefit packages, changes in (1) laws affecting employees and (2) the business environment. All these will impact upon the company in future. Many professionals believe that this is the critical area of corporate communications in this decade and, alas, many organizations take employees for granted. Once an organization has lost the faith and goodwill of its employees it faces an uphill battle. The Japanese have shown that getting employees involved in running the business leads to greatly improved productivity and creates an atmosphere of respect for all employees. The best way to achieve this is through good business communications.
>
>                                                          adapted from Argenti (1994)

## Employees – an integral element of good communications

As large organizations have undergone considerable change, there has been an increasing awareness of the need for overall consistency in the communications message. If employees are a precious organizational resource they must be listened to in the same way that other audiences are heard. Everyone within the corporation needs to be an integral part of an integrated and consistent internal and external communication process. White and Mazur (1995) report case studies which suggest a strong link between improved communication with employees and corporate performance – good internal communications must lead directly to improved competitive advantage.

## Significance of the internal audience

Lindo (1995) suggests four reasons why the internal audience might be important:

- Internal communication gives employees an interest in corporate objectives. The greater that interest the more likely employees are to be enthusiastic about the long term objectives of the corporation
- Internal communication enables an organization to gain acceptance for corporate policies and culture
- Internal communication provides a means by which the organization can win respect for the communication department
- Internal communication assists in establishing, maintaining and re-inforcing positive relationships with internal customers (as Lindo refers to them)

Lindo observes that internal communication amounts to a total communications effort – the aim of which is to inform and influence all the various internal publics. Quirke (writing in Hart, 1995) echoes this, saying that the flow of information and knowledge around the organization is crucial to success. He says that the role of communications as the process by which this is achieved is central to the management of the organization.

The communication executive of one major television station expressed the view that internal communication was a function of his department but was not an elemental part of corporate communications. He referred to it as 'A connotation to PR which is inherited from yesterday'; a view with which few other communication executives would agree.

> The need for internal communication increases by the day. Within organizations, people not only want more information, they want it faster. Organizations have long given lip-service to the idea that staff are their most important asset. Now a lot more of firms are doing something about it. In today's commercial climate – and almost every day someone announces that there is no longer such a thing as a job for life – staff feel very uncertain about their prospects. Accordingly, employees need information to put their minds at rest; not forgetting that insecurity increases considerably at the time of a merger or takeover.
>
> adapted from Gray (1996)

In a seminal piece of academic work in this field, Wright (1995) comments that too often employee communication is carried out by junior and inexperienced staff – suggesting that it might be an afterthought. Many senior executives say how much the approach to internal communications has changed since they first entered the communications field. Speaking of the time when he first joined Avon Rubber plc in 1972, their Group Promotions Manager recalled how the primary task then – and certainly that for which he was hired – was to give an external message. At that time, he continued, it was quite the normal thing to treat employees as second-class citizens. In fact, he said, the attitude towards communicating with employees was to 'Feed 'em shit and keep 'em in the dark.' Today, 40 per cent of the work of the communications department at Avon Rubber is devoted to communicating internally.

van Riel (1995) suggests that one of the manager's roles, in what he calls management communication, is to persuade colleagues that the goals of the organization are desirable. Yet, Wright (1995) claims that most communication authors ignore this importance. He quotes D'Aprix (1984) saying that 'one of the great ironies is the tendency to short-change the employee audiences in our organizations'. This is well summarized by the Director of Group Public Relations at Vaux:

> It would be supremely arrogant to impose decisions upon people.
> You see them first. You tell them about strategy before you go
> public on any major issue. This breeds commitment and loyalty. You
> go to your employees and tell them where you are and where you
> are going. It is critical to thank people. You must make people
> internally aware. That is the importance of good internal
> communications.

Today's high performance companies recognize that no organizational relationship is more important than that with employees. In fact, the then director of corporate affairs at Storehouse believes that the success of internal communication 'has its full reflection in the share price'.

> The communications industry has to stop thinking of internal
> communications as a branch of welfare and it needs to focus on
> ensuring that employees are not misunderstanding the corporate
> brand. Research reports that 50 per cent of employees say that they
> are not clear about what their company strategy is. However most
> employees will try to guess at what the corporate strategy should
> be – and they then act accordingly. 'People follow the strategy they
> believe to be right whether it is or not', said Quirke.
>
> adapted from *PR Week* (1997c)

As the communication manager at Avon and Somerset Police remarked, 'It is essential that you communicate your messages and themes. If staff do not provide good service it undermines your strategy. You have to make sure that you win the hearts and minds of your own people first. Do not tell the public something until you have told your employees; because the public is so important.'

Both J. Sainsbury and Storehouse echoed this, the former commenting that 'If your staff know what is going on they can follow a story through and see what their role has been in any particular project.' To this the practitioner at Storehouse added, 'It is important that our people project the values that we have ... in retail business anyone who deals with the public is in a public relations role. I regard this as a part of brand management.'

J. Sainsbury also regard internal communication as 'a way of motivating staff' and B.A.T. Industries (frequently the butt of hostile criticism because of their exposure to two controversial industries – tobacco and financial services) regard internal communication as 'a supporting and enabling process'.

> If you work in the tobacco business, where any company employee
> can suffer frightful grief, you must help your employees handle the
> criticism. Your employees are important ambassadors.
>
> Corporate Communications Director, B.A.T. Industries,
> in conversation with the author

This is a theme running continuously through many organizations that have undergone enormous change. 'It is now part of the culture that our managers and supervisors are meant to understand their ability to communicate', said the Head of Corporate Communications at Lloyds/TSB. He went on to add that 'public relations is practised by our branches. That is where our PR people are.'

'We make heroes of people,' said the then director of corporate affairs at Storehouse. 'Employees are the best ambassadors for any company', remarked the communication manager at Tennent Caledonian Breweries. As noted, a number of organizations refer to their employees as 'ambassadors'. However, the Director of Corporate Communications at Whitbread remarked on the very real danger 'in seeing your people as potential ambassadors for your organization and giving them only good messages'. He remarked that it was 'really very important that internal communications were not just concerned with gloss', saying, 'I feel very, very strongly about this.'

> Most professionals are capable of communicating with a wide variety of audiences, whilst others specialize in only one area, such as employee relations. A specialist of this nature can impact on a company's bottom line by improving employee morale, thereby increasing productivity and decreasing absenteeism.
>
> Johnson (1994)

The strategic purpose of internal communications is to improve staff morale and thereby to increase competitive advantage. Undoubtedly 'internal communication plays a role in the idea of good service ... good service output is critical', commented the Director of Group Public Relations at Vaux Brewery. At Storehouse, where the corporate affairs function is concerned only with financial communications and internal communications, the then director was able to remark that 'at Mothercare we have a reputation for being more knowledgeable about the mother and her baby needs'.

There are internal communication specialists – the Halifax Building Society is an example of an organization with a separate internal communications director. Strategies for the internal audience differ greatly from one typology of organization to another. Communications may well be an organization's competitive edge in tomorrow's market place; carefully tailored internal communication programmes will play a key role in the process.

# Stakeholders – who and where are they?

> Stakeholders is a concept that we feel uncomfortable with – you cannot be accountable to everyone.
>
> Director of Corporate Affairs, Boots plc,
> in conversation with the author

Some external publics assert their self-interests by seeking and granting stakes. A stake is something that an individual desires to have and it is something that can be given or withheld. Thus, a stakeholder is anyone who has a stake in the success of the organization and implicit in the nature of the stakeholder relationship is that there is the concept of interdependency (Hart, 1995). Few audiences have assumed as much importance for communicators and politicians alike as this new constituency. The sound practices of stakeholder management – understanding others' concerns, listening, collaborating – are integral to managing an organization's image and reputation (Post and Griffin, 1997).

Stakeholders are one example of that growing number of publics towards which successful organizations target their communication programmes; yet their existence is questioned by some and their significance debated by others. Many corporations are uncertain where they are or how they should be approached. Organizations no longer have to justify their actions only to shareholders, the internal audience and consumers. They face an ever growing demand to be seen to be practising high corporate standards of behaviour in all the markets in which they operate.

All those who have relationships are dependent upon one another and have expectations of each other. Because of this it is important that the organization understands the issues that are important to stakeholders for they may well impact upon an organization's strategies and performance. Indeed the achievement of sustained competitive advantage might well depend upon successful communication with key stakeholders.

Defining stakeholders has become one of the most difficult problems facing the communication executive (Brody, 1988). Brody suggests that they are 'those groups of individuals whose interests coincide in one or more ways with the organization with which the communication practitioner is dealing'. Corporate stakeholders – legislators, regulatory bodies, specialist interest groups, political groups, women's organizations, health and safety groups, consumer activists, environmentalists (who have become a major force in many parts of the globe), local police, even agitators – are all fresh publics for an organization and the perceptions and opinions of each and every one has to be understood.

Certainly companies have become aware that their organization must incorporate a consciousness of – and attention to – those who believe rightly or wrongly that they have a stake in the organization. This has become unavoidable with so many political, social and ethical influences bearing down upon their corporate performance; not to mention the impact of intervention from aggressive pressure groups.

Through their actions, rhetoric and graphics, organizations seek to communicate with stakeholders. They do this to identify with them and to show that they understand their concerns. They try to communicate in ways which develop a relationship with them – for organizations face an ever growing demand that they should behave as good corporate citizens.

> What I can say is that open and direct communication with all its stakeholders is more important for an airline than for almost any other business.
>
> Marshall (1997)

Communication executives need to have a far wider knowledge of socio-economic concerns than ever before. More sophisticated and well managed corporations have long realized that ecological and environmental issues impact on their operations and that a key element of their task will involve successful communications with all those groups that might put the organization under pressure in some way.

Fombrun and van Riel (1997) suggest that firms with strong, coherent cultures and identities are more likely to engage in systematic efforts to influence the perceptions of stakeholders; but the views of professionals concerning stakeholders vary widely. There are some practitioners like the Director of Corporate Communications at Whitbread who do believe in the 'stakeholder principle'. The then Acting Director of Corporate Affairs at W.H. Smith held the same view but opined that 'the order of importance of individual groups of stakeholders varies according to the time of the year'.

Some companies understand the impact that their organization has on its immediate locality and appreciate that local residents feel they have a stake in the organization. (Consider the recent impact on the town of Halifax of the conversion into a fully fledged bank of the Halifax Building Society – a large proportion of the residents of the town were stakeholders in the society.) A large international company, Avon Rubber (based in a small country town in rural Wiltshire), feels that 'Avon is a huge company in this part of the world'. Accordingly, it recognizes the principle of stakeholders and has regard for its responsibilities to the communities in which its businesses are located.

Some organizations accept the principle of stakeholders as an audience but are less than comfortable with it. It is up to the organization to ensure that all stakeholders have a realistic image of what they can and cannot expect (de Segundo, 1997). Boots is a big presence in the City of Nottingham, just as Avon Rubber is in Bradford-on-Avon. Boots has an equal record of caring for those whose interests it shares. However, its Director of Corporate Affairs notes that 'Stakeholders is a concept that we feel uncomfortable with; you cannot be accountable to everyone.' He added, 'It is important that the Nottingham community understands that the organization cannot spend money indiscriminately.'

Other companies, B.A.T. Industries is one example, are untroubled by the concept, simply finding that, at group level, 'stakeholders are not one of our audiences'.

# A vast new global audience

In an era of increasing globalization there is firm evidence that an ever growing number of organizations have to address an international audience. As the number of truly global companies grows daily the international community has become the latest public. Communicators who successfully create cross-border communications are in the vanguard of those who enable their organizations to present a coherent and consistent communication programme.

> An investment of effort up-front is needed in (1) deciding those common themes that may transcend national borders and (2) coming to grips with the national and regional cultural variations that influence markets. So your communication strategy just has to be developed at an international level.
>
> adapted from Lancaster (1995)

The communication executive faces a real problem with this new constituency. International communications are necessarily also intercultural. Different countries have different national, cultural and behavioural characteristics. Accordingly this vast new global public is a fast developing specialism. It is a part of the communication strategy that has to be tailored to meet local conditions, cultures and practices. Avon Rubber regards it as a prime and fast growing public, for a majority of their factories are overseas. Sometimes when an organization needs to be involved in an issue abroad it hires overseas consultants to act for it – they will understand the cultural and local conditions better. International communications are discussed in greater detail in a later chapter.

> One has to ask what people in the media think Hyundai is about? Their answer might be bargain-basement prices. However, people who buy Hyundai cars do not see themselves as bargain basement buyers. Hyundai owners consider that the treatment they receive and the reliability of their car are much more important than the initial cost. In a way this summarizes the problem with international communications. Countries not only have different national and cultural characteristics, they are also made up of different consumer segments. If you do not attempt to follow an international communications strategy without taking into account local interpretations your organization risks communications suicide.
>
> adapted from Kitson, quoted in Miles (1995a)

# The financial publics

Many management scholars suggest that financial publics have assumed a critical importance – certainly communicating with them has become more significant. It is now widely understood that communicating with financial publics has an increasing impact on corporate strategy. The financial audience may be subdivided into:

- the City – including analysts
- the financial media
- institutional investors and private investors.

> The high street group, Storehouse, has announced the appointment of a new director of corporate affairs to replace Richard Dixon, who has retired after eight years with the company.
>
> Mr Stephen Pain will join the company in November and he will be responsible for building the Bhs and Mothercare brands. The corporate relations role at Storehouse concentrates primarily on investor relations and analyst communications. Internal communication is another core function.
>
> The communications challenge for Storehouse must be to regain credibility with the finanicial community for this is a year in which its share price has dropped by 33 per cent.
>
> adapted from Bailey (1997)

To Storehouse, 'Shareholders are the most important group.' Their then Director of Corporate Affairs commented that 'Investor relations is by far the most important audience that the Group has.' Boots' Director of Corporate Affairs remarked that 'From a Group perspective the investment audience is the most important.' Accordingly, communicating with the City is a specialism that is too significant to be treated lightly, for without communication with the City a major corporation may lack credibility in the eyes of this key audience.

The financial audience is now established as one of fundamental importance and is dealt with in many different ways, by many different organizations. The Director of Corporate Communications at Whitbread remarked, 'Most senior communication executives regard financial communications as significant.' He continued 'The ultimate measure is the share price,' which, he said, 'I watch all the time.' The Director of Group Public Relations at Vaux echoed this, saying 'It is important that views are given to brokers and analysts so that they understand corporate strategy . . . the share price can fall or rise according to the perspective created by communications. Shareholders are a key audience.' This point was summarized well by the Director of Corporate Communications at Whitbread: 'Essentially shareholders own the place,' adding, 'the confidence of shareholders is fundamental.'

Financial communications are considered in some depth in a later chapter.

# The media – is it the number one audience?

> Creating good relations with the media requires constant effort and attention; but forward thinking organizations developed strong relationships with the media.
>
> Goodman (1994)

In the past some academics might have considered the media as the most critical public for a professional communicator. Certainly, 'Good media coverage can help you beyond your wildest dreams' (Jackson, 1995). Nowadays no organization can afford to ignore the potential concerns of the general public, consumers and other stakeholders in their operating policies. The media offer their audiences a perspective every time they refer to the activities of an organization. Key management must appreciate just how significant the media can be and the role that they play in how the organization is perceived by key constituents.

> The press will do its job with or without your company's help and a little co-operation goes a long way. To be able to co-operate in an appropriate manner, there first has to be a knowledge of the media as an audience that most often serves as a conduit for reaching various audiences. You have to understand how to use the media.
>
> Flanagan (1995)

In years gone by, the media may have been considered the main audience. L. A. Grunig (1992) suggested that communication practitioners might well come to regard communities, government agencies, stockholders and financial analysts, employees, labour unions, competitors, suppliers, clients and pressure groups as at least as important as the media. In 1998, they certainly do so; but the media remains a significant audience. The then Acting Director of Corporate Affairs for W.H. Smith admitted that, in the past, 'There was a feeling that you avoided talking to the press ... a bunker mentality. The company felt that they were out to get us. This is definitely changing.'

> It becomes increasingly pointless to practise fortress building and leak prevention. It demands a rethinking of how to deal with a hungry and amazingly diverse collection of journalists who

themselves have audiences to satisfy . . . it is no good hoping that
the media will go away.

White and Mazur (1995)

The media will find and follow up stories whether an organization likes it or whether it does not. Therefore, it works to the advantage of the communication executive to develop good relations with them; they will probe for weak spots, will see through things that are false, and come up with a story that can impact on corporate reputation and activities (White and Mazur, 1995). An organization that chooses not to be accessible may well end up with a poor reputation by default and certainly the media will not be well disposed towards it. The development of trust between an organization and the media is of vital importance. It is a relationship that can only be built up over time and will serve both interests well.

With the exception of more traditional companies such as Wm. Morrisson and Avon Rubber, there is a general understanding at the top of industry that good media relations do pay off – especially so where corporations desire to communicate the culture and persona of a complex organization, perhaps when the company is not easily understood.

Many of the largest corporations have separate media sections within their communication departments. British Airways are very pro-active in this area and is an example of a global organization that has a large media operation. It is one in which all staff are former journalists. Peter Jones, then Director of Public Affairs with BA, now filling a similar role at BUPA, commented that this situation might be unique. He explained that this situation arose for historical origins, rather than from some deep philosophical position. But he added that it was a help rather than a hindrance because former journalists are better equipped 'To suss out a good story and to be able to place it to the advantage of the organization . . . and to see a negative story coming.' He said 'A good journalist knows how to defend well as a journalist.' Jones made the point that his journalists are trained to find good stories from within the company's activities and to sell them to the external publics. In short, they are always on the lookout for a good in-house story they can turn to the company's competitive advantage.

The importance of good media communications, particularly in the context of complex organizations, is without doubt. Media relations are a vital part of the communication process. Those organizations that are household names understand the significance of excellent media relations. The Director, Corporate Affairs at GlaxoWellcome described it as 'crucial'.

## Opinion formers

Over the last ten years opinion formers have become a new and highly significant constituency. The work of the communication executive is heavily drawn towards this audience, for one of the most important functions of the corporate communicator is to provide an opinion barometer for corporate management – scanning the environment and tracking those issues which may impact upon the organization.

Nine out of every ten senior communicators regard opinion formers as a public of the utmost significance. The following are typical comments:

- This audience is deeply important
- I consider this public constantly
- I consider this audience all the time
- Considering this public is ALL I DO
- I regard this public second only to employees.

The practitioner at London Transport referred to opinion formers as 'The main focus of my job.' British Telecom spoke of them as 'very, very important – second only to employees'. Storehouse (which concentrates on internal and financial communication to the exclusion of almost all else) added 'There are issues that I will take on board – Greenpeace are having a campaign over the use of PVC. This issue has wide group connotation. I am very involved in the group's strategy.'

## Customers and consumers

> My firm belief is that the customer and customer service must be absolutely at the forefront of every business activity; and that the key to success is the setting up of a dynamic relationship based obviously on communication.
>
> Marshall (1997)

The layman might assume that consumers are an audience of prime importance. In reality customers and consumers are not regarded as a priority public by most organizations. They do not rank as the first, or the second, or the third audience. They could, of course, count as a duplicate public; increasingly critical and sophisticated consumers may well number among opinion formers as well as among consumers.

Consumer communication has evolved from being a narrow specialist function to one that plays a key role in the formulation of corporate strategy. It is sometimes referred to by marketing people as *relationship marketing*. Accordingly, it is no surprise that two supermarkets do regard customers as very important indeed. Wm. Morrisson regard them as the premier audience; J. Sainsbury commented that, 'as Tesco smartened up a bit', there was a need for good communications to be used to help them consolidate their position with their customers. Sainsbury remarked that they are using communication to emphasize their competitive advantage. This is an approach frequently used to reinforce marketing communications. It is aimed at developing not only commercial relationships with, but also the understanding of, customers. Consumer communications can take many forms and are used with increasing sophistication, for example, consumers can now log on to Carling Black Label Lager on the Internet at www.fa-carling.com

# Government and politicians

Relationships with government at both macro and micro levels are often referred to as *public affairs* or *corporate affairs*, and sometimes as *political affairs* or *government relations*. This is another area of management science where definitions both among academics and professional communicators are unclear, and, perhaps, a little confusing. Some communication professionals dismiss communicating with this audience as 'lobbying'. Some organizations spend much time soliciting support from government departments, which they seek to influence – what the Americans call the 'politics of the pork barrel' (i.e. performing actions in exchange for political favours). Lobbying is referred to in more detail in another chapter.

Some practitioners who specialize in communicating with government, especially at macro level, consider that theirs is a superior craft (compared to those involved with consumer or media audiences, which are historically associated more with publicity). Communication executives who function in this specialized area need a deep understanding and familiarity with the ways that both national and local government works.

Both national and local government are an important audience to the majority of organizations. Botan (1992) reports that many African countries see government as the primary audience. Communication with government at macro level may be concerned primarily with developing policies which in turn might impact profoundly on the organization. It may involve dealing with the constantly increasing amount of intervention and regulation of commercial activities. These policies may impact upon the way in which the organization is authorized to operate – this is particularly relevant to organizations like B.A.T. Industries, which has major subsidiaries in the heavily regulated financial services sector. Among other examples are organizations such as British Airways and London Transport, both of which are subject to much regulation and to policies that can impact directly upon profitability (and, in the instance of BA, on competitive advantage).

> In 1983 a takeover bid was made for the British fine arts auction house Sotheby's. The company, in a widely reported move, which brought public affairs practitioners to prominence in the UK, used lobbying effectively to have the bid referred to the Monopolies and Mergers Commission. This had the effect of killing the bid and protecting the company's interests.
>
> White and Mazur (1995)

## Corporate abstention

One matter little addressed by management scholars is corporate abstention. Some corporations – among them international corporations – ignore their publics altogether. A number of firms, Lonrho is one example, have no in-house practitioners. These organizations call on help from outside consultants if they feel they need assistance with communications. This approach (clearly stemming from the top) may demonstrate the general perception of the CEO and the executive committee of the communication function. It also demonstrates the corporate view of the real power of strategic communication.

> Surprising as it is there are still a number of quite large companies that prefer not to lift the veil on what they are doing. Great Universal Stores, one of the fifteen companies in the FTSE-100 which does not retain a consultant, has a reputation for reticence. Some companies retain consultants, but use them to act as a buffer between themselves and the press. Other firms prefer to maintain a low profile, believing that when their financial results are good they provide adequate evidence that the corporation has performed well.
>
> adapted from Davis (1995)

Evidentially, some companies make no attempt to promote themselves with key publics. This is their strategy in spite of the apparently overwhelming evidence that a favourable corporate reputation is a pre-condition for creating a sound corporate foundation on which to build competitive advantage. One has only has to consider some of the colossal public relation blunders of recent times:

- British Gas – Cedric Brown's salary
- Cunard – QE2 repairs
- Hoover – US air ticket promotion

to wonder why some corporations are, apparently, unconcerned with or unworried about corporate reputation; or perhaps they simply lack common sense (which is a rare enough commodity as it is, in the opinion of the author).

One in ten organizations make no appreciable attempt to communicate with external audiences. The then Director of Corporate Affairs of the Mothercare/ Bhs holding group, Storehouse, commented quite frankly that his company had no corporate promotion at all – a commercial approach echoed by global rubber company, Avon Rubber.

Avon noted that they had made no investment in national communication or promotion since 1977. Their group publicity manager remarked, with obvious regret and frustration, that his organization 'had not promoted itself at all' in that time. He added that his organization had 'a good story to tell', but that the story had not been told to any external organization 'for whatever reason'. He commented how very strongly he felt that a company of Avon's size should have an annual corporate campaign. He emphasized that many people would simply not be aware that 'Every house in the country contains at least one Avon Rubber product.' His company is one of the few organizations that could justifiably make such a claim – yet few people will be aware of the fact. Such is the effect of *not* communicating with one's audiences.

> 3M's public relations people chose to promote an understanding of their company with a new corporate identity strategy. Many people only associate 3M with Scotch Tape and floppy disks. But 3M believe that many of their customers may not know that the company is involved with many diverse industries and no less than 66,000 products. Such lack of information about the company and its products could, 3M felt, be a real corporate liability.
>
> adapted from Skolnik (1994)

Corporate identity (discussed in the next chapter) is the presentation of a clear picture showing what a company is and what it aims to be. It requires the integration of advertising, internal communications, packaging and literature. This is a strategic approach that must be developed through every layer of management, for people have come to realize that the various instruments of communication will have to be integrated better (Nessmann, 1995). There is abundant evidence that communicating with key constituencies gives added value to overall competitive advantage. Corporate strategy can only benefit if an integrated approach is used in doing so.

## *Case study*

# On successfully communicating with an audience – the media

### American Airlines – giving corporate communications a flying start

Communication departments have suffered, just as other functional departments have suffered, from the general restructuring that has affected the airline industry worldwide over the past decade. For those externally, this has meant less access to airline executives and fewer opportunities to understand an airline's internal workings. For those on the inside the result of this downsizing is that the corporate message may have been destroyed – because there may be fewer writers to craft it and messengers to deliver it.

Fortunately, this has not happened at American Airlines and its parent AMR Corp. Under MD-Corporate Communications, Timothy J. Doke, the company employs a large communication staff comprised of enthusiastic and highly capable people – all of whom speak with authority about all aspects of the airline's activities including technical, operational, marketing, cargo and financial subjects.

The department numbers about one hundred employees, of whom forty-five deal specifically with the media. The airline maintains communication offices in Dallas, Chicago, and Miami; as well as in Europe.

The philosophy of American Airlines is that working with the news media is a whole lot better than working against them; accordingly, the corporate communication department puts this belief into practice every working day. In addition, the airline management believes profoundly that the communication function is an essential core component of the corporation. Accordingly, the department participates in the decision making process at the highest levels.

American's communication staff do an excellent job in conveying American's thoughts on pressing issues to the media. Whether you agree with them or not, it is never difficult to identify American's views on current issues.

Of course, this willingness to communicate works in both directions. American goes out of its way to make its officials available to the press; both on a formal and informal basis; and each year the communication department organizes a visit to a city served by the airline so that key executives can meet the local media.

In addition to all that, American goes the extra mile helping journalists to understand the dynamics of the airline industry. It hosts an annual Media Day – actually 1½ days – consisting of seminars and discussions on the workings of the airline and of the airline industry as a whole.

The communication department peppers the press with position papers, consultants' resports, newspaper articles and speeches by senior airline executives – all of which reflect American's thoughts on issues that are important to itself and to the industry.

American also publishes a quarterly Corporate Fact Book that provides a wealth of statistical and analytical information about the airline's operations; and it provides an annual crisis management manual for use by its executives, outlining the airline's media relations philosophy. This provides guidance to managers, allowing them to talk directly with reporters in the event of an emergency.

Interestingly, American is one of very few airlines that maintains its own staff aviation photographers.

American also observes an aviation esprit de corps. This is exemplified by its anniversary's celebrations which mark important dates in the airline's development as well as its commitment to remembering the past. In 1993 American opened the $8.7m C.R. Smith Museum which includes a fully restored DC-3 among its exhibits. The musuem was funded through gifts from nearly 12 500 employees as well as through donations from more than one hundred corporations. It stands as a monument to an aviation pioneer and to one of the world's greatest airlines.

American's commitment to the future, and pride in its heritage, sends very powerful messages to its stakeholders saying that it believes in the importance of commercial aviation. Its corporate communication department does a superb job conveying this message. In doing so it also proves that good public relations are a benefit to any company.

adapted from *Air Transport World* (1995)

# Key terms

**CEO**   Chief Executive Officer, Managing Director. The senior executive responsible for running an organization from day to day.

**THE CITY**   Generic term for the major financial centre in a major country (e.g. The City of London).

**COMPANY SECRETARY**   Officer of an organization who is ultimately responsible for the legal and administrative functions.

**CONSTITUENCIES**   See Audiences, External and Internal.

**CORPORATE COMMUNICATIONS**   Communications between a corporation or other large organization and its internal and external audiences – the purpose of which is to create greater understanding for, and perception of, the ideals and purposes of the organization.

**CUSTOMERS**   Those groups of people who purchase the goods or services offered for sale by an organization.

**EXTERNAL AUDIENCE**   Those groups with whom an organization desires to communicate that are external to the organization.

**EXTERNAL CONSULTANTS**   Those who offer a specialized professional service in particular disciplines (e.g. communications) who are independent of the organization and who are hired by the corporation to provide those services on a fee-paying basis.

**FINANCIAL COMMUNICATIONS**   Those external communications concerned with sending a financial message to (a) the City, (b) shareholders, (c) financial analysts.

**FINANCIAL DIRECTOR**   Senior officer of the corporation responsible for the finance function – 'The Treasurer' in the USA.

**INTERNAL AUDIENCE**   Those groups with whom an organization desires to communicate that are an internal component of the organization (e.g. staff, colleagues).

**OPINION FORMERS**   Growing external audience made up of those who have a direct interest in an organization and who have opinions to express about it which may affect its commercial well being.

**PUBLICS**   See Audiences, External and Internal.

**STAKEHOLDERS**   Those external to an organization who are not stockholders but who nevertheless – and for a whole variety of different reasons – have come to feel that they have a stake in the enterprise. Sometimes referred to as the shadow constituency, because one cannot always be certain who they are or where they are.

# Chapter 3

# Corporate identity – the role and value of corporate identity programmes

Changing a corporate image can be fraught with difficulty for it is not easy to persuade the media to appreciate the finer details of corporate repositioning. It can be even more difficult to get consumers to understand why an image change needs to cost millions of pounds. BA added to its communication problems with its decision to stop flying the flag on its entire fleet, except Concorde.

The move by BA to replace the Union Flag with bold 'images of the world' won praise for its commercial foresight and for a distinctly more international feel from much of the media. However, the minders of British patriotism – the *Sun* and the *Daily Telegraph* – were not impressed. Both a reader poll in the *Sun* and an indignant *Telegraph* editorial sparked a storm of hostile letters from readers.

Filtering the 'white noise' of letters revealed a media broadly understanding and supporting BA's bid to be seen as a global airline – and leaving the *Sun* and the *Telegraph* isolated. They obviously had not heard BA's new strapline – 'the world is closer than you think'.

adapted from *PR Week* (1997d)

# Introduction

We now consider the essential differences between corporate identity and corporate image. We note that promoting corporate identity is one of the vital tasks of the corporate communicator and that transmitting the desired perception of an organization has become an essential part of corporate strategy. Few management subjects are more confused than corporate identity and corporate image; writers often refer to them interchangeably. Although the two can sometimes be one and the same (the image *may* match the identity), in many cases the image of the corporation is sharply different from its actual actuality. How corporate identity reveals itself – and how it mirrors the way in which an organization desires to be seen by its audiences – is discussed. We note that in the course of corporate communication, the image can become blurred or distorted. As a result, publics sometimes question whether the image matches the reality. We note some of the tools and mechanisms used in shaping corporate identity and how important it is to keep that identity under constant review and, where necessary, to bring it up to date.

# Defining corporate identity

## Confusion

> What is still remarkable is the extent to which people agree on the importance of corporate identity yet differ in their definition of what it is. It is almost as if corporate identity is something that fills a vacuum.
>
> Ludlow in Ind (1992), quoted by Balmer (1997)

van Riel (1995) drew attention to his finding that virtually no one knew exactly what corporate identity meant. Balmer (1997) notes the confusion that persists regarding the nature of corporate identity; a view echoed by van Rekom (1993), who observed that an unambiguous, generally agreed definition of corporate identity does not exist.

## No accepted definition

Most writers agree that there is no accepted definition for corporate identity. There is, however, a clear difference between identity and image and they should not be used interchangeably. That difference is fundamental to an understanding of corporate communication and to the successful performance of the corporate strategist.

## Difference between identity and image

Identity is how the organization really is. Identity concerns the presentation of the corporate persona. Image is what the organization *appears to be* – the identity having been established and communicated to various audiences. Unlike image, identity does not change from one audience to another. Until such time as it is altered, it remains consistent. One of the fundamental issues facing a communicator is whether it is more important for the communication practitioner to convey the organization's identity to its publics; or to convey the image to them.

Balmer (1997) notes the number of writers who have argued that the key distinguishing feature of an organization's identity is its corporate personality. There is the underlying presumption that the corporation has worked out how it does wish to be seen. There is also a presumption that it cares about how its audiences see it. There are instances where neither is the case. However, most organizations do assert a persona to which external publics react either positively, negatively or indifferently. van Riel (1995) suggests that identity is associated with the way in which a company presents itself to various publics, whereas Albert and Whettan (1985) propose that it can be defined as those organizational characteristics that are most central, enduring and distinctive – in short its innate character (Balmer, 1997).

Corporate image, however, is the way in which various audiences see an organization. Corporate identity is not just corporate image. The image is the perception that audiences have of an organization based on the identity as it is communicated. Image, van Raaij (1986) suggests, is a form of favourable impression management amongst target audiences. Identity concerns the individuality of the organization – the way that it actually is – in short, corporate personality. If you understand the personality you understand the identity.

Goodman (1994) believes that companies which enjoy a positive image in the minds of the public and their own employees are generally good companies. In short that the identity and the image are not too far apart from one another. If communicators succeed in their task the image and the identity may be one and the same. Argenti (1994) considers that communicating image and identity is the most critical aspect of any corporate communicator's work. He believes that determining how a firm wants to be perceived with different audiences, and how it chooses to identify itself, is the first function of corporate communications.

Accredited academic and professional journals regularly confuse identity and image. Balmer (1997) suggests seven reasons for uncertainty surrounding the subject of corporate identity (a management area which he suggests empirical research has largely failed to address):

- confusion caused by terminology
- influence of fashion

- association with graphic design
- limited amount of academic research
- lack of dialogue between researchers
- inappropriateness of the positivistic research paradigm
- weaknesses in available models.

## Creation of identity

A corporation is an artificial person in law. Thus its identity necessarily is created. That identity is experienced through everything that an organization says, makes or does; accordingly, it is experienced through total corporate communications. Management academics are increasingly aware that in order for the organization to secure a favourable corporate image and reputation they must (a) know and (b) manage their organization's identity (Balmer, 1997). Both reputation and identity are definitions of organizations from the perspectives of outsiders and insiders respectively (Fiol and Kovoor-Misra, 1997). Organizational identity is thus created as part of a corporate plan by communication strategists. Once created that identity is encoded by communication executives and transmitted to key publics.

Identity is what makes up the corporation and how it behaves. In exactly the same way as humans are unique in some way, an organization is unique and cannot be replicated. It is those singular qualities of the organization that shape and make its identity. Every organization has its own persona and many make a conscious attempt to communicate that individuality – with all it nuances – to key constituencies.

# Revealing the identity

## Identity revealed through strategic communication policies

Corporate identity is revealed through organizational communication policies. Organizations define strategies in order to solve external adaptation and internal integration problems. The ability to create external images and internal identities depends on strategic decisions enacted to make sense out of the present and the future (Marziliano, 1997). Strategic communication policies involve a long-term view of how the organization wishes to be judged by its key constituencies; so, inevitably, they reflect how an organization actually sees itself. It may wish to be seen as powerful, or as the brand leader in its market, or simply as the maker of the most reliable car on the market or, as was the case with BOAC (British Overseas Airways Corporation) simply the airline that 'took good care of you'.

## Importance of the mission statement

There is a core proposition in the identity literature that a person's response to an identity crisis yields highly reliable insights into his or her identity (Elsbach and Kramer, 1996). The first communication policy must be the creation of the corporate mission statement – the first formal act in the development of an organization's identity (Goodman, 1994); this defines the corporation, its goals and its operational principles. Until quite recently, many people thought of corporate identity in connection with the way that the organization used symbols to represent itself. These were often used with the intention of creating a good first impression.

## Use of various tools

In this era of global markets corporate identity is concerned not just with symbols. It involves every way in which an organization communicates. It also concerns the way in which it behaves. Accordingly, an organization communicates corporate identity to its various publics using a variety of tools. It is communicated with the intent of transmitting a corporate philosophy in tune with the organization's overall strategic plan.

# The sense of self

Identity equates to a corporate sense of self – all those qualities and characteristics that make an organization unique; its history, beliefs and philosophies – it is the very backbone of reputation (Fombrun, 1996). Identity is not something cosmetic, it is the core of an organization's existence (Hart, 1995). A well-established identity is hard to change. Corporate communication is the process that translates the identity into an image.

Investors are a critical audience. Institutions are not likely to consider risking capital if the integrity of the organization is questioned or if the corporate personality appears flawed. In the same way customers are more likely to trust a corporation that displays a clear identity and inspires their confidence.

The corporate identity must be monitored and updated continuously. By adopting a new identity an organization can altogether change its relationships with key publics (Fiol and Kovoor-Misra, 1997). It can alter the perception that key publics have of the organization – for example from being perceived as a national corporation to being seen as a global organization. Brand names must be part of a clear policy for strategic corporate identity. If the organization offers different goods or services under different names it must have a clear corporate identity policy.

# Integrating corporate identity into the communication process

> As a communicator, each company seeks to combine many efforts so that they speak as one, with one persona in one Voice . . . that outcome assumes that what employees do and say will be similar and complementary.
>
> Heath (1994)

A sharply honed and co-ordinated message communicates the identity of the organization to key publics to whom an organization needs to send clear messages. Thus the corporate message needs to be well integrated. The effectiveness of the message is influenced considerably by the level of co-operation between those at the decision-making table. The process inevitably enhances the credibility and reputation of the corporation. The message must be well integrated with both internal and external communication. A strong sense of corporate identity (here Virgin Atlantic Airline is a good example) is likely to impact favourably on *esprit de corps* within an organization.

# Transmitting the identity

Messages are received as well as sent. A skilled communication executive recognizes that the recipient will use both eyes and ears to decode the various communications that are transmitted. From these messages the recipient forms an image of the organization and this image represents the recipient's perception of the organization. The experienced and skilled communicator uses symbols, communication and behaviour as a mix in conveying the identity of the organization. All play a part in the communication strategy, which is concerned – at least in part – in the transmission of an organization's identity.

The strategy may fail to transmit a good image. If it does not succeed – if the perceived image of the organization is poor – audiences *still have an image of the organization*. But the received image may well not be that which the communication strategy intended in the first place.

Corporate identity is demonstrated in the various ways by which an organization reveals itself. It does this through the use of the following.

### 1 Symbols
A sign that causes one to feel, or to behave, in a certain way may be called a symbol. There has been much recent interest amongst management scholars into the use by organizations of symbols for the purpose of building harmony with stakeholders (Heath, 1994).

A symbol is a powerful corporate tool. Its strength lies in the increased attention that it may attract to the communications output. A symbol can convey a signal to those to whom it is communicated – in effect a short, sharp message. This can cause the recipient to recall something instantly. This process can bypass a long message from an organization and it can convey something that the company is trying to communicate in a very simple, quick form.

Symbols are signs that are intended to reflect the way in which an organization wishes to be pictured by its audiences. The Holiday Inn signs assures a home from home anywhere in the world. Symbols are signs with which the organization seeks to communicate images to audiences: images that strengthen and support its activities. When we speak of symbols we are considering:

- the corporate name
- logos
- colours
- icons
- heraldry
- flags
- brand marks
- corporate headquarters
- employee uniforms.

The corporate logo can be a powerful tool. It is a symbol whose value lies in the associations that people attach to it (Hart, 1995). It needs to be crafted with special care, for by giving a non-verbal message it seeks to convey the spirit and culture of an organization, for identity and culture are related. Identity describes core, enduring and distinctive features of a firm that produce shared interpretations among managers about how they should accommodate to external circumstances (Albert and Whettan, 1985). The logo sets out to explain the organization and to demonstrate what it has to offer to all its various audiences. It should reflect accurately the character and the ethos of an organization and the way in which it desires to be perceived by its constituents.

If the identity of the corporation is not recognized immediately, the logo has performed graphic communication badly. A new logo can result in a shift in the way that people perceive an audience; but it cannot of itself change the organization. White and Mazur (1995) note at least one company reacting to a take-over threat with a change of logo. They also report that, with the change of identity and name from British Telecom to BT, that corporation was signalling its determination to become a major player in the fast-growing global telecommunications market.

House style can be important. House style promotes a collegiate feeling. It helps employees to have a feeling that they belong. It assists in giving them a sense of recognition. It also enables the organization to increase its self-esteem and self-awareness. House style can impact considerably, creating a feeling amongst employees for consistent high quality performance.

Many symbols are referred to as being *cognitive*, that is to say they convey a meaning about which one thinks consciously and which then causes audience members to act in a certain way.

## 2 Communication

As noted communication involves both verbal and visual messages.

## 3 Behaviour

This relates to what the organization does and the way in which it does it. At the end of the day an organization is judged by what it does.

These three identity carriers taken together produce the identity of an organization; they represent the personality of the organization and the totality of all its desired perceptions.

# The types of corporate identity

A problem faced by many companies is whether or not to keep all communication under one roof. A complex multinational organization, for example, may well have many separate divisions. So, should corporate communication emerge from corporate headquarters – with a clearly focused identity for the whole – or should it be decentralized, so that subsidiaries are able to have their own perceived identities?

Ind (1992) suggests that organizations rarely attend much to this issue and that where they do not do so there can certainly be confusion. He notes this because communications that originate from a subsidiary may not be identified with the parent company (Hart, 1995). If communications are under one roof it is easier for the organization to maintain consistency of the message. On the other hand a decentralized approach does allow subsidiary companies to respond to the specific needs of the local audiences and to develop cultural factors pertaining to the local business.

Olins (1989) distinguishes three kinds of corporate identity:

## 1 Monolithic

Here the whole corporation uses one visual style. It is a style that is recognized instantly – all goods and services are associated with a known reputation. It is a style employed where the corporation is in a narrow field of activity and where tight guidelines are imposed from the top. It is a style enabling economies of communication and a consistent message. Lloyds/TSB is an example. Its present identity was established almost 30 years ago – at the sign of the black horse – it is an identity which you see wherever Lloyds Bank is represented in the world, as residents of New Zealand are very well aware.

## 2 Endorsed identity

In this typology the parent company remains pre-eminent; but the subsidiary companies each have a recognizable identity with their own style – culture – traditions and brands. This is well illustrated by Bass plc. Their subsidiaries (of which Tennent Caledonian Breweries is one example) all have their own style and the individual history of each is very much impressed upon the local audience. In this typology, financial communication is typically dealt with at holding company level. Tennent Caledonian not only have a distinct (and very effective) identity but they also have brands that are unique to the company.

## 3 Branded identity

Here subsidiaries have their own style and the parent company is not recognizable. Brands have no relation to each other and indeed compete with one another. Olins (1989) gives Unilever as an example of this typology; certainly it is typical of fast-moving consumer goods and conglomerates like Lonrho and Williams Holdings.

# The importance of corporate identity

People learn to identify with a company by noting everything that it does. A company's identity may be one of few things that differentiate it from another. The impression that Tesco gives of being innovative, customer oriented and not complacent could be critically important. It is the communication executive who has the responsibility for conveying these impressions to key audiences.

Referring to the mergers and acquisitions of the 1980s, and the downsizing and restructuring that have followed in the 1990s, Goodman (1994) notes that changes and upheavals have treated corporate reputation roughly – making the need to develop an excellent corporate identity more important than ever to an organization's survival. In the 1960s Watney's had the reputation for being a brewer that produced fizzy, tasteless beer (witness Watney's brand keg Red Barrel), and for years the company was identified with such a product.

A communication executive has to develop a programme for corporate identity that not only is coherent but also encapsulates what the organization believes it stands for. That identity needs to represent how employees feel about the organization and how the customers and investors wish it to be perceived. It is a process of giving the organization confidence in itself and of inspiring the confidence of its various publics.

# The importance of corporate identity from a practitioner's perspective

> The enhancement and protection of a company's public face is a fundamental corporate responsibility which all good managers will instinctively understand and grasp.
>
> Marshall (1997)

Major organizations were asked how important corporate identity was in the context of their jobs. The responses given reveal that eight out of every ten practitioners at the summit of industry do regard the communication of corporate identity as a key part of their job. Their view was summarized by the then Acting Director of Corporate Affairs at W.H. Smith who remarked that 'It is a prime function of this department.' Those confirming that they are involved in shaping corporate identity say how important a part of their job it is.

On being asked about the extent to which he was involved in helping to shape corporate identity, the Director of Corporate Affairs at Boots commented 'totally'. But it is agreed that as a corporation is an artificial person in law its identity has to be created. It is with this concept of creating an identity that some communicators are uneasy. Some executives see themselves as projectors of an image rather than creators of it. Certainly, senior executives today are more conscious of their corporate identity than ever before. It is a dominant influence and they regard the process of conveying corporate identity to key constituencies as a primary communications function.

## Corporate identity programmes

Organizations commission identity programmes for a variety of reasons. They may not have had one before or they may feel that they need to change or update their identity. Typical reasons for commissioning an identity change might be:

- change in consumer perceptions – Dr Barnado's desire to be seen as more than an organization that rescued orphans
- mergers/acquisitions – Glaxo merging with Wellcome
- new strategy – British Airways' desire to be perceived as a global airline
- privatization – British Telecommunications, a whole change of ethos since public ownership
- restructuring of the organization – management buy-out of Fisons horticultural products and the subsequent change of name.

# How the communication executive creates corporate identity

- Conduct an identity audit with both internal and external publics.
- Establish how the organization is presently viewed — gain an understanding of core values and the organization's culture.
- Research perceptions of the organization among target audiences.
- Check if existing perceptions of an organization are wrong.
- Analyse if the results reflect the desired perception.
- Question if the perception is up to date. Do people still regard the organization as it once was?
- Decide if the perception is favourable.
- Set objectives.
- Design a programme that is coherent throughout the organization.
- Position the organization correctly.
- Establish the desired identity as part of an integrated strategy.
- Ask if a name change is necessary.
- Check if a new name will be acceptable globally.
- Develop new logo.
- Test new corporate identity in the market place.
- Apply the new identity consistently right across the organization.
- Research the views of various audiences.
- Communicate the programme.

## Communicating – corporate image

> Perceptions are facts because people believe them.
> Epictitus, 1st century slave-philosopher, quoted by Worcester (1997)

How do you think of image?

- a likeness
- a copy
- the living embodiment of a particular quality
- a mental picture
- a persistent mental conception
- the impression given to others of someone or something's character
- the figure of an object formed through the medium of a mirror lens by rays of light.

# Definition of corporate image

Image – often used as a synonym for reputation – is becoming the single most significant point of differentiation between competing companies and their brands, because other differences have simply eroded or disappeared (Chajet, 1997), yet you cannot always control your image (Jackson, 1995). If identity answers the question 'who/what do we believe we are?' then image answers the question 'who/what do we want others to think we are?', for images are in the eyes of those that receive them (Albert and Whettan, 1985).

A good dictionary defines an image as the visible representation of a person, while Argenti (1994) refers to image as a reflection of the organization's reality. Kennedy (1977) believes the corporate image is based primarily on our total experience of the company. This is echoed by van Riel (1995), quoting Ford (1987), who says that image is the sum of experiences that someone has with an institution.

The image is the picture an audience has of the organization through the accumulation of all the messages that it has received and decoded. Marziliano (1997) proposes that an organization creates an image to be managed and controlled in order to survive and project a good perception of itself. Balmer (1997) argues that positive image and reputation should be built on an organization's identity – which needs to be managed and understood. Perhaps image is the total impression of an organization. An organization can be found out if stakeholders experience the organizational reality and find that it does not measure up to the decoded image.

Images are external manifestations of people's mental pictures and they are subject to interpretative processes. Images of organizations can be interpreted in numerous ways depending on peoples' cognitive filters (Fiol and Kovoor-Misra, 1997). The process is an individual-level phenomenon which exists in the minds of individuals and may be different across individuals (Brown and Cox, 1997).

> Not long ago Chrysler Corporation announced its 'first corporate advertising campaign in years'. The primary objective was to show that Chrysler as a corporation had changed; and that it is a different company from what it had been a few years before. The company reported research which revealed that many consumers still remembered Chrysler for its dependence on government guarantees and its dull product range of boxy K cars in the early 1980s. This was the first campaign to concentrate on changing the company's image as a whole – rather than just selling a single car or truck brand – since a year long campaign in the early 1990s. Research reflected the sad fact that few consumers associated some of Chrysler's most successful brands with the parent company. It was truly amazing how many people thought that JEEP was a company.
>
> adapted from Chajet (1997)

## Transmitting a picture

Jackson (1995) recalls that the term used to describe how people perceive us is a term used in the art and photographic world – an image is a snapshot of a given moment. The image may change the next moment. You cannot make people see you in a certain way. An organization cannot order itself a good image. The existence of corporate communication teams and strategies confirms that image matters – and of course it does. A good image sells; it sells both the corporation and its products or services. Jackson says that the only way that the British Library can reach its potential users – and acquaint them with what the Library can do for them – is by communicating; by painting a picture of what it is and what it can do and by transmitting that picture.

An image is developed and formed into a picture. By interpreting this picture the viewer can form a judgement of what he or she sees pictured. Corporate image results from a series of impressions communicated by an organization to its key publics. The images that are projected by organizations reflect the different ways the organization perceives itself (Fiol and Kovoor-Misra, 1997).

## Decoding the picture

The sender encodes information in the form of the projected image. The receiver takes in the message and decodes it in the form of the received image. Each audience may see the organization in different ways, but from these impressions publics come to know the organization as they perceive it. On the basis of those impressions – made over a period of time and gradually accumulating, each building one upon another – an image of the organization does develop. Based on that image audiences remember the organization and react to it.

> Every organization has an image even if it does nothing to create one consciously.
>
> Argenti (1994)

## Role of corporate advertising

Images – whether they are an accurate reflection of reality or not – may be created by advertising. Corporate advertising is designed to create a positive image of the corporation itself in the minds of all those groups who might be considered stakeholders in the organization. Decisions have to be made about how to present certain messages and the tone may need to be changed to accommodate different audiences. This is the task of corporate communications (Hart, 1995). A series of advertisements over a period of time may convey a particular image of an organization. Carlsberg really may be the best lager in the world; perhaps Carlsberg is the best brewer of lager? One dimension of corporate image is the degree to which the company is perceived as possessing qualities that make it successful (Brown and Cox, 1997).

> Communication is the bridge between what we are and the image that others have of us.
>
> Jackson (1995)

## Managing publics' expectations

Image is the momentarily shifting and adjusting visible representation of a company (Rindova, 1997) – it concerns the impression that various audiences have of it. That representation may differ from one audience to another. B.A.T. Industries may have a bad image with the anti-smoking lobby – but it may be have a wonderful image in the eyes of Americans who smoke and enjoy Lucky Strike cigarettes. But publics do have to consider the reality. Corporate communication is concerned with conveying a favourable reputation of the organization. It is concerned with managing publics' expectations. A good image is the backcloth for organizational success be it in the for-profit or non-for-profit sector.

## Developing the persona

There are very many definitions of image – most complement each other. In corporate terms numberless diverse acts, influences and messages emerge from an organization and reach target audiences. It is on the basis of these messages and impressions that the organization develops a persona. This persona reflects the reality of the corporation. On the basis of that reflection audiences judge the organization and its people. They make decisions about what they imagine the organisation is. A good corporate image can powerfully help a corporation to enter a new market. Ultimately it is on the basis of these images that publics decide whether or not they wish to have relationships with an organization.

Individuals are all different. Each person is likely to have a different image of one and the same organization. Heath (1994) recalls that Chrysler Corporation spent $30 million creating a new persona after it discovered that one of its critical publics (namely, its customers) disliked buying automobiles from pushy salespeople. Some persona are developed with great care and considerable investment. GlaxoWellcome is one organization that has invested heavily in the publication of admired and respected academic papers (relating to a number of its products), which it publishes to benefit the medical profession.

The impact of various acts, influences and messages passing from an organization to its publics must be considered. Any one of those communications may be adjusted at any time – either in content or emphasis; so the image can be adjusted. Just as the revenue from petroleum tax in the USA can be adjusted by putting an extra 10 cents a gallon on – or by taking 10 cents a gallon off – it may be necessary for the communications executive to take action to adjust the perceived image. For this reason the practitioner will conduct market research to ascertain exactly what perceptions publics have of the organization.

## The mirror function

van Riel (1995) believes that much of corporate communication is geared towards bolstering corporate image. He identifies this as the reflection of the identity of the organization with its stakeholders. He perceives the mirror function – monitoring developments and anticipating their consequences on audiences so that the image will be built over time.

# The image maker

## An impression

*Cassell's Concise English Dictionary* defines an image maker as:

> a public relations expert employed to improve the impression that someone makes on the general public

Although reality (the identity) is significant – the corporate image is critically important too and it is a prime responsibility of the communication department. As noted, image is a result of how an audience feels about the organization. These feelings are grounded in impressions that the organization has made as well as what an audience has come to believe about it. The impression that many American citizens had of President Richard Nixon was that he was Tricky Dicky. Watergate may or may not have altered their perspective.

## Impression management

van Riel (1995) suggests that identity is associated with the way in which a company presents itself to its various publics; but that image is the picture by which its various audiences see an organization. van Raaij (1986) suggests that image is a form of favourable impression management amongst target audiences (in contrast, defensive impression management is a reaction to an unexpected accusation – it attempts to attribute negative events to happenings outside the organization and thus beyond its control). Favourable impression management is, he says, an organization's way of presenting itself to target groups in such a way that it succeeds in giving them a favourable impression of itself. But not all scholars are happy with this proposition. Rindova (1997) refers to the move away from image management (which he sees as organizations taking superficial actions to make themselves look better) and towards reputation management (which is seen as firms taking substantive and responsible actions to gain the esteem of key publics).

# Does the communication executive create an image?

van Riel (1992) believes that the aim of corporate communication is to improve the image of a company and that an orchestrated communications strategy facilitates the process of creating a favourable corporate image. Not all practitioners agree with him. However, although communication programmes are about presenting an organization to its key audiences they are certainly not about presentation, image and reputation alone. Aaker (1996) argues that marketers may leverage the corporate image in their marketing strategies. The fundamental question is whether or not the communicator practitioner is an image creator; and, if the executive is, does this suggest manipulation? Newsom and Scott (1976) underline that communications deal with reality not facades; and this brings echoes of Heath (1994) who reports Cheney (1992) as saying that some companies groom their images so carefully that they are nothing but image.

The communicator's job is to communicate an image; but not to create an artificial one. But perhaps some communicators do contrive to create an unrealistic image? As identity is involved with actuality, with the corporate persona, with organizational individuality, conveying that to one's publics *is* part of the task. Conveying an image that might, or could be, contrived is another thing altogether.

## Divergence amongst professionals

> Getting it right can be a real source of competitive advantage, but only if the image matches behaviour to reputation.
>
> Marshall (1997)

Amongst senior communicators there is an almost total divergence of opinion. Some – rightly or wrongly – see image creation as a negative concept. Speaking of image creation, the then communication manager at Tennent Caledonian Breweries remarked 'it is the essence of the art'. However, the Director of Group Public Affairs at B.A.T. Industries said, 'I am a reputation engineer'. This, perhaps, carried an undertone of Woodcock (1994) who remarked that if a crisis situation was handled in a professional and competent fashion it could present real opportunities for the enhancement of corporate image and values.

This will be considered in a later chapter.

> The image—reality gap can play havoc with a company's reputation.
>
> Energy spent contriving to present an upbeat image rarely works backwards into reality.
>
> White and Mazur (1995)

However, not every communication executive does see him- or herself as an image creator. Perhaps that role carries undertones of improving an impression, which might be described as massaging the truth – or embellishing the facts. The Director of Corporate Affairs at Boots summarized the general view when he said that 'I am not in the business of creating a reputation which cannot be sustained by actuality', a view echoed by Cheney (1992) who advised his readers to beware the potential danger of an unreflective corporate discourse. van Riel (1995) quotes Boorstin who, writing as long ago as 1961, criticized American society. He said that it was excessively influenced by pseudo-events and that he believed that 'apparent reality' was emphasized; in other words it was the image of a non-existent reality. Heath (1994) discusses the danger of a corporation merely being an image, a creation that exists in the mind of the beholder, lacking substance.

## Actuality versus image

One has only to recall the unpopularity of British Gas to recognize that public perception of an organization – how it presents itself – impacts on commercial success. Competitive leadership in an age of declining product differentiation is gained not only through the quality of corporate performance but may also be achieved simply as a result of the superior way in which the organization is perceived by its constituencies (White and Mazur, 1995). Organizations set out to acquire a good image for a variety of reasons – it may help promote its products, convey a good impression of its services or simply to create awareness of the company. As noted elsewhere, few consumers realize that they have Avon Rubber components in their home, because the company does not promote its image.

---

- The financial audience is one of the most important. A favourable image is more likely to encourage would-be investors – who are after all the lifeblood of an organization. As the Director of Corporate Communications at Whitbread summed it up, 'essentially they own the place'.

---

- If a commercial decision has to be made and essential information is missing which would allow a considered decision to be made, an executive might be more likely to come down in favour of the side that has a good image. This may be what used to be called giving someone or something the benefit of the doubt.
- Any organization that is well thought of in its market place is likely to have happy employees, satisfied customers and be well regarded by its audiences. These are all factors that contribute towards desiring a favourable image.
- As has been noted, corporate image is concerned with a mental impression. If a public thinks well of an organization it is more likely to wish to do business with it; and it is more likely to encourage others to do the same. Certain controversial areas such as those found in the tobacco industry require image bolstering and special presentational skills to increase the level of their acceptance to their various publics.
- An organization that is well regarded by its audiences is likely to be positioned to do well. It is the more likely to have a good foundation on which strategic success can be built. The feel good factor (much beloved of politicians) is clearly generated from the very top of an organization – not from the bottom.
- An organization with a good image is likely to be one step ahead of the competition – increasing market share – the very image itself is likely to be an added value factor.

To create a favourable image is not a good thing if it is an artificial one, but the transmission of a sustainable favourable image is a fundamental part of the communication executive's job. Promoting a favourable corporate image is now one of the executive's primary strategic tasks, for none of the differences between companies seem more effective than image; organizations will increasingly rely upon it as a powerful business tool (Chajet, 1997).

Skolnik (1994) quotes the Public Relations Director of Atlanta-based UPS opining that normal commercial excellence is not enough to make an organization stand out. He believes that senior executives of other organizations are influenced by what they hear about a company, what they know about its capacity to deliver and what they know about its ability and image. He goes on to say that corporate communication has a major role to play in the process of communicating those good images and messages.

These days the significance of corporate image cannot be debated. As most successful politicians would admit, there is a general belief that a good image is the best foundation for success in the polls. John F. Kennedy was the first to put this belief into practice in his remarkable and successful 1960 Presidential campaign. Thus an organization also desires to have a favourable image.

But, why does image matter? van Riel (1995) quotes Poiesz (1988): he considers that if customers have no corporate images on which to base an opinion they may have difficulty in making purchasing decisions. He considers that knowledge, expectation and consistency are all factors that are influenced by the existence of a good image.

# Image not matched by actuality

When actuality fails to live up to the image it can damage the organization. The image and reputation of the shipping line Townsend-Thoresen were destroyed in the aftermath of the sinking of the *Spirit of Free Enterprise*. When those who study communication process discuss corporate image – and the fact that it has become one of the essential responsibilities of the corporate communicator – this divergence between reality and what is imagined is one of the issues with which they are concerned.

Does the image sum up the whole organization? B.A.T. Industries might be regarded as a global tobacco company. In fact it is as much involved in financial services as it is tobacco products. Sometimes the identity of the group as a whole can enhance the reputation of its subsidiaries.

## Conclusion

Corporate communications have become a strategic framework embracing all types of communications – marketing, organizational and management. Taken together these diverse forms of communication produce the total business message. The production of this message assists the process of defining the corporate image and inevitably helps to impact on and add to an organization's overall competitive advantage. It adds value. There is a difference between helping to define a corporate image and actually creating one and, as noted, not every communications executive sees him- or herself as an image creator. The first priority is to determine the corporate vision – then to fashion a communications strategy that drives towards that vision.

Brown and Cox (1997) argue that a better understanding of what makes up a company's image, where it comes from and how it can influence important audiences would allow marketing managers to utilize corporate assets more effectively. Corporate image could be thought of, and treated, as a valuable business investment – an investment that could potentially show greater returns than almost any other corporate venture (Gregory, 1997). Trying to impact on their environments, organizations spend millions of pounds on corporate identity programmes and they do this to gain acceptance and to enhance their corporate reputation.

## Case study

### Corporate image studies

Robert Worcester defines corporate image (from the consumer's standpoint and from that of other external audiences) as 'the net result of all experiences, impressions, feelings, beliefs and knowledge that people have about a company' and he sees this as more subjective than objective. The importance of this is that it may or may not be true. However, Worcester's company measures not truth in some abstract way, but perceptions.

It was in 1969 (in its first co-operative corporate image study in Britain) that MORI asked the public 'What two or three things do you consider that it is most important to know about a company in order to judge its reputation?' MORI discovered that industrial relations and the treatment of staff came first. 35 per cent volunteered this factor. Following not far behind was the quality of a company's products and services at 33 per cent; in the rear were factors like customer service at 13 per cent or profitability at only 7 per cent.

The answers to this question have changed a great deal over the years; for example, staff treatment has fallen as low as 13 per cent in 1983, it recovered to around 20 per cent over the past four or five years; quality of products or services stayed high through the 1980s, but fell off in the past two or three years and now at 19 per cent is down a third; while profitability (of concern to only 7 per cent in 1969) moved into the teens during the 1980s – went to 21 per cent last year – and is now (at 24 per cent) the most frequently mentioned factor.

Since those pioneering days a quarter of a century ago, the British public have lost some of their confidence in large companies. In 1969 MORI found a staggering three in four people who believed that company A, that had a good reputation, would not make products of an inferior quality; which, of course, was palbably not true; it was nevertheless the perception held by three quarters of the British public. That figure has now fallen to 60 per cent (which is still remarkable) but a drop of a fifth. Nearly half were confident that old established companies make the best products; now a sixth fewer, 40 per cent, have this confidence. In 1969 37 per cent believed that 'I never buy products from companies I have never heard of', which Worcester describes as another nonsense. Now 31 per cent say that this is what they feel. Then 37 per cent also believed that new brands on the market were usually improvements over long established brands and that has now dropped to a third. These are the public's perceptions, but as the slave philosopher Epictitus said in the first century 'Perceptions are facts because people believe them'.

Worcester's second law is that 'Familiarity breeds favourability, not contempt'. Almost all of the time the better known a company is, the more highly thought of it is. This is more true of the public at large than of more sophisticated and elite audiences studied by MORI (such as the City, editors of national daily and Sunday papers, or Members of Parliament). It is certainly a fact that many companies become well known by doing good things for people. By so doing they earn esteem.

The acquisition of esteem affects:

- their recruiting and keeping staff
- what the City thinks of them
- their ability to catch the ear of the media
- what the customer – and potential customer – thinks of them

- what politicians and government feel about them
- how stakeholders view them

The majority of people in Britain think that 'As they grow bigger, companies usually get cold and impersonal in their relations with people'; this is a view which has been held consistently by about three quarters of the British population for a quarter of a century. Yet 70 per cent or more consistently believe that 'Large companies are necessary for the nation's growth and expansion'. So the population at large thinks that businessmen and women are a necessary evil, they cannot live with them and they cannot live without them. The public are sick to death with politicians and journalists and only 10 per cent of the public say that they can trust what journalists have to say; sadly only 11 per cent say that they can trust what government ministers have to say. 'The good news', writes Worcester, 'is that over a quarter say that they can trust what business leaders have to say and that over half say that they trust pollsters!'

adapted from Worcester (1997)

# Key terms

**AUDIENCES**   Those groups of people – representing a wide variety of different interests – whose concerns and interests an organization seeks to address.

**BRAND MARKS**   Identifying signs, symbols, logos, which differentiate one brand of good from another.

**CORPORATE HEADQUARTERS**   Location of chief office of the organization.

**CORPORATE IDENTITY**   Those characteristics, traits and qualities which taken together make up the persona or individuality of an organization.

**EMPLOYEE UNIFORMS**   Uniform dress code worn by all employees.

**HOUSE STYLE**   Uniform typology of dress and behaviour
– 'the way we do things here'.

**ICONS**   A picture, image or mosaic representing an image of the organization as a whole.

**INTEGRATION OF MESSAGES**   The process of ensuring that all messages to all audiences carry a common theme and do not contradict each other.

**LOGOS**   A symbol or simple design typifying a company.

**SYMBOLS**   An object typifying an image of the organization as a whole.

# Chapter 4

# Strategy

According to a survey of top US companies carried out by The Conference Board in 1993 a growing number of senior managers view communication as strategic; and a strategy that can confer competitive advantage.

White and Mazur (1995)

The new role for communications for the next century has to be strategic. It is when – and only when – corporate boards, CEOs and other senior executives become fully committed to the vital role and to the strategic value of communications in practice that there will be any confidence in the long term future of any major corporation.

adapted from Finlay (1994)

'Communication is being harnessed as a strategic resource in many major corporations' reported Kay Troy (author of a May 1993 report based on a survey on this topic by The Conference Board) (a research organization based in New York City). The report concluded that:

- press relations and corporate advertising assist firms to build and maintain favourable reputations with key audiences.
- communication executives frequently report enhanced responsibilities and status, particularly with greater involvement in policy and long-range decisions.
- at least 80 per cent of the respondents are 'aligning their communication programmes with the company's strategic goals'.
- communication executives are resolved to produce significant results in order to secure their role as a strategic resource in top management.
- communication can confer competitive advantage.

adapted from Skolnik (1994)

## Introduction

Strategy is essentially the process of long-term planning by an organization towards sharply defined organizational goals; above all strategy provides priorities. Corporate communication is at its most powerful when it is at the core of an organization's overall strategic plan. A well-developed, cohesive communication programme arrived at through a careful process of environmental analysis and evaluation plays a vital strategic role – for communication input is one means of achieving corporate goals. This input is needed at the very earliest stages of the development of the strategic process and it needs to be maintained and developed throughout by strategic design and execution. Yet corporate communication is often sidelined by less successful organizations and treated as a peripheral management discipline – one unimportant to the overall functioning of the successful corporation. Over the last decade some organizations have planned increasingly sophisticated strategies with communication harnessed as a strategic resource. Corporate plans should consider the communication aspects of any action that the organization takes, for communication is a process that promotes, and helps to protect, the interests of the corporation. It assists the development and enhancement of those relationships upon which an organization's competitive existence, prosperity and survival depends. It enables an organization to lead, motivate, persuade and inform those numerous constituencies which it identifies as important for strategic purposes and it assists the organization in one of its essential functions – gaining and maintaining an advantage over its competitors.

> As a tool to access and manage the intertwining of business
> performance and social change the communication function is
> quickly becoming one of the most important assets of a company.
> Finlay (1994)

## Corporate communication's unique qualities as a management discipline

Information is a crucial commodity in any company so management scholars have long recognized the importance of communication policies within organizations; they understand that good channels of communication add to an organization's success. In reality really effective communication programmes are, by definition, created for strategic purposes.

> International distribution group Inchcape has restored
> communications to the boardroom. Inchcape's CEO said 'The
> appointment reflects not only the value Inchcape places on its
> corporate communication activities, but also the wider contribution
> that I expect the corporate affairs function to make in the day to
> day running of an international company'. The communication
> executive said that 'the move would ensure that corporate
> communication implications were considered in every business
> decision that we make'.
> adapted from Bevan (1997)

## Working in conjunction with the CEO

How information is conveyed can help or hinder the corporation's goals (Goodman, 1994) so a communication strategy is a priority for the organization. Assuming a strategic role in the execution of the organization's business plan, the communication executive needs to fashion that strategy in close conjunction with the CEO and the executive team (the more reason for the communicator being *part* of it) all of whom need a clear vision of their corporate values, culture and mission. In shaping such a strategic programme the organization needs to consider the nature of the organization itself and its impact on its key constituencies.

> In the broadest sense, Storehouse considers corporate communication to be an important element of all decisions that it makes. When setting budgets we think 'what will the City think about this plan?'
>
> The then Director of Corporate Affairs, Storehouse plc,
> in conversation with the author

# Supporting other management functions

Marketing activities may be judged a success if they succeed in developing confidence and goodwill for an organization with many different audiences. The way in which marketing can work in conjunction with corporate communication underlines the essential supporting role which communication plays, for it underpins the more traditional marketing processes of sales promotion, selling itself and advertising. Thus organizations can gain synergetic benefits from a communication strategy that exploits the inherent strengths of these disciplines (Moss, 1990).

### Integrated communication programmes

It is in this supporting role that corporate communication comes into its own. It helps to create and sustain coherent communication strategies with all those publics that the marketing department perceives to be important to it. Marketing and communication may on occasions use very different techniques; but they work together in parallel towards the same corporate target. The objective is corporate success and the overall competitive advantage of the organization.

> The primary task of advertising is to aggressively promote the sale of a company's products. The primary role of corporate communication is to manage a company's reputation and to help build public consent for its enterprises.
>
> Osborne (1994)

As with marketing, advertising and corporate communication are management disciplines which complement each other. All three have an essential role, working alongside each other and supporting management communication strategies. These developed and intertwined communication tools enable the promotion of the organization and its products as part of a total integrated communication strategy. This is a strategy which can be used effectively, for example, to generate public interest in – or to win support for – the launch of new products or the addition of a new brand.

## Communications inform you about other organizations

> Corporate communication is used to communicate your messages and themes. If staff do not provide good service it undermines your strategy. You have to make sure that you win the hearts and minds of your own people first. Do not tell the public something until you have told your employees; because the public is so important. That is why the internal public is so important.
> The Public Relations Manager, Avon and Somerset Constabulary,
> in conversation with the author

Skolnik (1994) refers to the Communication Director of Atlanta-based UPS, who suggests that normal commercial excellence is not enough to make an organization stand out and that senior executives are influenced by what they hear about a company, what they know about its capacity to deliver and what they learn about its ability and image. The UPS executive added that corporate communication has a major role to play in the process of communicating good images and messages.

The language, customs and traditions of an organization influence the creation of new relationships. Thus, transmitting corporate image and culture through well-constructed messages and themes becomes an important strategic tactic, facilitating, as it does, understanding with external constituencies. Through these strategies important publics come to understand the organization, its goals, its aspirations, its missions and the quality of its services, products and people.

Thus communication becomes a powerful tool when it is generating an effective dialogue with key external publics. It assists organizations in the creation and development of harmonious relations with those who see themselves as its stakeholders. Any one of those stakeholders may hold a plethora of opinions about the organization and may, at some time or another, adopt a position that impacts on corporate operations and represents the key to corporate success or failure.

Moss (1990) referred to British Telecommunication's severe image problem and suggested that this largely stemmed from a failure by the public to appreciate fully the nature of its business or the huge investment that the company was required to make to maintain and upgrade its services. BT concluded that, in order to improve its public image, it had not only to effect the promised improvements to the payphones service but it also had to develop a strategy whereby it communicated that it had taken note and acted accordingly.

> Communications are the key enabler to business strategy today –
> far more than, say, finance
> > adapted from Larry Snoddon, Burston–Marsteler Europe
> > speaking at a Conference Board Seminar in 1990,
> > quoted by White and Mazur (1995)

> Relevant data must be gathered before any strategy can be
> developed. First stakeholders must be identified and then their
> perceptions and behavioural inclinations must be discovered. After
> that you should ask 'can we take a position that is mutually
> beneficial both to our organization and to those stakeholders and to
> the greater public good?' Strategies which are designed for mutual
> benefit hold the greatest potential for generating widespread public
> support.
> > adapted from Tucker and Shortridge (1994)

# Strategic value of scanning the environment

> Company decisions which ignore public imperatives will almost
> certainly run afoul of public consent.
> > Osborne (1994)

## Boundary scanners – the eyes and ears of the organization

> Whereas scanning discovers information, managing the business
> context requires making information actionable through integration
> into strategy.
> > Morris, quoted by Lauzen (1994)

Communication with stakeholders – and all those who form opinions about the organization – is an essential plank in corporate strategy; but the Communication Executive of Atlanta-based Home Depot sees his sphere extending beyond communication. He believes that it is his responsibility to help his organization to understand the impact of its various activities on its audiences (Skolnik, 1994). Certainly, predicting how an issue will move – and what that issue may affect – can be critical in developing strategic communications (Bodensteiner, 1995). The ability to predict the impact of corporate decisions on critical audiences is one that the communication executive must have honed sharply.

Corporate communication is a management discipline which provides the technical and speciality skills that other disciplines simply cannot provide. It is the discipline which acts as the eyes and ears of the corporation – watching out for every threat and opportunity presented to the organization. Its importance as an early warning system is beyond dispute (Lauzen, 1995). Accordingly, practitioners are involved in a process of two-way communication with their constituencies and in this way they differ from other organizational decision makers. They are exposed not only to the organizational values of their own corporation but also to the values of their external publics as well. Consequently they become what Lauzen (1995) calls organizational boundary scanners. In this role, communication executives are in a unique position to provide cultural cross-fertilization – that is, they relay organizational values to external constituencies and *vice versa* (Cutlip et al., 1994).

As noted the organization's image can be fundamental to commercial success. Whether or not an organization is considered credible can depend on how it is perceived by key audiences. These perceptions can be a matter of real significance in the development of a cohesive and integrated communication strategy. Once public perceptions of an organization are set they can be difficult to change and communication specialists cannot hope to effect a change in public opinion unless they have a wholly credible story to communicate. Environmental scanning can give an organization an objective view on how it is perceived by those key publics. It can give the organization a wider knowledge and comprehension of those key audiences; how they feel about it and what they want from it. Organizations exist in the context of their ever widening environments and they become more fiercely competitive as more and more organizations assume a global presence. These environments can – and do – impact on the way in which the organization performs and upon its corporate objectives. Hence it is essential that the organization gathers information not just about its environments but also about itself.

## Both a simple and a complex process

Environmental scanning is a macro theory of organizational communication process. It is both a simple and complex process. It is an essential information and communication procedure for re-orienting organizational strategy. It is easy because critical information required to analyse the underlying dynamics of a market is readily available. It is complex because the number of areas that an organization needs to monitor may be large (Goodman, 1994).

## Two levels of scanning

Scanning and monitoring the environment has become a key function for the corporate communicator. Environmental scanning is the managerial activity of learning about events and trends in the organization's environment. Lauzen (1995) suggests two levels of environmental scanning:

- FORMAL
  - media content analysis, surveys of publics, focus group studies of key stakeholders
- INFORMAL
  - media contacts, monitoring written and telephone complaints.

## A process which enables better corporate decisions

Through boundary scanning, practitioners participate in strategic activities throughout the organization in addition to operational activities solely concerned with the public relations department (Lauzen, 1994). It is a process involving not only the practitioner but other senior management to whom the communicator gives advice. It is a means by which organizations gather information (particularly concerning interest groups who may perceive themselves as stakeholders), which enables them to interpret their environment better. It is an enabling process because it provides key personnel with information which allows them to make better informed decisions. Those decisions can – and often are – essential ingredients in strategy formulation.

## Market research

Conducting market research among key audiences is an essential function of the communication department. The importance of research lies in the fact that it is an enabling process. Study of market research conducted among critical constituents gives an organization greater knowledge and understanding of the relationship that exists between an organization and its key publics.

> 'Finding out what people thought about the company was vital to developing a group communications plan', says Tim Blythe, Director of Group Corporate Affairs at W.H. Smith plc. Improving internal communications was an immediate priority followed by increasing communications between different countries – he is very keen on increasing awareness of the group's international operations both internally and externally.
>
> Nicholas (1997)

Market research facilitates an exchange of knowledge about how the one feels about the other. It is a means by which an organization may learn how significant constituencies feel about it and what they consider to be the strengths which give it competitive advantage. It is also a means by which the organization can learn about its perceived weaknesses. Market research enables a corporation to gather perceptions about its management; as well as about its position in its market place. It permits an organization to have a better understanding of itself. From this greater comprehension the organization is better placed to adopt strategic positions which enable it to gain competitive advantage.

> Good business leaders will gather around them the means to draw a fairly accurate map. That means communications, in the form of research and market intelligence. Such services do not come cheap, but they are as essential to progressive business as meteorological forecasting is to flying an aircraft.
>
> Marshall (1997)

# Strategic value of communicating with key constituencies

> There is a broad, growing recognition among corporate executives and corporate boards that the 'ability to succeed will depend upon the corporation's ability to effectively communicate with its employees, customers, shareholders, suppliers and the public at large. This recognition of the importance of good communications is good news for all of us. Communications professionals and the communications function in the future will be increasingly recognized as an absolute, integral part of the top management function'.
>
> Graham (1994)

## Internal communication can be a powerful morale booster

Corporate communication with the internal audience can also play a powerful role in corporate strategy. Here, the object is to ensure that employees are given proper information – and in good time – about what their organization is doing, its vision and purpose. It is good sense as well as good manners – communication with employees is a powerful morale booster. As many organizations have discovered (and particularly in a time of crisis) it is important strategy to have your people on your side.

## Having the City on your side

One principle objective of financial communication strategy is to enhance shareholder value.

Communication can play a major role in ensuring that the City, analysts and shareholders are on your side – and this can assist the process of bringing about a rising share price; just as the opposite can facilitate a falling share price, as Laura Ashley Holdings have found to their cost.

# Strategic input to CEOs and key senior executives

Strategic value-added communications must begin with highly qualified input from the communication executive at the decision making table; and there must be a receptive environment for that contribution. The executive will need to produce strategically-focused recommendations for action. He or she must bring to the attention of top management a broad understanding of those issues which may affect and impact upon a company's image and reputation.

adapted from Osborne (1994)

Strategic value-added communication starts with highly qualified input to the highest levels. So, it becomes the more important that communication input is welcomed at that level (Osborne, 1994). The more senior-level commitment you have the more strategic your corporate communication will be to your company (Skolnik, 1994). Flanagan (1995) notes that the task of the communication executive is to present the company in the way that the CEO requires. However, in some cases the CEO does not know what he or she wants – and sometimes the CEO is disinterested altogether in the potential strategic power of corporate communication.

Whitney (Goodman, 1994) quotes Koten (1984) as saying that excellent companies have communication policies that are the concern of top executives. When communication executives are involved at the decision-making table, information about relations with priority publics gets factored back into the process of organizational decision making and into its policies and actions (Lauzen, 1995).

Top management must have a clear perception of its communications strategy. This means that corporate communication needs to be a part of the planning being done by CEOs as they examine where they want their business to be three or five years from now. In order to achieve this they will have to work with the communication executive; together sharing thinking, perceptions, ideas and visions.

adapted from T. Gelder quoted in *Management Review* (1995)

Most communication executives regard advising and guiding their board of directors on their communication strategy – and on the consequences of their policies – as a critical function. They understand that communication helps to ensure that senior management is equipped with the relevant information that it needs to enable it to make important decisions.

> In February 1992 Keith McKennon took over as Chairman of Dow Corning. He changed the reporting structure and had corporate communications report directly to him. By putting a high profile executive in charge of Corning and by moving the corporate communications function into the ranks of senior management, the company was better positioned.
>
> Adapted from Argenti (1997)

## The board originates communications policy

In some instances the board itself generates communication policy. At supermarket chain J. Sainsbury the family ethos is still very strong – possibly almost suffocatingly so. Their communication direction emerges from their board. As their Acting Director of Corporate Communications commented, 'they decide the level of corporate communication input'. At Storehouse – where the group are controlling two separate, major operating companies (Bhs and Mothercare) – the then Director of Corporate Affairs had a 'non-hierarchical say in ... developing group strategy'. At GlaxoWellcome the Director, Corporate Affairs inputs to the strategic process by reporting only to one person – and that person is the Chairman. This is the mechanism by which he perceives that 'he inputs to the decision making process'. It is also his 'way into the information flow'.

> If leadership and management mean anything at all, they mean communication. Good and effective communication must begin at the top of the company – in the boardroom – permeating throughout the organization, manifesting in all its different forms along the way. Communications ... is the very essence of enterprise and endeavour and the first tool of leadership.
>
> Marshall (1997)

## Communication leadership from the CEO

Evidently many major organizations already recognize the wide implications of the impact of communications on corporate strategy. This recognition sometimes stems from the very top. Mr Frank Nicholson at Vaux Brewery and Mr Bill Cockburn at the time of writing Managing Director of W.H. Smith plc are examples of CEOs who have a heightened respect for communication performance and visible communication flair themselves, illustrated by strategic moves originating from their organizations. The then Acting Director of Corporate Affairs at W.H. Smith remarked that 'Cockburn recognizes that . . . corporate communication is a tool that you have to use.' A similar example is the CEO at Whitbread where, with the communicator sitting on the strategic communications committee, the two instigate strategy.

> At British Airways communication plays an enormous part in corporate strategy. This organization has a high profile because it is such a 'sexy' industry. Everything that it does has a huge impact. This industry is regulated like no other. We operate in a goldfish bowl. The company has always been sensitive to the public relations impact of every decision. We would be expected to recognize corporate communication aspects of any proposed move. Corporate communication should provide the early warning system.
>
> The then Director of Public Affairs, British Airways, in conversation with the author

## Departmental strategy

Not all communicators are involved in strategy considerations (van Riel, 1995). Some communicators simply consider their departmental interests rather than the strategic interests of the whole organization; their function being simply that of transmitting good information so that the community is aware of the organization and its programmes. Their organization's view is that publicity alone increases public understanding of an organization's goals and attracts consumers (paraphrasing Bedics et al., 1987).

## The power of communication is often not fully appreciated

Rice (1991) is critical of the effectiveness of communications by some managers while White and Mazur (1994) suggest that there is evidence that some corporations do not make full use of communications in pursuit of their strategic objectives.

Evidence confirming this suggestion comes from organizations like Avon Rubber – and Lloyds/TSB (the latter having 'no group view on corporate communication'). In companies such as these it depends very largely upon the CEO whether communications impact at all on corporate strategy. As noted, there is considerable lack of understanding of – and a lack of commitment to – communications amongst some very senior managers and there are senior executives who do not believe in the importance of corporate communications.

Some senior executives do not recognize corporate communication as a management discipline ranking alongside HRM or Corporate Finance. At Lloyds/TSB, the head of corporate communications (speaking of his CEO) said 'the strategy is his'. The CEO at Avon Rubber is 'very ambivalent about the whole thing' and is not sure 'what he wants or how he wants to get there.' In many cases senior management have not been made aware of – or simply do not understand – the strategic power that corporate communication is capable of unleashing.

Yet those successful communication executives surveyed by America's *Fortune* magazine emphasized the importance of the CEO as the main communicator of the company's positions and policies to target publics (Skolnik, 1994). Skolnik notes that the J. P. Morgan CEO, together with other Morgan senior executives, discuss frequently with their communications people and that it is their belief that they make better decisions because of the communication input that they receive.

The CEO at Lloyds/TSB 'is a powerful figure'. His Head of Corporate Communications says of him that 'he has clear views on what banking is all about. If we have a reputation for being hard nosed then that will be something of which I am conscious and it will affect how I run the corporate communication strategy'. Lloyds' communication executive continued 'I will explain why we take a hard nosed attitude. We will not write off debt to the Third World. That is a public relations headache.'

## The strategic role of the communication executive

While all strategic decisions are the responsibility of the board of a company, those decisions are taken following the advice of the functional experts (Harrison, 1995). Thus the role of the communication executive becomes more important than ever; embracing so many different management disciplines and playing, as it must, an integral role in corporate strategy. The executive is developing a strategic communication process that earns respect and acceptance for company policies from the organization's publics.

The role has widened. At the highest level the director plays a pivotal part in communicating with a wide and growing range of audiences. In fashioning strategy the director needs a profound knowledge of his or her organization. In turn the corporation as a whole must share a deep understanding of, and shared belief in, the essentiality and power of excellent communications. Skolnik (1994) cites the communication director at Sverdrup Corporation in St Louis, Missouri, saying that the communication executive should be in such a position that he has a better sense of public opinion and shaping of public policy than other executives in the corporate structure.

Some organizations have strategic planning committees (tobacco and financial services giant B.A.T. Industries is one example). A number of those committees have a communication presence; others do not. The communication executive at B.A.T. Industries commented, 'I do not sit on the committee, what matters is that I understand the arguments that are going on and that "this and that" will have "such and such" an impact'. Brewery and leisure group Whitbread has a strategic communications committee – described by their communication executive as 'a driving force' – which meets twice a month. It is in that forum that their executive talks 'about the perceptions of our various audiences'. 'That body', he continued, 'is quite critical to the function of corporate communication. They understand the messages because they help to form them.'

Organizations are becoming increasingly aware that communications as a function are not being fully exploited (van Riel, 1995). But many influential executives demonstrate clarity of strategic intent. One of their strategic objectives is to bolster a rising share price (W.H. Smith), others are excellent relations with opinion formers (GlaxoWellcome) and a better understanding with their public (the Avon and Somerset Constabulary). As part of that objective a few do eye the 'halo' effect (Wessex Water and Lloyds/TSB are examples of companies who are demonstrably conscious of the benefits accruing to their organizations from charitable and community involvement).

Communications are used increasingly as a tool in the development and implementation of the competitive strategy of many corporations. An integrated corporate communication programme can help considerably to raise the profile of an organization – or of its brands – and it can help sustain interest in them. It can impact considerably on sales and on competitive advantage. The communication executive plays an increasing role in the formulation of that strategy; but the input could in some cases be greater and at a higher level. Few organizations of any size are unaware of the importance of good communication; but some choose to use the tools to a greater extent than others. Perhaps the more traditional an organization – and the less that it has changed its structures – the less likely it is to make full use of all the powers that good communications are ready to unleash.

## Strategic objectives of corporation communication

- Advising senior executives
- Arousing interest in the corporate brand and products
- Assisting the CEO to overcome rumours and threats
- Carrying out market research into the motivations and attitudes of target publics
- Communicating corporate strategies and positions
- Ensuring that questions from significant publics are answered
- Establishing and nourishing relationships with significant publics
- Establishing a dialogue with media over important issues

- Helping to recover losses in corporate credibility
- Helping to handle crisis situations and creating sympathy for the organization
- Joining in the promotion of new products and services
- Lobbying government at macro and micro level
- Offering reassurance to publics concerned about an issue
- Producing a defence for corporate views and positions
- Projecting a corporate image and boosting reputation
- Promoting the corporate brand
- Providing an explanation of critical issues to important opinion formers/ stakeholders
- Transforming negative situations into corporate opportunities
- Winning support for organizational positions and goals.

# Formulating the good communications strategy

- Decide upon the desired corporate image
- Allocate the budget
- Carry out research to identify key audiences
- Carry out market research to ascertain the perceptions and beliefs held about the organization by those key audiences
- In conjunction with the CEO and the executive team develop an appropriate communication strategy
- Considering desired messages and themes, decide communication content, select appropriate communication tools and forms of delivery
- Create and deliver an appropriate, communication programme integrated with the total corporate strategy.

---

## The communication strategist needs to take the following steps:

- identify/prioritize the most critical publics/opinion leaders important to advancing a position
- clarify desired behaviours ... for each
- develop a goal describing the ... end result that the organization is seeking
- develop messages that reflect the desired behaviours.

Tucker and Shortridge (1994)

---

# Case study

No organization is too small to have a communication strategy; indeed, some one-man businesses have well-developed strategies. Certainly it is not unusual for a charity or for a police force to plan strategically. Essentially when the strategy is drawn up communication must be a key component. This case concerns a small village church in the west of England which burned down. It shows how a sharply focused and successfully implemented communications strategy ensured that it was re-opened by its diocesan bishop 18 months later (to the general astonishment of most local people who all thought that it was doomed to closure). It is a powerful example of the use of integrated communications in a developed strategy.

After West Hatch parish church was destroyed by fire the Friends of St Andrew's formed – it was to have a co-ordinating role working alongside the parochial church council. The Friends realized that necessity forced them to market the local church throughout the worldwide Anglican communion. They recognized that they would need to advertise the great work that they were undertaking. Their Communication Director perceived at the outset that excellent communications would be needed to draw the marketing and advertising strategies together in an integrated global communication programme.

First the Friends identified their key constituencies; these, they saw, were not located solely in the hamlet of West Hatch; they were in the county of Somerset, in the rest of the British Isles and they were scattered around the world. Further, they noted the make-up of their external publics. They were members of the worldwide Anglican communion. As not all of these publics could be approached individually their bishops and archbishops would need to be targeted as figureheads. Thus, both target market and target constituencies were identified.

Then the Friends considered their budget. As they had no money at all they realized that they were going to have to generate their own resources as they went along – raising money and reinvesting a small proportion to fund their outgoings.

Next they decided upon their corporate identity. The Rector developed the concept of The Phoenix Fund. Henceforth the phoenix – the fabulous Arabian bird which rose from the ashes in ancient mythology – would be the symbol with which this campaign would always be identified. The Rector, his wife and the Communication Director then scoured libraries and other information sources trying to track down a phoenix logo. They even tried the offices of the Sun Alliance insurance company (who had taken over Phoenix Assurance some years before). Finally, they came up with three very good representations of the mythical bird. They selected the best. The Rector had a rubber stamp made bearing the chosen image. It was used throughout the campaign. The phoenix symbol appeared on all letters and publications originating from the campaign headquarters. This identity helped to encode a message that was transmitted throughout the world. The message that it transmitted was that St Andrew's was going to rise from the ashes like a phoenix and that it was going to reopen – and reopen it did.

Next, the Communication Director had to commission research into important audiences. The only problem was that he was without a budget to pay for the commission! So, as he had no budget, he did it himself! He spent hundreds of hours of his own time doing it. Essentially he concentrated on two main tasks:

1 He identified the *Directory of Grant Making Trusts* – listing every charitable trust which might help a deserving cause. This was a critical audience. He carefully identified every single trust which might be a potential donor.
2 He identified directories that listed key figures (bishops and archbishops) in the worldwide Anglican communion.

Armed with this research material into two key audiences, the Friends were in a position to develop a communication strategy.
They produced:

1 a strategy of communicating with the director of every single grant-making trust who, it was thought, might be willing to make a donation.
2 a plan of writing to most Anglican bishops and archbishops around the world asking for their prayers and support – each was also asked to send a message for the parishioners in West Hatch. Each was sent a personal letter and details of the fire. None of these was expected to send money and none was asked to do so.

Then the mode of communication with other audiences was chosen:

1 A racy, humorous and light hearted newsletter would be published each month by the Friends to feature (a) news of the restoration and (b) news of the fundraising (both by the church and by the Friends themselves). This would be sent to all those from whom support was solicited as well as to all subscribing members of the Friends.
2 All relevant media (in this case local newspapers, television and radio) would be briefed regularly – both on the restoration and on the progress of fundraising. Every time a big story broke (such as a message from the Archbishop of Canterbury or the arrival of flowers from world figure African Archbishop Desmond Tutu) the media were informed and coverage obtained. West Hatch, it seemed, was never out of the news. This tiny hamlet of 257 souls had never such achieved fame before. It was the focus of attention everywhere.

The communication programme was an enormous success. Many donations were received from those grant-making trusts who were approached. Messages of encouragement and support – and the prayers of those sending them – were received on a regular basis over the 18 months that the campaign ran. The monthly *West Hatch Phoenix Courier-Tribune (The Voice of West Hatch to the World)* regularly trumpeted news of the progress of the restoration to delighted Anglican brethren all over the world. Success built upon success. Messages of encouragement and support were received from two successive archbishops of Canterbury and from the Archbishop of York (who was moved to send encouragement subsequent to the fire at York Minster). The Archbishop of New Zealand wrote and asked if he might visit the village and give his support at first hand. Within 18 months the church was rebuilt – and over £225 000 of repairs were paid for. The Bishop of Bath and Wells reopened the church in person and well over a dozen international Anglican archbishops sent personal greetings to mark the occasion.

# Key terms

**BUNKER MENTALITY** A colloquialism originating from World War II referring to a frame of mind in which an organization keeps its head down, chooses not to be seen or heard (and, in short, 'stays in the bunker').

**CULTURE** The language, customs and traditions associated with an organization – 'the way we do things here'.

**EARLY WARNING SYSTEM** Use of corporate communication to give advance warning to an organization about factors building up amongst the audiences that impact upon it. Factors about which it needs to have knowledge – a direct result of cross-fertilization.

**ENVIRONMENTAL SCANNING** Referred to by some academics as the managerial activity of learning about events and trends in the organization's environment – see Boundary Scanning in Chapter 1.

**GOLDFISH BOWL** Reference to a bowl made of plain glass in which fish are kept. By its very nature it is possible for an onlooker on the outside to see everything that is happening inside it.

**GOODWILL** The respect and appreciation given to – and felt towards – a person or organization (NB this word has a different meaning in financial terms).

**MISSION** The expressed purpose and commercial intent of the organization. A Mission Statement is a fashionable business technique which emerged from corporate communicators in the US in the 1980s. Considered by some management gurus to be an essential communication tool; and not by some others!

**PIVOTAL ROLE** A management position providing the executive concerned with a position of such significance that many other executives depend upon him or her.

**RISING SHARE PRICE** The increasing value of the price of the company's shares on the stock market; a price which goes up almost every day; this might suggest that the organization is well regarded by the stock market; also it might suggest that it is being chased up for other reasons (some, occasionally, dubious).

**STRATEGIC RESOURCE**  A reference to any management discipline which contributes substantially to corporate strategy, corporate performance and ultimately to overall competitive advantage – as well as to the bottom line.

**SYNERGETIC**  If for example marketing and communications are said to be synergetic the comment means that one matches the other and that they work well together; the two in tandem enhancing and adding to corporate performance, to overall competitive advantage and to the bottom line. All this in a way that each would not achieve on its own.

# Chapter 5

# Using the tools provided by corporate communications

What role does public relations play in helping an organization win the admiration of its peers?

Skolnik (1994)

In many organizations communication executives are becoming involved increasingly in the decision making process – a process that results in corporate policies and strategies.

'Partly because we are such a visible company, management appreciates communications more than any place I have been involved with' said Gary McKillips, Turner Broadcasting Systems. 'Our chief function is media relations, but we are broadening to include community relations and issues management. We put together a voluminous strategic plan for issues that we thought might develop around the Goodwill Games, the first international sporting event in the new Russia.'

Some corporate executives undoubtedly feel a sense of frustration at not being able to make an input into decisions that affect the reputation of their corporation. Gaining a step on the ladder towards holding a key management role is often far from easy. Apparently, making a big media splash is one way that communicators feel that they can attract top management attention, according to McKillips.

'The key things are performance and professionalism', he advised. He added that this was easy to do at TBS for 'we have a visible CEO and we do not have to break down doors to get placement. We are successful in the media and management recognizes how important we are'.

Too often management does not understand corporate communications, McKillips acknowledged. 'People become complacent. But that is wrong. If you score big you can break through and become a major part of what's going on in your company'.

adapted from Skolnik (1994)

A lot of communication executives discuss the need for integrated corporate communication programs. But, the question is, how many of them put this into practice? How do they convince their colleagues of the benefits that communications can make? HRM is one example. Most executives recognize the value of taking a strategic approach when communicating with their workforce. However, relatively few think this through for their external audiences. How much strategic thinking is done about communicating best practice HR messages using best practice communications techniques?

In our experience, the brochure used to attract graduates to an organization is often used internally and externally as the definitive guide to an organization. However, many executives do not seem to realize the necessity of striking a fine balance between presenting the corporate personality (which must reflect accurately the recruiting organization) and attracting and informing suitable applicants in a way that deters unsuitable ones.

The responsibility for graduate recruitment – and its associated marketing communications – is most frequently put in the hands of HRM people. Because it is seen as an HRM function it is separated from mainstream corporate communication; thus its marketing potential gets overlooked. HR managers see their colleagues in communications as mere guardians of visual identity – not as people who can add value by coaching them in communication principles.

Perhaps communicators are doing a poor job at marketing their own skills. Recruitment marketing – and the communications which are associated with it – must be part of the overall strategy if truly integrated corporate communications is to become a reality. For certain, communications and the rest of the marketing mix can be used to benefit recruitment.

adapted from Spencer (1997)

# Introduction

In this chapter we consider some of the varying ways in which corporate communications can impact upon organizational success. Communication executives are concerned with presenting their organization to key publics and winning their admiration. Thus influencing them has become an important part of their task. Communicators help to define the organization's mission, objectives and strategies; explaining its role within its social, political and economic framework; scanning environmental boundaries (organizations believe that they can achieve marketing advantage by having advance knowledge of those public policies which are likely to impact upon it) and transmitting messages internally and externally.

Lobbying is a communication process which seeks to bring views to bear on those who might be influential to an organization. In contrast, sponsorship (a powerful communication tool) is used to impact on external groups by contributing financially to social activities. It has the commercial objective of raising the profile of the organization and creating a favourable corporate image. Corporate communication has developed as a supporting role for marketing and advertising; creating messages and themes which aid the promotion of branded products; playing a significant strategic role in helping the organization gain competitive advantage. Likewise, financial communication now plays an important role in communication strategy – some academics feel that a measure of the growth of financial communications is that it has given public relations in general added respectability.

Fostering the goodwill of key stakeholders is at the heart of successful communications. Yet some organizations make no effort to manage external communications – preferring them to develop naturally. As corporate brand manager the CEO is largely instrumental in deciding whether the organization invests in communication strategies designed to enhance and develop the corporate reputation. Fostering a good reputation is equally important to many communicators. It can be facilitated considerably by the use of modern research techniques, which enable the organization to discover the thoughts and beliefs of key constituents. But they are expensive, and unsophisticated management regards the cost of corporate communication as an undesirable drain on scarce resources. In reality excellent communications can impact favourably on corporate profitability by ensuring contented customers, better informed financial analysts and by reducing the possibility of misunderstandings with opinion formers.

Communication (by definition a process of changing attitudes and understandings) can powerfully enable the management of change by conveying the values and perceptions of the organization to the internal public. Finally, we note that many stakeholders expect the chief communicator to be invisible – and some are – but a small minority of company spokespeople do, we note, envisualize themselves as 'the face' of their organizations.

# Lobbying

Lobbying is that means of communication by which an organization seeks to influence – and to bring its views to bear on – those external groups of people which, it perceives, may be of potential influence to it. Lobbying involves the communication executive communicating facts and information to a third party in such a way that the opinion of that third party on those matters may be influenced and its support gained for particular issues.

> British supermarket giant J. Sainsbury is hunting for a European public affairs consultancy. 'We are doing it essentially to improve our level of communications with the European institutions', said the head of group public affairs.
>
> The importance attached to consumer protection and public safety issues is one important reason for this strategic move. Sainsbury's believes it can derive marketing advantage from providing input for, and getting early interpretation of, EC directives.
>
> adapted from *PR Week* (1997e)

That branch of corporate communications variously referred to as Corporate Affairs or Public Affairs is sometimes referred to as lobbying. Goodman (1994), in referring to Government Relations, remarks that it is what some refer to with a smirk or a sneer as lobbying. He goes on to describe it as the meeting with local, state, federal, and in some cases international, agencies to advocate for the corporation on matters in its interest. It is, he notes, an area of corporate communication which demands the highest ethical standards.

> Calling on the government to restrict the 'potentially corrupting activities of lobbyists', Paul Flynn MP, demanded greater transparency. The MP was commenting on what he saw as a depressing influx of new lobbyists all convinced that alcohol is essential if researchers are to be persuaded to influence MPs to do the bidding of the affluent commercial organizations that employ them.
>
> adapted from Dowman (1997)

Successful lobbying involves corporate communicators in:

- Identifying those people or groups in public life who may be helpful in the pursuit of your cause.
- Carrying out research to establish the opinions, positions and desired behaviour of those whose support you hope to elicit – thus gaining the knowledge that will enable you to win the support of those target groups.
- Recommending the stance that the organization should take upon the issue.
- Soliciting the support of potentially influential external groups such as members of parliament and government ministers – those who you consider may be potentially sympathetic and who might be prepared to seek to influence their colleagues on your organization's behalf.

## Lobbying – TMA's bid to stub out smoking ban

One election pledge which the government was able to implement was a tobacco advertising and sponsorship ban; a White Paper on smoking will follow.

The cigarette manufacturers' trade association (TMA) wants to ensure that new legislation excludes any ban on advertising and sponsorship. Their objective will be to convince MPs that advertising does not encourage children to smoke; that such a ban would not reduce smoking consumption; and that statutory regulation in this area would not produce the desired results.

The TMA has been lobbying the public health minister for several months in an effort to ensure that the industry's viewpoint is listened to. TMA sent an eight minute video to all MPs in the hope that it would persuade them that an advertising ban would not achieve the government's aims.

A TMA spokesman said 'we hope to influence MPs because we feel that the minister is under a misapprehension. The campaign will continue. Some MPs have requested further infomation from the TMA, but the response has at best been muted.'

adapted from Lee (1997a)

The lobbying industry is undergoing great change. It is believed widely that a new climate of open government is sweeping through Westminster and Whitehall. Lobbyists who hope to survive will have to adapt. Lobbying will become more the art of providing clients with the information and strategy that they will need in order to carry out the lobbying of MPs and civil servants themselves.

adapted from Lee (1997b)

# Sponsorship

Sponsorship typically refers to the financial support given by an external organization to a leisure or sporting activity: this financial support is given with a definite commercial objective in mind – if only with the intent of creating goodwill and good public relations. Typically, without this external financial support there would be no available funding for the proposed activity. Sponsorship may be an approach to communication which penetrates consumer perception filters in an indirect way – overlapping between corporate and marketing communications (Kitchen, 1993).

## A powerful communication tool

The sponsor will expect a measurable commercial return in exchange for its investment. The organization receiving the sponsorship funds will provide valuable publicity and helps to create goodwill (getting the message across) for the sponsoring organization. Goodwill generated in this way can be a powerful tool in the development of a communications strategy aimed at image building and raising the profile of the sponsor's organization. Sponsorship is a communications medium that can reach many people very easily and very quickly, and it can be highly cost effective. But the sponsorship must be sharply focused on the key publics whom the organization seeks to influence.

Although sponsorship can be a highly effective – and can certainly help win competitive advantage – it can require a large initial investment. This investment may well extend far beyond the initial sum handed over to the event being sponsored. The sponsor may need to allocate a substantial sum from its marketing budget to cover the ongoing costs of supporting the sponsorship programme so that the organization obtains a full and perceptible return for its capital outlay.

## Sponsorship fulfilling obligations to society

White and Mazur (1995) refer to the value of sponsorship as an effective communications tool. It is a tool that provides the organization with the 'halo' effect (Kitchen, 1993) – the benefits derived from charitable or community involvement. Major corporations have become increasingly concerned that they are seen to be fulfilling their societal obligations responsibly (Brown and Cox, 1997). Sponsorship is now a powerful communication tool used by organizations to convey their messages and themes to key publics. It has come to play a useful role in the communication process; but it is a specialist tool and not one that ought to be used indiscriminately.

## Creating a favourable image – building the brand

Part of the power of sponsorship as a communications tool is that it can assist the process of creating a favourable corporate image – as it can also help raise the awareness and profile of a particular brand. This can be reinforced by the sponsorship of a series of events. Carling Black Label Lager, for example, sponsors the Football Association premier league programme at a cost of £12 million (Bond, 1995a). Extended sponsorship programmes of this nature help to promote the corporate image as the sponsorship programme unfolds. Sometimes companies sponsor several different activities at one time, building the corporate image in two places at once. Tennent's Lager, for example, sponsors both the Tennent's Scottish Cup (soccer) and Tennent's in the Park (music throughout Scotland).

## Raising the profile

Just as a full page advertisement in a newspaper may raise public awareness of a particular issue, so also sponsorship can be a powerful tool, raising the profile of the corporate brand or of the corporate goods or services. Sponsorship of English test matches was responsible for transforming the sizeable but little known Cornhill Insurance company into a household name – the central purpose of the sponsorship programme was to raise the company's profile and thus to make its name better known.

Corporate sponsorship can – and does – extend into very many cultural and leisure areas; from Fosters' sponsorship of The Oval cricket ground in London to the sponsorship of the choir in Bristol Cathedral. Sponsorship of a local nature can impact powerfully on key regional audiences, creating a favourable impression, raising the profile of the organization with local media, customers, opinion formers and stakeholders alike. It can also assist where advertising is not a viable option. In early 1998, B.A.T. Industries were discussing possible sponsorship of a motor racing team in the world championships to overcome the ban on cigarette advertising.

In this context the communications department has a key responsibility ensuring that the organization conveys one message and speaks with one clear, co-ordinated Voice (Heath, 1994). The task will be to ensure close co-ordination between the communications programme and the marketing and advertising departments – making certain that the policies of all three departments are dovetailed so that the core strategy of the sponsorship programme is effective in promoting the desired messages and themes.

## Helping gain entry to overseas markets

There are very many ways in which sponsorship can facilitate the communication process; one is in the context of international communications. Here sponsorship can be a powerful means of enabling a corporation to reach and gain entry to international markets; for example it can facilitate the process of crossing new frontiers. In fact sponsorship (especially in the context of supporting brand and product PR) may well be chosen as a key tool to help shape the image of the corporation in international markets.

> The Public Affairs consultancy Political Context is about to launch a sister company. This new firm will advise organizations on community relations. Its aim is to help them to create links between businesses and communities. It will achieve this through initiatives such as sponsorship, staff secondments and educational programs. It will also advise charities and other voluntary organizations on matters of concern such as politics, public affairs and issues management. The founder said 'we believe that there is an

opportunity to better integrate community relations as part of
corporate communications'

adapted from *PR Week* (1997f)

# Consumer public relations

Consumer communications has evolved. It was a narrow specialist
function and it has become an indispensable component of overall
marketing strategies.

adapted from Mazur (1994)

## Corporate brand manager

The concept of a brand is not limited to an individual product line but can be
extended to an entire company (Srivastava et al., 1997). So in an era of global
markets, and the ever increasing pursuit of overall competitive advantage, the
corporate brand has become all important. One of the few tools of differentiation remaining to competitors is corporate reputation (Chajet, 1997).
Likewise the CEO is now recognized as the corporate brand manager. It may
well be that the corporate brand is now a deciding factor when a corporation
makes a choice between one supplier and another.

## The brand is king

As the brand manager has assumed a role of greater significance so also have
the brands for which the manager is ultimately responsible. Over the past
decade an increasing number of major corporations have included the value of
their brands in their balance sheets – just one visible manifestation that the
brand has assumed increasing importance. The brand has become a key
strategic weapon in increasingly competitive market places.

## New role in marketing strategies

The Commercial Director of petfoods for Quaker believes that
Consumer PR is changing. 'We had a fairly traditional view – we
looked at it as a narrow specialist function we now look to our
agency to be part of the broader mix and have a point of view on
the most appropriate type of communications that do not
necessarily stay in the box of what has been traditionally called
public relations'

adapted from Mazur (1994)

Accordingly Brand PR and Consumer PR have assumed key roles in the corporate communications mix. It is part of the function of the communication executive – working in tandem with the marketing and advertising departments – to create carefully tailored promotion programmes. Information about a new product – and a media relations campaign to excite the interest of identified journalists in such a product – has become a legitimate part of PR activities (Harrison, 1995).

Harrison makes the point that a consumer PR campaign, together with advertising, may well be more effective than advertising alone. She lists three circumstances in which marketing can be assisted powerfully by brand public relations:

- building and maintaining awareness
- repositioning
- overcoming negative perceptions.

> British Airway's PR offices are also an arm of the airline's marketing efforts.
>
> *Air Transport World* (1996)

> By utilizing carefully-targeted and bespoke promotions much greater flexibility can be brought to bear when your messages are complex. The Managing Director of Burson-Marsteller points to the example of the Wall's Ice Cream brand *Too Good To Be True*. This was a product with a complex set of messages all of which conflicted with each other. On the one hand was the message indulgence, food values, and ice cream. On the other hand the message was that the product is low in fat, healthy and so on. What Burson did was to use different magazines for different messages; some emphasizing the quality and value; some concentrating on low fat and health; and *Family Circle* was used for food lovers generally. In that way the problem of how to communicate a complex and seemingly conflicting set of messages to different audiences with different priorities was solved.
>
> adapted from Mazur (1994)

## Increased sophistication of consumer PR techniques

There has been an increasingly sophisticated use of Consumer PR over the past decade, which Mitchell (1994) attributes to:

1 increasing sophistication of the available communicating techniques – targeting the right messages to the right audiences at the right time and subsequently evaluating their effectiveness.

There is so much more space in the Sunday papers. So many
dedicated sections on food, drink, gardening, travel and so on. It
is just a wonderland for PR. There are so many more
opportunities for PR in this media mix.'

2 media fragmentation prompting many clients to rethink their attitudes towards
  advertising.
3 a new desire for marketing integration.

Adapted from Mitchell (1994)

## Key role for consumer PR

Consumer PR has taken on a key role as an indispensable part of the overall
marketing strategy using advertorials, advice lines, reader's offers and
sponsorship among many other marketing tools. Until quite recent times
Consumer PR was used to enhance the role of advertising. Today it plays a
role of increasing dominance in the marketing mix. It is often used to round
off the meaning of major media advertising campaigns.

Gillette is not a company that is normally bashful where its
advertising is concerned. But last May it found itself in an
embarrassing position. It had to withdraw the centre piece
(heavyweight TV advertising) of the planned launch of its new
product Gillette Sensor for Women. The American launch was so
wildly successful that Gillette simply could not keep up with
demand.

So, when it came to the UK launch, Gillette proceeded with a
small amount of brand public relations; taken together with a
little bit of women's press advertising. Countrywide
Communications added the usual spice – research on what men
and women thought were a good pair of legs – and there was
additional research covering social trends in hair removal and
beauty for the upmarket media. Within three months the Sensor
for Women product accounted for 40% of all razor sales both
male and female. Gillette's marketing manager remarked that it
really demonstrated the role that PR can play in building a brand.

She went on to say how very difficult it is to quantify the
different elements of the marketing mix – when the whole
purpose of the exercise is to integrate them. Many marketers
within Gillette have, in the past, not placed much emphasis on
PR. They feel that this has been an amazing case study for the
entire Gillette organization.

adapted from Mitchell (1994)

## Working alongside sponsorship

Consumer communications can work closely alongside sponsorship deals. As noted, Bass plc product Carling Black Label sponsors the FA premier league. The Consumer PR campaign, which supports the sponsorship deal sets up events designed to bring together key media with players and fans. There are monthly Carling Number One awards for players and managers. This is a regular opportunity to get photo-branding in football media, which simultaneously underlines Carling's position as Britain's Number One Pint (Bond, 1995a).

This is all about targeting in an age of tight budgeting and fragmentation of both media and audience. Nobody wants fluff any more. Everything must be very focused, targeted and tight; this is particularly due to the recession. Organizations require effective consumer communications and they are looking for strategies that get the product brought to the attention of the public. A lot of communication today needs to be (1) based on very strong information and (2) linked to issues confronting key publics.

adapted from Mazur (1994)

Whitbread's intentions were to distract us from political fatigue with a taste of America. Brewing Boston Beer under license from Sam Adams in the US, Whitbread set its sights on the growing hybrid beer market.

Communique Public Relations brand PR tactics involved using a variety of media:

- regional press
- men's lifestyle magazines
- radio

... all meshed in with American dates and events aimed at drumming home the American connection ... all to promote brand awareness.

The trade launch kicked off with a survey to gauge attitudes on contemporary culture in the UK and the US. Communique PR set up ten radio competitions with Boston Beer prizes – to run in tandem with the Boston, MA celebration of St Patrick's day.

Cinema goers – seen as a key Boston Beer audience were also targeted through Flick's Magazine with a competition run around Patriot's Day.

The biggest challenge was to reach ABC males. A full page Boston Beer feature went in Sky Magazine's 10th birthday issue.

Communique PR also arranged 4 July parties for eight outlets across the UK to run Boston Beer Independence Day parties.

Then Communique PR switched to men's fashion arranging for Boston Beer to be the sole tipple at the June launch of USC clothing store in Manchester.

It is too early to gauge the full impact. However, so far coverage has included the *Mirror* and *Independent*, five regional newspapers and BBC Radio and the radio competitions have amassed a reach of 5 000 000 listners nationwide. Whitbread PR Manager Mandy Macleod is very happy so far.

adpated from Smith (1997)

Consumer PR can play a major strategic role in preparing the ground for the Brand PR that is to follow; this can be done in the shape of carefully formulated advertising campaigns. In the case of Redoxon, the brand campaign came 24 months after the public relations campaign.

In some cases it is simply timing that matters. With the launch of Roche's Redoxon the Quentin Bell Organization prepared the ground for advertising. It communicated through the press about how anti-oxidants might be the key to protecting our bodies from free-radicals ... but the ads were not launched until two years down the line.

adapted from Mitchell (1994)

British Airways have an enormous corporate communications budget, much of which is taken up by Brand PR – of which 28.5 per cent is consumed by free seats given to the media.

A major part of British Airway's public relations effort is aimed at ad hoc events. However, major efforts are constantly required when launching new brands (examples of which are the recent relaunch of club world business class *and* its new first class service). The promotion of these new products resulted in BA getting more than one hundred reporters to London for briefings. This was followed up by a worldwide tour which introduced the products to (lucky) members of the international press.

adapted from *Air Transport World* (1996)

As noted later, cross-border communications present special challenges to the corporate communicator. Cross-border communications play a critical role in Brand PR where the global brand and the global identity has to be co-ordinated by the world headquarters. In reporting that international communications are growing, the MD of Shire Hall Communications points out that today a strategy can be formulated in the US, adapted for the UK and then modified for local markets, each learning from the other.

You can accept that the communications trategy can – and should – be developed at an international level, with brand guidelines PR, advertising, corporate identity, set and policed at an international level by the corporate brand owner. Given these agreed brand messages and values you then have the messy job of implementing them in countries overseas.

adapted from Lancaster (1995)

A Brand PR campaign communicated across borders faces the special challenge of finding what works in each country and integrating cultural differences into particular communication strategies. Mazur (1994) notes that consumer communications seems to be much less the junior partner in the marketing mix. Its practitioners are able to offer more sophisticated, targeted and creative solutions to their brand plans which, she suggests, are implemented alongside areas like direct response, sales promotions and advertising.

For international marketers the corporate brand is only part of the story. There is also the additional challenge of communicating brand values across geographical boundaries.

Seagram International is a distiller on a global scale. It is a diverse business both in terms of product range and geography. As a company it puts heavy emphasis on developing both character and heritage of individual brands. One such product is Chivas Regal which is sold in over 150 countries.

Last year Seagram used 'the Spirit of the '90s; A Chivas Regal Report' in an attempt to position the brand as 'the most prestigious and the highest quality premium spirits brand'. Seagram developed a PR campaign to run in conjunction with its worldwide advertising campaign.

'We use a "360 degree approach" to our global marketing' commented the media and brand manager at Seagram UK 'I provide PR expertise alongside brand directors as part of our global marketing initiative'.

She added that 'It's possible to have a single international program but at the same time to take into account different market needs. We provide the PR companies in each country with details of our research they are then encouraged to implement the campaign using their knowledge of the local market'

'People want a neat solution but you need to build from the bottom up and find out what works in each country.'

adapted from *PR Week* (1997g)

# Financial communications

We noted in an earlier chapter that financial communications have emerged over the last decade and become the fastest growing, and perhaps the most increasingly influential, growth area in corporate communication. This has arisen largely as a result of the globalization of financial markets following the Big Bang in 1987. Over the previous 30 years institutional investors had largely taken the place of private investors as the main source of capital for corporate investment. As large amounts of available capital began to flow into the markets from overseas, companies realized the importance of communicating with institutional investors and of enhancing their appeal to them.

Many communication scholars feel that the measure of the success of financial communications is that it has done a great deal – some suggest more than any other area of the communications field – to give public relations in general added respectability. There are risks attached to communicating with the City (which some corporations regard as the key financial audience) and it is an area of intense interest to many major corporations. It is the one communication field in which many corporations choose to employ the services of specialist external consultants. This is almost certainly because financial communications require a degree of sophistication.

However, while acknowledging that financial communication does require a degree of specialist knowledge, the Director, Corporate Affairs at Glaxo-Wellcome commented that whilst the content of financial communication 'is highly technical – with a degree of detail – an awful lot of it is in common with other communications; and, therefore, with due diligence can easily be mastered by a senior communication executive'. 'Financial communication', he added, 'has a significant impact on our key audiences. The flow of information through the department is a continuum.'

One management writer has suggested that financial communications began with GEC in 1950s. Certainly communication with key financial audiences has become a central plank of corporate strategy. Major commercial organizations understand the need to be understood by publics who provide their capital (and who need to appreciate their potential from the point of view of earnings growth) and whose perceptions and opinions can impact on their share price.

As the percentage of stocks held by institutional investors increases, the more incentive they have to raise their voices challenging the conduct of top managers and, in turn, the greater are the incentives for managers to create subunits to liaise with institutional investors, provide them with information and hoping to win their approval (Rao, 1997). Fashion retailer Laura Ashley is one company which has lost much credibility with financial audiences and, in early 1998, is seeking to reverse this situation by communicating with financial analysts and the financial media. City institutions have become a critical audience – their purchasing and selling decisions can impact dramatically on the share price – witness the price of Laura Ashley stock which fell from £2.20 to £0.30 in 18 months.

## Keep the City informed

A key factor in successful communication with financial publics is not only seeing that the City is kept informed but that this done in a timely way. The City does not like to receive bad news nor does it like being taken by surprise by unfavourable news. Today the professional communicator is very much aware that the essence of his or her craft with City publics is to see that they are informed – and kept informed – on a regular basis.

## Responsibility for financial communications

Communicating with key financial constituencies has become an increasingly demanding role often requiring specialist knowledge and skills. We noted earlier that organizations structure the financial side of their communications in very different ways. Financial communications may be handled by:

- the Director of Corporate Communications
- the Financial Director
- the Company Secretary
- by a mix of all three.
- or, indeed, by external consultants.

In some organizations financial communication is dealt with by the communication executive. At Yorkshire Tyne-Tees Television, for example, the Group Director of Corporate Affairs deals directly with City journalists with whom, he says, he has a 'synergetic relationship'. White and Mazur (1995) consider that many organizations allocate this responsibility to the Financial Director, with the communication executive merely playing a presentational role. Other organizations, they suggest, hand the task to the communication executive, with the financial director working alongside him or her. Management students might think it essential that financial communications are co-ordinated by the communication executive and the financial director (or Treasurer as he is styled in some countries) working in tandem; whoever takes the presentational role.

In some instances, financial communication is dealt with separately by the company secretary or by the financial director. Some organizations segregate financial communication. At J. Sainsbury there is a separate department dealing with this function – they report to the company secretary. At the Avon and Somerset Constabulary the limited amount of financial communication is dealt with by the corporate team.

At Lloyds/TSB financial communication reports to the finance director. Lloyds handle the function this way because they feel that 'Financial communication sits more sensibly with the finance division.' Interestingly at Lloyds, where the CEO is reputed to be agnostic about the full power and use of communication strategy, he nevertheless takes a very great personal interest in financial communication and enjoys, says his Head of Corporate Communications, 'a session with the analysts'. British Airways is another organization at which both investor relations and the City are handled by separate departments.

In the summer of 1996 financial communication at GlaxoWellcome had just been moved – the remit had gone to the finance director. While this decision departed from a long established Glaxo tradition of integrating financial communications with the broader remit of corporate communications, the group public affairs director was nevertheless sanguine. He had ensured that communications with the investment community remained, de facto, fully integrated with the wider corporate communications function so that messages were consistent.

Perhaps major corporations need to examine corporate communication from a more interdisciplinary point of view. However, where the financial and communication functions are separated, it is not unusual for the communication executive and the finance director to work closely together with the former particularly advising on presentation.

At tobacco and financial services giant B.A.T. Industries (where financial communication is dealt with by the financial director in liaison with the communication executive), their communication executive has an advisory role. But the company has always believed that the greater part of the task is 'a communications sort of job rather than a finance job'; so their communication executive feels that it makes sense that the person talking to the analysts should also be the person talking to the press.

## Financial communications to the exclusion of all else

In some organizations financial communication is dealt with by the communication executive to the virtual exclusion of all else. At Storehouse, for example, the role of the director of corporate affairs is limited almost entirely to financial communications and to internal communications. Here the CEO and finance director have other responsibilities. So their communication executive carries bigger responsibility than is usual in this area.

The significant role that he plays in connection with financial PR is demonstrated by his major role with the *Annual Report* – at least half of which he writes himself. He has considerable autonomy – with a very free range to speak about the organization and to project it to key audiences. He was brought in when the organization was facing a severe financial crisis and was hired because of his particular skills and experience. Storehouse is one example of an organization where sophisticated use of financial communication has been understood by those who make up the dominant coalition. Communicating with key financial audiences is a central plank in their corporate strategy.

## Financial communications dealt with by external consultants

As noted elsewhere financial communications are often dealt with by external consultants working in tandem with the communication executive. Essentially there are two reasons why this may occur. On the one hand, a company (and here Vaux Brewery Group is an example) may feel that consultants are able to offer specialist – and often sophisticated – advice of a sort which is not available in-house. Secondly, the organization may prefer to have its financial communications handled by external practitioners who may have a wider range of influential contacts in the City.

Davis (1995) described financial PR consultancies as a 1980s growth industry, but he described them as 'one of the least deserving' and he went on to question exactly what contribution financial communications makes. Many senior communicators might respond by commenting that financial communication consultants contribute enormously to a better understanding – and perception – of the organization.

## Key financial publics

The following publics are those generally regarded as the ones which make up the financial audience:

---

- analysts
- the City
- financial journalists
- institutional investors – investor relations
- merchant banks
- private investors – investor relations
- stockbrokers.

---

## Investor relations

> In many ways we treat investors just as though they are our customers. When we go to a meeting, we make a note of what we are asked most frequently and what appear to be the major issues of the day. Naturally, we make sure that these issues are specifically addressed in detail in our next quarterly report.
>
> adapted from Halliday (1992)

As financial marketers, investor relations departments seek to educate investors and financial analysts and recruit and retrain investors (Rao, 1997).

> If shareholders occupied management time at all before the 1980s, Investor Relations was often taken care of by the Chief Financial Officer. In those days it involved little more than public relations and

occasional crisis management. By 1990 the investor relations office
had developed into a full-time professional operation and the
manager occupied an office adjacent to that of the CEO.

adapted from Useem (1993)

White and Mazur (1995) suggest that there is an ongoing debate about the
way in which investor relations are handled. Some organizations subdivide
their communication departments to handle different publics. Wessex Water,
for example, has separate departments for both institutional investors and
private investors; other organizations have separate departments for communicating with analysts. Many large organizations (of which Viridian plc is an
excellent example) employ an Investor Relations Manager whose primary
function is to communicate with the company's shareholders.

Private shareholder loyalty cannot be bought – it should be sought.

Gummer, writing in Hart (1995)

In many ways investor relations is still maturing as a management
skill. It developed in the 1980s when companies recognized that
investors needed to learn more about the businesses in which they
had made investments. This management area is now en route to
achieving similar focus and importance as it has long enjoyed in the
US.

The increasing emphasis placed upon shareholder value within
large companies has simply highlighted the importance of good
investor relations. More and more corporations seek to excel in this
field as they compete for the funds of prospective investors.

Communication executives involved in investor relations are
responsible for managing their company's relationships with the
financial media. A company's investor relations efforts could be seen
as one way in which it impacts upon how the market determines
the cost of its capital.

Institutional money is concentrated increasingly into a few very
large fund management groupings. Consequently there is growing
interest in corporate governance. Further, increasing emphasis on
investment performance has accelerated the growth and the
importance of investor relations.

Institutional investors now take it for granted that they will have
regular direct access to corporate management teams. By this
means, they can assess for themselves the competence of the
management and they can judge the merits of their corporate
strategies.

Investor relations professionals represent their companies in the
investment community but they also have important internal roles
to provide strategic input and participate in takeover activity. They

(1993) suggest that corporate reputation may function as an intangible asset – providing a sustainable positional advantage for firms who enjoy a strong and positive reputation. But some organizations (for example, Williams Holdings) choose not to attempt to manage relationships – allowing them to emerge, unmanaged and unfocused – naturally – as the business itself grows. Dow Corning had done little to try to build awareness for itself (Argenti, 1997) until it became involved in a crisis – and it ended up filing for Chapter 11 bankruptcy in the US in 1995.

> Early publications focused on a narrow definition of image and identity. This definition was rooted in the world of logos and design. It was not a strategic approach to the area defined in the term *reputation*. More recent books (Fombrun, 1996) have demonstrated the important part that reputation plays in the overall success of organizations; and this applies from business schools to large corporations such as Dow Corning. Corning could not be bothered to consider its reputation as a strategic tool until after its crisis developed.
>
> Any organization has to consider its reputation as a potentially powerful means of measuring its overall performance in its marketplace. At the end of the day its ability to manage its reputation may well determine its very survival.
>
> adapted from Argenti (1997)

## Reputation affected by local involvement

Organizations need to realize that almost all actions that they take – or with which they are involved – can impact on the environment in which they operate (for example, many decisions made by Boots plc have an enormous impact upon the population at large in the city of Nottingham) and resultantly upon its reputation. Accordingly, those organizations which have an awareness of corporate responsibility can hardly escape entering into dialogue with those key publics affected by their actions.

> Regardless of how companies are chosen by would-be investors, it is difficult to imagine that corporate reputation will be ignored in the process. It is a mind boggling thought to imagine what anti-tobacco lobbyists might say about investing funds in Philip Morris or what the human rights lobby would think of companies who trade with China; and just consider what the anti-abortion groups would say about drug companies who produce abortion-related medications.
>
> So, as management comes to appreciate – and reacts to – these forces, a strong correlation between corporate profitability and corporate reputation will be drawn with both precision and clarity. Then the management of corporate reputation will come to be seen as a mainstream and vital discipline; and one which will need to be integrated into the entire business management process.
>
> adapted from Chajet (1997)

As noted earlier a large number of people in the community in Halifax consider themselves stakeholders in one form or another in the Halifax Building Society. Thus the society could scarcely avoid noticing that it is affecting the economic climate in its locality in many differing ways – giving it a position of leadership in its social and economic environment. Corporations with a global presence recognize that well-orchestrated communications with external audiences bring great benefits and they use them to underline their sense of corporate responsibility. Oil-producing giant BP is a topical example. It is having great difficulty in sustaining its deserved reputation for corporate responsibility in the face of ever growing attacks from Greenpeace over its drilling operations in the North Atlantic.

## Impact of boundary scanning on reputation

Corporate communication units are responsible for understanding current and emerging issues affecting the organization's reputation (Post and Griffin, 1997). As a management discipline which plays an essential role in environmental scanning, corporate communication is an approach which enables corporate responsibility to be an essential part of a two-way communications strategy. ASDA plc is one example of a company which actively involves itself in strategically focused local promotion – enabling the organization to make better commercial decisions, because they take into account the perceptions and views of local stakeholders and those who form opinions of it.

When considering audiences we noted that management of dialogue with stakeholders has become a critical function of the communication department. Corporate dialogue has risen on the agenda because the organization and those who regard themselves as its stakeholders are dependent upon each other in many different ways. This state of dependency is likely to grow as the economic environment and the global market become increasingly complex. The views, priorities and aspirations of those who feel that they have a stake in the company will have to be listened to with ever increasing care as corporations accept responsibility for managing relationships with key external constituencies by whom they wish to be regarded as good corporate citizens and with whom they desire to have a good reputation.

## CEO's responsibility

Heath (1994) stresses the need to consider the body corporate as a communicator and suggests that once we do so certain assumptions and conclusions follow. Corporate reputation – thus corporate responsibility – is the concern of the CEO, as corporate brand manager, and of the communication executive. It is just common sense that a company's reputation is often coloured by the reputation of the CEO who is managing it – so there are valid reasons for the intermingling of managerial and corporate reputations. The recognized ability of the CEO is an important clue to the company's prospects (Meindl et al., 1985; Wade et al., 1997).

Heath continues that the quality of the goods and services is a corporate statement and that if the company cares about its reputation and customers it provides a level of quality of goods or services to foster positive regard by its customers. The really essential point, he continues, is that the organization tries to match the quality of its products or services to the expectations of its consumers. Heath notes that the expectations of most key publics are likely to result from marketing and advertising sponsored by the organization – and this will be the concern of the communications department.

Shoddy goods and services communicate that the organization does not care about its customers. Hart (1995) refers to a growing appreciation of the importance of customer retention to the success of the business. Gaines-Ross (1997) notes that the equity in a corporate reputation is the organization's most enduring and lasting asset; it requires thoughtful management and communications. It can be no surprise that research is beginning to reveal the correlation between an organization's overall reputation, the reputation of the CEO, the financial performance of the firm and the level of brand loyalty (Fombrun, 1996).

## Construed image

Management scholars suggest that yet another type of image is constructed in interactions between firms and constituents – construed image. It is defined as 'what organizational members believe that outside observers think of the organization' (Dutton and Dukerich, 1991). Construed images arise because firms attend to reputations not only as valuable assets but also reflections of themselves in the institutional mirrors. According to social identity theory, individual identity is formed through interactions with others. In the same vein, firms' identities incorporate institutional feedback about how they are perceived, and to what degree they are meeting the expectations of various constituents. In the absence of reputational rankings or other explicit success measures (Fombrun and Rindova, 1996), construed images may be a primary mechanism through which firms sense the changing expectations in their institutional environments.

Rindova (1997)

## Researching the attitudes of key publics

The public relations person should be in a position where he or she has a better sense of public opinion and shaping of public policy than do others in the corporate management structure.

Skolnik (1994)

## Need for research

Consumer research techniques have become an increasingly important tool for communication professionals in recent years. In communicating with key constituencies, successful organizations set out to alter the perceptions of influential publics and to create favourable images of the organization in their minds. Resultantly, publics come to think about the organization in new ways. Audiences form new images – and have new perceptions – all of which, as the communication executive at Boots plc noted, need to be based upon actuality. In order that the organization may bring about a sea change in public perceptions it needs to be informed of the perceptions and beliefs held by key publics; and it needs to be aware of things happening in its wider environment which might impact in some way upon its economic performance and competitive advantage.

## Reasons for research

Modern research techniques are used to discover the thoughts and beliefs of members of those publics perceived to be important to the organization. Another use is to identify whether or not those thoughts and beliefs represent reality. If they do not do so, that becomes a problem which the professional communicator has to resolve; for it is a communications problem.

Heath (1994) suggests a simple but effective model to underpin research in this area. First he proposes that current perceptions of key audiences are ascertained. Then he suggests that the objectives of a communication programme will be to alter those perceptions. Lastly, he considers what activities might be needed to achieve those objectives.

## What research reveals

Being aware of the thoughts and perceptions of key publics is part only of what research needs to discover. The organization needs to know what is required of it by key publics. The corporate communicator may desire to discover what image those audiences have of the organization, for promotion of the corporate identity is a key function of the communication department. Market research is an important means of establishing what image important constituencies have of the organization. When the results of the research are to hand promotion of an improved image can be facilitated if it is felt to be necessary. This is a central part of communications strategy.

Market research may be used also to ascertain if the strategy proposed will be effective – thus whether or not it will achieve desired corporate objectives. Research can evaluate if the proposed communications medium will be the most suitable one – for the success or lack of success of the communication strategy may well depend upon the medium selected. Research is also capable of deciding by what yardsticks the communications strategy can be deemed to have achieved its strategic objectives.

## What research can achieve

As noted research enables the corporation to explore perceptions of key audiences. It can also ascertain what is required from communication between the organization and its publics. Therefore, it is important that the organization tailors the programme to fit the needs and typology of those key audiences. The communications programme will form part of the overall corporate strategy so the research which helps to devise it is itself an important part of the total strategic process.

Not only does research serve a purpose, finding out if the means of communication are appropriate, it can also establish – beyond reasonable doubt – what messages and themes may be required to bring about a new perception of the organization or to establish a new image. Research is capable of identifying the perceived characteristics or traits of the body corporate and establishing if they are the ones that are desired. Supermarket Tesco may, for example, have a reputation for putting the needs of their customers first. Research could establish the veracity of this reputation. It could also ascertain if Tesco's reputation needs to be brought up to date in any way and, if so, how perhaps it should be done.

Train operator Stagecoach may, for example, have a reputation for running late and unreliable commuter trains in southern England. Research is capable of identifying if this is really so and, if it is, which messages might help to bring about an improved public image. Sometimes segments of a large audience may need to be specifically researched. In the autumn of 1996 there were particular problems with trains run by Stagecoach between Salisbury and London. This fragmented part of a wider audience (comprising the whole of South East England) might need to be the subject of focused research if it is thought important that the communications strategy brings about a major shift in the local perceptions of a regional train operator.

## Have results changed?

Market research programmes need to be conducted on a regular basis – so that that they can track and monitor changes in the perceptions of key publics as and when they occur. If communication programmes – aimed at changing the perceptions of those constituencies – are to be effective, further research needs to be carried out to see if perceptions have changed and whether they have resulted in desired actions. So the strategy continues: researching audiences; establishing if the message has got across; researching to see if perceptions have changed. The communication strategy will only be seen to be successful if it achieves its aim of bringing about changes in the perceptions of key publics.

# The bottom line – how corporate communication adds to economic performance

> Our findings showed that corporate brand image impacts stock
> price in two ways. One is in business results (sales generated and
> the earnings and cash flow that comes from those sales). Image also
> affects the way that the stock market evaluates the company in
> terms of the price/earnings ratio (the premium the market puts on
> earnings when setting the stock price) and the cash flow multiple
> (the premium put on cash flow). Business results and stock market
> evaluation in turn influence shareholder value.
>
>                                                        Gregory (1997)

Pincus et al. (1994) refer to a belief commonly held among senior management that they believe that communication adds little to corporate performance. Yet Heath (1994) notes that communication executives can only become part of their organization's dominant coalition when they contribute to management strategy in ways that affect the bottom line.

Shortsighted management see the cost of communication as a drain on corporate resources, in reality it is the opposite. The communicator's argument for a healthy and consistent budget has bottom line validity (Gregory, 1997). One senior communicator spoke of the power of corporate communication in terms of its ability to improve economic performance, and (reported Fleisher and Burton, 1995) 'what most of our colleagues do not know or understand is how critical our role is to the bottom line'. Alas, some do not even care.

## Difficulty of CEO in understanding economic impact

When reputation is treated as a genuine form of social capital (an intangible resource) senior executives recognize that corporate communications does generate real value for the enterprise (Post and Griffin, 1997). This may be because most CEOs acknowledge the importance of communicating; but have difficulty in measuring the impact that it has on the bottom line. Senior executives who cannot see the strategic value of effective communications are short sighted. Finlay (1994), referring to CEOs who question the bottom line *cost* of communications, says that they only have to look at the millions of dollars *lost* by corporations who have disinherited the trust and confidence of one or more of their audiences.

## A form of insurance

In the same way that an insurance policy offers intangible benefits ('it may never happen') communication might be thought of as a safeguard; offering in its own shapes and forms insurance against all manner of happenings and eventualities that may never happen – but could very well do so. In reality corporate communications can impact dramatically on the bottom line. Senior communicators with multinational corporations are aware increasingly that an essential part of the increasingly complex and involved role that they are expected to play is promoting the bottom line (Heath, 1994).

This can be achieved by preventing:

- law suits – misunderstandings leading to legal action can be avoided if both sides are able to communicate better with each other
- industrial actions – by enabling better communications with the internal audience
- misunderstandings – by communicating with opinion formers
- disputes – by enabling dialogue with key stakeholders

and the drain that they can all be on the profit and loss account.

## A measurable impact

Goodman (1994) notes that good corporate communications can improve the company's financial position. A good rapport with the press can benefit the organization through more objective and balanced reporting. Although the dollar value of good communications has been notoriously difficult to quantify and measure (Post and Griffin, 1997), excellent communications impact beneficially on the bottom line, contributing to profitability, by ensuring the existence of:

- better informed government, and other stakeholders, in the public arena
- better and informed, and thus happier, customers
- better informed investors who are thus more willing to invest in the corporation
- better informed analysts who rate the company more highly – helping the price of the stock to rise – thus increasing the underlying value of the corporation.

Perhaps the fault lies with the communicator. Johnson (1994) comments that communication executives have failed sometimes to demonstrate their own value to their own senior managers.

# Communications facilitating the management of change

The rate of change is increasing in many organizations. Heath (1994) notes that corporate communications have increasingly come to play a positive role in the management of change itself. He points out that communications have been used not in a response to change but as part of the actual process of implementing change. A greater number of channels for communication have come into existence as the rate of change has gathered pace. The Director, Corporate Affairs at GlaxoWellcome is one senior professional who refers to the important role that communications played in helping to facilitate enormous change in the aftermath of the take-over of Wellcome Foundation by drugs giant Glaxo.

## Role in changing attitudes

Communication is a process of changing attitudes and understandings. It can facilitate the organization of change itself when organizations are undergoing alterations to fundamental business processes. This is particularly beneficial when large organizations are merging; as is happening in early 1998 with Guinness and Grand Metropolitan Holdings. Communications help ensure that parties to a merger are aware of: what is happening; why it is happening; and why it is beneficial that it should happen. Employees not only become aware of what is going on but feel included in the process. Internal communications can enable the process by persuading personnel that changes are implicitly for *their* long-term benefit. Communications assist the process, rewarding personnel through the use of carefully developed and properly communicated incentive programmes.

# Communications facilitating culture change

Each organization has a culture of its own – 'the way we do things here'. Corporate culture can be interpreted by detailed research and analysis. Change programmes can help to modify or change corporate culture, or can facilitate the creation of an entirely new one. Communicating and developing corporate culture is a vital part of internal communication programmes, for it is part of the function of internal communication to convey the values and perceptions of the organization to the internal public.

When a large corporation such as BT merges with fellow telecommunications corporation MCI (as had originally been proposed in the summer of 1997) a new culture has to develop; corporate communications facilitates that process. Following the merger of BEA and BOAC in 1973 it was a full decade before sustained efforts were made to blend the differing characters and cultures of the two large organizations into one – to the competitive disadvantage of the then newly formed British Airways.

## Gatwick enters the fast lane

London Gatwick has invested a lot of time and effort into trying to change people's perceptions of the airport. Until quite recently, some travellers still thought of it as being locked in a 1960s timewarp, when it was used almost exclusively for holiday charter flights. These days scheduled flights account for more than 60 per cent of services.

Gatwick Airport (1997)

# Communication facilitates a new identity

In an earlier chapter the importance of corporate identity was explored – as was the image that can be developed from it. As an organization undergoes great change it may be felt that a new identity is required. BT and MCI (who had, as noted, planned to merge at the end of 1997) were to have emerged as a global telecommunications giant to be known as Concert. Concert would have required its own identity as a means of demonstrating to key constituencies what the new organization stood for.

## Communicating the new logo

The proposed Concert identity would have played an essential part in the process of change resulting from the creation of the new corporation. This new identity would inevitably be much more than a new symbol or a freshly created logo. Nevertheless, the new logo would have been an important communication tool – being the means by which the very core – the essential corporate nature and personality of the company – would have been conveyed. A logo defines the spirit and character of an organization and what it intends to stand for.

> Proving the point that geographical location is no hindrance to implementing national public relations programmes was the challenge for Greenwood Tighe Public Relations ... when it was charged with the task of handling the launch of MFI's redesigned stores across the UK. ... The overall aim was to upgrade the profile of the stores and to promote MFI's image as well as extending MFI's traditional customer base to include new groups of store users.
>
> But as the new concept was to be rolled out across 53 stores up and down the country, the overall objective had to be translated

into specific local activity relevant to each area. The task was therefore to 'localize' the PR program creating individuality for each particular store launch.

Greenwood Tighe first carried out research in each locality, liasing with locally based media in advance to discuss promotional opportunities for the store launch.

GT consultancy provided details of investment, appointments and training to the local press. They also liased with media contacts, region by region. They did this before and after every part of the program, thus ensuring that they built and maintained awareness of each re-launched store.

The consultancy ran competitions with local media titles the aim of which was to involve the local community and to position MFI home works as a part of that community.

It held a sneak preview evening and for the official launch ceremony the winner of the newspaper competition was invited to open the store in that area. Photocalls featured local figures and representatives from local schools, groups and fundraisers. MFI home works also gave support to local charities.

This strategy succeeded in generating at least two opportunities for local coverage each day. At the same time the release of information was staggered and this helped to extend press coverage. This also maintained awareness over the allotted time.

'We had to make sure that everyone in the catchment area knew about each launch', said GT

adapted from PR (1997h)

Marketing strategy needs to support – and be supported by – the vision at the heart of the corporate identity. The marketing department will be in the driving seat, but the design company should come in very early on and they should obtain an in depth understanding of both what the organization is and how it works. The visual identity will be the third or fourth stage.

Many companies have taken a pounding from the press as they announce expensive new corporate logos – more than demonstrating how many senior marketing departments have failed properly to grasp the concept.

Staff, from receptionists to directors, must know what an organization is trying to achieve – for corporate identity is as important as any financial, property or technology tool. Indeed corporate identity needs to be managed at board level. Another element in managing an identity change is the importance of communicating it effectively to staff – for you must take them with you. This is a job that is also affecting the way that identity change is managed. Quite obviously specialist communication strategies could iron out some of the communications problems posed by corporate identity changes.

adapted from *PR Week* (1997i)

One way in which 3M's communication executives promoted understanding of their company was with a recently initiated identity strategy. Those people who identify the company with Scotch™ tape and computer diskettes may not know that 3M is involved in many other – and various – industries. That lack of knowledge might be a liability for 3M. 'We want to hire the best and the brightest and they do not want to work for an unknown company', Davis explained.

'Hence the identity strategy to help people understand who we are and what we are about', Davis explained. 'An integrated approach to communications ties in advertising, internal communications, packaging and literature, grouping discreet divisions under rubrics such as 3M Health Care. It communicates that we are in that business', Davis explained.

This identity strategy was developed jointly by all layers of management. Once the philosophy behind it was in place the professionals took over and began to implement it.

adapted from Skolnik (1994)

## Communicating a change of perception

Organizations may choose to adopt a fresh identity with the intention of retaining their competitive advantage. A new identity may concern a change in the desired perception of the organization. Change may be a necessary step towards redefining the present role of the organization. The organization may have grown and have developed into an international company or it may have expanded its range of activities. Stimulus for a change of corporate identity may come from an awareness that what the organization presently stands for is not matched by the present perceptions of key publics – it may attract perceptions which no longer reflect its current activities.

Dr Barnado's homes underwent an identity change because its trustees realized that the public at large still perceived it as a Victorian organization which rescued abandoned children; this perception was out of date; it did not represent the wider social values of the organization. Earlier, we noted that the Avon Rubber company manufactures rubber goods which are found in every home; yet consumers are unaware of the fact. A change in the way that key audiences perceive an organization can be facilitated powerfully by communication of a changed identity.

British Airways is undergoing considerable change following the appointment of a new CEO in early 1996. As we saw, BA introduced a new identity in the summer of 1997. The purpose of this new identity was to facilitate a changed image amongst key publics. It believed that this new image was required to underline the corporate strategy of translating the corporation into a global airline.

## New corporate identity is part of £6b investment programme

British Airways unveiled its radical new corporate identity to thirty thousand top customers and staff in sixty three countries. Amid the subsequent hype there was more than a note of sadness – BA was shedding its national cloak in favour of a distinctly global look. The airline vigorously denied that it is turning its back on Britain by dropping the Union flag – an emblem which has graced its tail fins for decades. The CEO denied such an idea. He said that the airline was building on the very fact that it is British.

Some commentators perceive that BA has a cold aloof image and that it is anxious to shed it. Instead it seeks to be seen as having a relaxed, friendly style, designed to appeal more to those customers who originate outside the UK and who now account for 60 per cent of its business. In explaining the recent decision the CEO said that the airline needed a fresh corporate identity that would enable it to be seen as a truly a global airline. The controversial new look is designed to reflect the international nature of the business. This new corporate identity is supposed to send an important message to customers around the world. BA desires to be the favourite airline, one responsive to passengers' needs. The new identity is that of a global, caring company, more modern, more open, more cosmopolitan, but nevertheless, proud to be based in Britain.

adapted from *Executive Traveller* (1997a)

## Furling the flag

According to British Airways CEO, Bob Ayling, the new identity is intended to present BA as a community and one passionately committed to serving and connecting the communities of the world. Behind this is the belief that BA is now a global carrier and must shed its cool and aloof British image. As a marketing exercise designed to maintain BA's dominance in the changing world of aviation (as well as flying it into the next millennium) the new identity is a bold, innovative and possibly brilliant concept.

adapted from *Executive Traveller* (1997)

Marketing communications practice Butler Cornfield Dedman was commissioned earlier this year to design a new corporate identity for Charlton Associates to mark a change of direction which it had taken; it had decided to chase the bigger Western European banking advice market – instead of just the Eastern bloc.

Changing the name to CA Consultancy would help to reinforce the organization's professionalism and convey its expertise to a new and more sophisticated market. This new identity faced potential problems as the decision had been made without involving employees.

Faced with a business selling an arcane set of skills in a very conservative market a design was chosen for the visual identity that used a typeface based logo and a distinct conservative blue/green colour scheme. This was designed to create an identity which was intended to inspire confidence.

The 'expertise' message was re-inforced by the strapline 'Consultants to the financial services industry' blazened across the firm's literature and stationery.

adapted from *PR Week* (1997)

## Communicated identity not matched by reality

The director of corporate affairs at Boots plc commented that an image needs to be backed up by actuality. Implicitly, a change programme that is not underpinned by performance may achieve a cosmetic effect; but it will achieve very little else – as British Gas found to their cost. If it is to succeed the new identity must draw on the core philosophies, beliefs and practices of the organization; it must represent the very essence of the organization itself. Of course, a change of identity might result in fresh perceptions which prove to be the opposite of those the organization wished to create in the first place.

When British Gas revamped its identity two years ago, its new logo featured a globe. This made reference to the company's international status and aspirations. But, alas, at the same time British Gas received a record number of complaints and its reputation took a severe pounding during the furore over Cedric Brown's salary.

Like so many newly privatized utilities it forgot about consumers. It was a case of the old British Gas wearing new clothes.

BG's problem lay not with its logo but within the business itself.

Corporate identity is misunderstood by senior executives. Often they see it as a magic wand which mysteriously and mystically creates change without really understanding the principles – and, indeed, the need to create change themselves.

In the opinion of Redhouse Lane MD, Jeremy Redhouse, the worst recent example of a mishandled identity is PepsiCola. It treated its corporate identity as just a visual identity when it relaunched on 'Blue Tuesday' in 1996.

They had lost the brand values and identities that they had built up over decades, so they tried to identify themselves with the values of a new generation. But there is no evidence of a link between the colour blue and the values of that generation and the strong visual activity obscured the message that lay behind it.

On the other hand, too weak a corporate identity lies behind one of the most damaging examples of mishandled identity. More than ten years after a gas explosion in an Indian factory that killed and blinded thousands of workers, Union Carbide has not invested in its image or identity and has chosen to remain invisible to the public. It risks being known only for its disasters.

adapted from PR Week (1997j)

Public relations have a role to play in changing Britain's image, according to a group of design consultants who this week suggested scrapping the Union Jack. They have also proposed re-writing the national anthem.

Wolff Olins reported that research showed that there is a gap between the perception and the reality of modern Britain.

The Chairman of PRCA was in favour of a rethink of the national symbols. She commented that 'We have constantly and consistently and regularly abused the flag. If Wolff Olson were to create a flag and guard it as jealously as most big multi-nationals guard the use of their logos and trademarks that would go someway to protecting the integrity of the flag'.

adapted from Garside (1997)

# The face of the organization

Whether Richard Branson (Chairman, Virgin Group – who reckons to devote between 20 per cent and 50 per cent of each working *day* to public relations; Fitzherbert, 1994) or Bill Gates (Chairman, Microsoft Corporation), it is the CEO/Chairman who epitomizes the Alter Ego of an organization – if any one person does so. Skolnik (1994) quotes Microsoft's communication executive as saying 'Bill Gates is our best spokesman, he is a charismatic leader.' Certainly the CEO should play a major role in communicating the message of his company (Osborne, 1994), for he ought to be the single most important – and potentially the most effective – communicator.

Most senior practitioners do recognize that they have a role in promoting senior executive colleagues. Many communication scholars underline the figurehead role of the CEO (van Riel, 1995). The public relations manager for the Avon and Somerset Constabulary said 'the Chief Constable is in effect "The Super PR Director" . . . he is the Alter Ego. He is a reassuring figure in uniform.' The Group Director of Corporate Affairs at Yorkshire Tyne-Tees Television noted that, of course, every CEO has a different style. He commented 'my job is to keep them happy. I am not the Alter Ego, I am very keen to get the CEO out there.'

Perhaps the communicator should be invisible? The Director of Group Public Relations at Vaux Group commented, 'I would not be so arrogant.' She continued 'Vaux is not a personality based company. Our Chairman fought against the "Richard Branson image"; although Frank Nicholson (Managing Director, Vaux Brewery Ltd, also Joint MD, Vaux Group plc) is a PR manager's dream. Public Relations helps others to be presented in the best possible way.'

Some corporate leaders are so powerful in their own right that their personality is inseparable from that of their organization. Could a similar thing happen to some communication executives – given that they may frequently be the spokespeople for their organizations. After all many people associated Michael Cole (communications spokesman for Harrods Ltd until his premature – and lamented – retirement in the early spring of 1998) with Harrods. White and Mazur (1995) comment that 'it can be hard to have an objective assessment of PR people when at their best they are almost invisible. There has long been an unwritten rule that PR spokespeople are never quoted, for example, though that is changing as in-house communicators have a much higher executive status.'

Howard (1992) comments that the communication director might be 'the face' of the organization. He conceptualized the communicator as 'the alter ego' of the organization. This is an interesting concept, but it is one that is not sustained by the views of most senior communicators. Practitioners over-whelmingly see their role as being invisible. Generally, senior communicators see the CEO as the face of their organizations, as the protector of the corporate reputation and as the corporate brand manager.

At one extreme, the Director of Corporate Communications at Wessex Water emphasized that she does not believe in the principle. Her view is that the person speaking 'is the person who understands what is being asked'. So, at Wessex Water, 'the public face could be any one of a number of people . . . there is no one person'. But, referring to her company, she added that 'this is a fairly unusual organization' and 'there are various aspects of the organization that become its personality'. Referring to Northumbria Ambulance, their communication spokeswoman noted that 'sometimes the CEO acts as his own PR manager', while the communications manager at Tennent Caledonian Breweries Ltd added, 'Angus Meldrum (Managing Director – Sales) is the face of TCB.

The Director of Corporate Communications at Whitbread thought the concept ridiculous. He commented that 'the whole idea emerges from 1980s "spin-doctoring" – to generate a lasting favourable impression. The whole idea was a con.' This was an opinion confirmed by the Director of Group Public Affairs at GlaxoWellcome, who remarked that 'this is a rather tired and worn out perspective on the role'.

So, many professional communicators do have strong views that their role needs to remain invisible. The then Acting Director of Corporate Affairs at W.H. Smith said 'no, I am the *éminence gris* – mine is a support role . . . and faceless'; his opposite number at J. Sainsbury stated 'the Sainsbury family is the Alter Ego'. The spokeswoman for ASDA (referring to their then CEO) commented 'the challenge for ASDA is that Archie Norman (now Chairman) is strongly associated with the company's turn around. We try very much to communicate a sense of team and involve all our colleagues in the success.'

However, there is a minority of very senior communicators who do see their role as representing the face of their organizations. The Head of Communications at BT commented, 'I represent the desired character of the organization.' The Group Publicity Manager at Avon Rubber echoed this, saying 'I am the public face of Avon. There is a certain personality side to it.' Two other senior communicators agreed with this view.

The Director of Group Public Affairs at B.A.T. Industries commented, 'Yes, I am the Alter Ego of the company. It is part of the job. It is my perception of the role. If you are in tobacco and financial services there comes a time when you have to stand up for the organization.' The Director of Corporate Affairs at Boots plc echoed this, saying 'only one person can stand up for the organization'. B.A.T.'s spokesman expanded his comments, saying 'I believe in standing up for the organization and doing these difficult jobs.' But, he concluded, 'When I was in consultancy I hoped that I should be transparent.'

Three conclusions suggest themselves from the views of communication executives regarding this issue:

- A family might be conceptualized as the face of an organization.
- Certain controversial areas require image bolstering and special presentational skills to aggrandize their level of acceptance to key audiences and this gives the spokesperson a higher than usual profile. The efforts of Harrods' spokesman Michael Cole in the aftermath of the death of Diana, Princess of Wales are certainly an outstanding example.
- A service industry such as water may well approach the issue of corporate personality from a different standpoint.

## Case study

A million people are attending music festivals and they are a captive audience for anything up to four days.

When it comes to brand penetration the youth market is highly illusive – music festivals offer an opportunity to influence this sector within its own environment.

FFI organizes PR and sponsorship acquisition for Mean Fiddler. Fidler is a group responsible for 75 per cent of the UK outdoor music Festivals. If their sponsorship is to prove effective sponsors must integrate with the event.

Pager brand Vodazap launched onto the youth market at the Big Love festival last year. They integrated with the audience through a message tower which sent messages around the site.

However, the most credible activities are often those which build on synergies between products and music.

At the Phoenix Festival computer giant Sega wanted to sponsor an area where people could play computer games. In order to achieve this, a key feature of the festival at Phoenix was its two dance tents. Research showed that the sort of people who enjoy dancing also enjoy computer games. Sega placed a Sega Saturn tent between two dance tents linking it to each with a tunnel. People came across it as if by chance. They were impressed.

Another example of credible sponsorship activity is when brands use festivals to extend advertising campaigns. Recently a Bud Ice promotion at the Tribal Gathering built on its Antarctica ad campaigns. These had featured ants carrying a bottle to an anthill. The company built a Bud Ice Chill Out Station – a giant tent with snowboard simulators, white foam seating, a bar, computer stations and models of ants climbing mountains.

Sponsors get value for money. In addition to the exposure which they obtain to their target markets there is usually massive media coverage both before and after the event; for example, at Phoenix there were over five hundred journalists present.

Adapted from PR Week (1997)

# Key terms

**BIG BANG**   A single day in 1987 when a series of reforms were introduced to the conduct of business in the City of London – including the introduction of new practices and regulations.

**BRAND PUBLIC RELATIONS**   A branch of public relations practice (used increasingly over the last 10 years), the main purpose of which is to support and publicize branded products. It is frequently used to support new product launches.

**CONSUMER PUBLIC RELATIONS**   Another branch of public relations practice which has become increasingly fashionable over the last 10 years. It has similarities with Brand PR. The essential purpose of Consumer PR is to communicate with members of the organization's buying publics.

**CORPORATE RESOURCES**   Usually refers to the financial resources (fixed and working capital) of a corporation; can also refer to human resources or any other attributes which contribute to enhanced corporate performance.

**EXTERNAL CONSULTANTS**   Firms of consultants outside an organization whose services are called upon when the organization requires assistance – either due to physical lack of resources or due to lack of expertise in-house in a particular specialized field.

**THE FACE OF THE ORGANIZATION**   An expression used by some academics to describe the one person (THE ALTER EGO) who may be seen to represent the perceived *face* of the organization.

**SPONSORSHIP**   Sponsorship typically refers to the financial support given by an external organization to a leisure or sporting activity. This financial support is given with a definite commercial objective in mind, if only with the intent of creating goodwill and good public relations. Typically, without this external financial support there would be no available funding for the proposed activity.

# Chapter 6

# Crisis communications – truth at all costs?

> No one can predict when the event will occur, only that sometime in the life of an organization a product will fail, your market will evaporate, the stock will fall, an employee may be caught doing something illegal, the CEO will retire, the workforce will go on strike, a natural disaster will occur or a terrorist will plant a bomb.
>
> Goodman (1994)

## A. H. Robins – a badly handled crisis led to bankruptcy

In 1970 A. H. Robins bought the rights to a plastic intrauterine contraceptive device known as the Dalkon Shield. Over the next half decade 4 500 000 of these devices were fitted in women. Problems with the product resulted in miscarriages, sterility and death.

Robins did not publicly acknowledge any problem with the Shield, nor did they order its recall. The company continued to market the shield aggressively for three more years after they first became aware of the problem. In 1975, as lawsuits against the company began to mount, the firm engaged in a 'market withdrawal' of the product. It still took Robins another nine years to advise women publicly to remove the device.

Here was an example of a firm attempting to avoid any appearance of liability. It tried to maintain the product's safety in spite of falling sales of the device. Moreover, women who filed lawsuits against the firm were subjected to an aggressive response from the company, who were trying to discourage such suits. At one point a federal judge in Minnesota became so angry with Robins' actions that he sent investigators into the company. They rummaged through its files and uncovered substantial evidence that senior executives had known of, or suspected, the problems years before the public was alerted.

Clearly Robins would have incurred huge costs due to the failure of its product, regardless of its disclosure policy. However, advocates of full disclosure contend that the financial losses suffered by the company were exacerbated because of the unwillingness of senior management to disclose problems sooner and then to assume responsibility. By the early 1980s more than 12,000 claims had been filed against the company. The resulting legal liability forced Robins to seek court protection. In 1985 it filed for bankruptcy.

adapted from Kaufmann, Kesner and Hazen (1994)

# How not to do a Cedric!!

Communication blunders do not just cause red faces for a few executives – they can do serious damage to a company's reputation. Companies must develop a wider perspective and they must start predicting what impact a corporate decision may have outside the boardroom.

'It could have been handled better'. That was the nearest that Cedric Brown, then CEO of British Gas, got to a grudging apology over the fabulous PR gaffe which vastly increased his salary – while at the same time cutting those of some of his colleagues.

To the PR industry it could not have been handled more ineptly. Brown's admission had been dragged out of him by a posse of tenacious Labour MPs at a Common's employment committee hearing.

Rest assured that Brown does not intend to be made to look such a big fool again; the full horror of BG's post-privatization policy of cutting back its in-house PR support has been made painfully clear to him. As a result, external specialists in issues and crisis management have been consulted, although the organization's press office does not seem aware of the fact yet!

Brown and his cohorts can at least claim some credit! They have helped the media to point a finger at an unattractive trait among some organizations – that is the trait of being arrogant, incompetent or both. Individual issues may blow over, but before they do so they invariably damage an organization's image – sometimes irreparably.

adapted from Bond (1995)

Are you listening British Gas? Not quite yet, apparently. In the wake of the media furore over Brown's salary the in-house newspaper headlined a story with a quote from their renowned chief executive 'the good messages have not come out – we have a good story to tell'.

Well, then what 'good story' did the press latch on to next? – a reduction in the number of free safety checks. Mr Brown has once again proved himself most prophetic – it could have been handled better. You bet it could!

adapted from Bond (1995)

# Introduction

Crises may occur at any time and they can come in all shapes and sizes. A crisis is never anticipated fully, however careful the advance preparation. It will impact on the organization because it contains elements of surprise. When the crisis occurs it brings with it the possibility of grave consequences. It can result in loss of confidence, it can damage staff morale and it may destroy the firm's reputation. It can have a lasting and altogether negative impact. But, if handled well, the situation can be turned to real corporate advantage and the organization may emerge with its reputation enhanced. Here we consider the essential role that communication plays in crisis preparations. Corporate communication must play a role as it is the discipline which attempts to anticipate events that might impact on key constituencies. We note that some organizations have mechanisms rather than formalized plans to deal with the unexpected. Accurate, skilful and truthful handling of a crisis can help to play a powerful part in bringing it under control and of returning the organization to normality. A good, experienced spokesperson will be needed to handle the situation; one who will understand the importance of expressing genuine concern and real sympathy for those who have suffered harm. Finally, learning from experienced professionals, this chapter explores the importance of speaking the truth at all cost when dealing with unexpected eventualities.

Ask yourself what action you would take the next time that you:

■ observe a Greenpeace boat being rammed by a Japanese fishing boat when it has tried to stop a shipment of nuclear retractor fuel at sea or
■ witness AIDS sufferers in ACT-UP in death costumes outside a drugs company protesting at the high price of the experimental drugs used for treatment or
■ see Pro-Life groups demonstrating in front of a global drug company that manufactures 'the morning after pill' available only in Europe

adapted from Goodman (1994)

# Defining a crisis

No organization is immune from fires, explosions, floods and other
natural and accidental disasters, not to mention scandal and
embarrassment.

Flanagan (1995)

A crisis is a major unpredictable event that has potentially negative results.
Quite often it is not what really happened in the incident, it is what key
audiences believe happened, that counts. It can damage its employees,
products, services, financial condition and reputation and image (Barton,
1995). It can severely damage the confidence placed in the organization by
its audiences. Above all it can seriously damage a company's share of the
market, it can damage its long-term financial viability, and its very survival
may be threatened.

One in three businesses which experience a major crisis never
recover to pre-incident trading levels – and some simply never
survive.

Paul Fox, MD, Grayling Group quoted in Cathy Bond,
*Marketing*, 1995

# What is a crisis?

'Crisis' is a relatively shapeless expression. When used in the
context of business organizations most of us think of disasters –
nuclear meltdowns – plane crashes – plant explosions – and so on.
In reality the term covers a much wider range of eventualities.

According to a former chairman of American Motors crises can
result from many different types of situations, which he thinks might
include the erosion of good feelings about an organization from key
publics, unexpected market shifts, the failure of products, upheavals
within top management, cash flow problems, industrial action or
inaction, undesired take-over bids, changes in regulation or deregula-
tion and adverse international events.

These are all vastly different in cause and consequences, but they
all have features in common. They could all escalate and get worse,
interfere with normal business operations, wreck the public image
enjoyed by the company, impact on corporate profitability and bring
about undesired scrutiny from media or government.

adapted from Kaufmann, Kesner and Hazen (1994)

A crisis is a situation characterized by surprise and high threat to important values; it has a short decision time (Holsti, 1978); and it can occur in many different ways. Every corporate crisis is unique so every situation has to be managed on its own terms (O'Rourke, 1997).

> Just before Memorial Day weekend in 1995 cigarette manufacturer Philip Morris discovered a problem with an ingredient that was used in the filter material for the cigarettes which they produce in the USA. They launched a product recall which brought back some 8b cigarettes from around the USA within a week. That was a crisis; and the defining characteristic of crisis is surprise.
>
> adapted from O'Rourke (1997)

Surprise creates the most dislocation. It is the thing that precipitates the behaviours that tend to compound the problem and makes it more difficult for the organization to extract itself (O'Rourke, 1997).

> Contamination of Perrier water led to the largest consumer recall in history. Perrier learned about the contamination when a public health inspector used a sample of Perrier to calibrate his testing equipment, figuring that Perrier was the purest water that he could find. He intended to use it as a base line against which he measured other water samples. Instead he discovered the benzene contaminant.
>
> His agency went to the FDA. The FDA went to Perrier in the USA. Perrier in the USA went to Perrier in France. Within six days the world's leading bottled water was off the shelves globally.
>
> That is what I mean by surprise.
>
> adapted from O'Rourke (1997)

White and Mazur (1995) note that a crisis may contain a high degree of threat to life, safety or to the existence of the organization; and that it contains elements of the unexpected. Certainly a crisis can put organizations into the forefront of unwanted publicity and may call into question the competence of personnel. So, crisis situations require management, and communication is an essential ingredient of that management. Guth (1995) remarked that one person's incident is often viewed as another's crisis. Crises can vary from the 1958 Munich Air Disaster (a disaster for a football club) to the 1996 *E-Coli* outbreak in Scotland (a commercial disaster for a small butcher's shop).

The Crisis Index was derived from the extent to which corporations who responded to a survey indicated that they had faced crises over the previous five years.

- Organizational restructure and change
- Hostile scrutiny from the news media
- Financial problems caused by budgetary cutbacks or a corporate deficit
- The threat of potential damage arising from a law suit
- The reappointment of CEO
- The Forced removal of the Managing Director
- Unwanted scrutiny from government regulators
- The impact of a natural disaster
- The geographical relocation of the organization
- Political controversy
- An allegation of wrong doing
- An employee facing criminal charges
- Questions about employment practices
- The death of an employee
- A corporation causing the death of non employee
- Protests from stakeholders
- A civil disturbance impacting on the firm
- The failure to meet corporate obligations
- The theft of corporate assets
- An accusation of corporate impropriety
- The arrival of a hostile takeover bid
- A public health warning against the organization
- Industrial action or inaction
- Being the focus of a political controversy

adapted from Guth (1995)

During the Tylenol poisoning crisis in 1983, Lawrence G. Foster, corporate Vice-President for public relations, explained the company's strategy. It was, he said 'to be completely open with the news media since they were helping us inform the public of possible danger, and helping us to protect them. The news media recognized early in the tragedies that we, too, were a victim. They recognized our plight, appreciated our openness, and treated us very fairly'.

adapted from Seitel (1992)

Whether the organization brought the crisis on itself – or whether it was a victim of circumstance – will affect the development of the crisis. If the organization is the victim of a crisis it is demonstrably in a different position to an organization that has itself precipitated the crisis.

In 1991 a psychopath drove his car through the front window of one of Luby's chain of restaurants and started shooting those inside. The gunman murdered 23 people before he turned the gun on himself. Within three hours a crisis team from Luby's was on the scene. This team included the company president and a communications expert was also present. Within twenty four hours the company had donated $100,000 to a fund for the victims. It also decided to keep the restaurant's employees on the payroll indefinitely. Further it held a press conference featuring the company's president. Observers commented that the speed with which Luby's acted – and the level of compassion that it demonstrated – were critical factors in their recovery from the incident. The company was seen to be a victim – not a culprit.

adapted from Kaufmann, Kesner and Hazen (1994)

The head of corporate communications at Norwich Union steered his organization through a sticky patch when it was heavily fined after falling foul of the industry regulator.

The problem is that so many managers see the media as fair-weather friends. They would prefer to slam the door when the storm breaks. A relationship with the media must be kept in good and bad times. You cannot have it one way and not the other. The only way for Norwich Union (when it was fined after falling foul of its regulatory authority) to ride with the bad publicity was to be completely open and honest. We had to be in there first with relevant and accurate information. Inevitably, there are rumours which could damage everything – the corporate name, customer perception and staff morale.

adapted from Bond (1995)

In the majority of great communication disasters something unexpected happened and the organization failed dramatically to handle it well. An organization cannot risk the harm done to corporate reputation from a badly handled crisis; and it may have little time available to make a judgement of what has happened or to carefully consider the questions asked by the media.

## Importance of reacting effectively

Effective communications may:

- reduce the risk of the problem escalating
- limit interference with normal business operations
- contain damage to the company's reputation
- contain damage to the company's bottom line

Kaufmann et al. *Business Horizons*, (1994)

Crisis communication strategies often involve expressing regrets to harmed publics. A well-handled crisis can powerfully develop an organization's image and may enhance its reputation. An appalling tragedy with well-handled communications in which the spokesman comes across as caring, genuinely distraught but willing to answer anything he can, is viewed differently (Jackson, 1995). Woodcock (1994) noted that crises handled in a professional and competent fashion can present real opportunities for the enhancement of corporate image and values. John Hall, CEO of Ashland's Oil, quoted by Kauffman et al. (1994), observed that if the public perceives that you are truly sorry and that you genuinely want to do the right thing, they will usually forgive you rather quickly. At a time of crisis the corporate image becomes all important – a good reputation is only gained over time and it can be lost in an instant.

# Do organizations prepare to handle crises?

Crisis preparation is absolutely vital for every company.
S. Aiello, *quoted in* Management Review, 1995

## Need for crisis planning

Crisis communication has become increasingly important in recent years. Planning for a crisis – and doing it as a matter of course – is the first step towards the resolution of the crisis and towards a subsequent return to normal operations. More and more (but far from all) organizations realize that to ignore a crisis is a strategic error. The tendency to ignore the worst scenario recognizes that people cannot control events (Goodman, 1994).

> At stake are opinions of people about the credibility and reliability of the organization involved ... that will influence people's reaction in the event of crisis.
>
> Goodman (ed.) (1994)

The communication executive is concerned with reaction communications. Crisis communications have as their key objectives (1) the appeasement of external stakeholders and (2) keeping employees informed (Ressler, 1982).

## Key role for communicators

Most large organizations cannot avoid dealing with a crisis at one time or another. The crisis may involve the late arrival of an ambulance, splinters of plastic in beer bottles, or worse. Loss or damage can occur in many different ways. They can include an accident involving an organization's lorry, they can originate from a decision badly made by an employee, they can be the result of the actions of others, such as saboteurs. Some concern loss of life, damage to buildings and their contents, financial disasters or scandals.

Major corporations have long recognized the importance of having crisis management plans in existence involving clearly integrated communication strategies. These strategies need to be capable of dealing with many different contingencies. The communication department has a key role in these plans so the strategy must be understood by all their people. Crisis planning ensures that when disaster occurs, the organization is prepared for what has happened and knows how to react to it. Crisis strategies must be revised and amended frequently as times and circumstances change.

## Absence of crisis planning

Guth (1995) found an alarming absence of crisis planning. But crisis planning should be a primary concern for communication practitioners. Guth suggests that there might be a link between the level of organizational crisis planning and the managerial role of its communication function – but his findings suggest that this might not be the dominant influence.

## Importance of responding

> In 1996 New York had its worst blizzard for half a century. The commuter railroad in New York spent most of the first day assuring commuters that everything was fine, that they had a plan in place to clear the tracks and that the trains were almost on schedule. Tens of thousands of commuters went to the train stations and got on the trains. They quickly stalled in the snow. They spent hours on freezing, dark and powerless trains. It was a fiasco for the Metropolitan Transportation Authority.
>
> On the front page of the of *New York Times* one of their senior executives said 'There is no question that we put together a plan that was overly optimistic. We underestimated how bad it would be'.
>
> adapted from O'Rourke (1997)

Few things impact upon – and concentrate – the organizational mind as swiftly as a crisis. Yet, some organizations seem unaware of the need for preparing to deal with emergencies. Attempting to conceal the truth or to withhold information is bad strategy as well as being intrinsically misguided. Either can lead to speculation and wrong assumptions about the situation. Failure to react to crises may prove a commercial misjudgement and is open to misconstruction. Some stakeholders may interpret a failure to react as an admission of guilt.

The organization must recognize the importance of responding to the inevitable media interest in a crisis situation. Its reaction will be judged by the media, just as it will be judged by all those who feel that they have a stake in the situation. The organization will have to face the damage that its reputation suffers if it fails to communicate with those who perceive that they have an interest in the crisis. Appreciating key audiences, understanding how they feel and communicating quickly and skilfully with them through the media becomes essential. Most communication executives favour a straightforward approach, dealing with problems as they arise. It may be that apologies have to be made on behalf of the organization to audiences who have suffered financial or personal harm as a direct result of what has happened.

# The form of crisis communication planning

There is no such thing as a universal crisis management programme and the nature of any crisis will vary from organization to organization. Thus, communication crisis plans need to be developed to meet the demands of each individual sector and organization. O'Rourke (1997) suggests that there are far too many experts in the crisis management field who are willing to propound rules that must be followed in every situation – many of which, he suggests, are difficult to apply in real-life situations. But crisis communication strategy does involve being seen to take control of an unexpected situation and it may have to be done in the face of high uncertainty – with the end intention of gaining the confidence of external constituencies. The communication executive must execute a thorough analysis of existing procedures and will not forget that successful crisis handling is more about attitudes than procedures. (Bland, quoted in Hart, 1995).

Bland (Hart, 1995) suggests that a starting point is to consider the experience of how previous crises were handled. He believes that much is to be learned about crisis handling from examining other well publicized crises. He proposes three questions that need to be asked:

1 What happened?
2 Why did the crisis get the amount and type of publicity that it did?
3 How did the management handle it? What seemed good and bad about their responses?

In his major American survey in 1995, Guth found that 56.9 per cent of those questioned had written communication plans for dealing with crises and emergencies. The level of preparation, Guth noted, appeared to be highest among for-profit organizations. Of those, 62.8 per cent confirmed that they had practised their crisis communication procedures within the preceding two years. Guth's survey confirmed that organizations with a high level of crisis experience are more likely to have written crisis communication plans than those with less experience.

## Three sources of reaction

In planning for a crisis, White and Mazur (1995) suggest that an organization has to prepare to deal with behavioural patterns originating from three separate sources:

1 Its own organizational behaviour.
2 The conduct of its own staff.
3 The reactions of those who perceive themselves to be its stakeholders.

## Reaction of stakeholders

Stakeholders may impact on the organization either:

1 because they themselves are affected by the crisis, or
2 because the way that they react to the crisis affects the organization.

In drawing up its crisis plans the organization needs to accommodate the prospective behaviour of all these sources. Planning for potential disasters (and thinking the unthinkable), White and Mazur continue, requires systematic, informed, organized monitoring and analysis on a multinational basis.

## Pivotal role for the communicator

Every day organizations face difficult decisions concerning the handling of complex emergencies – any of which might do irrevocable damage to a corporation and its reputation, and this damage can be done very quickly. For example, the executive may be attempting to contain a drop in orders leading to a collapse in turnover; and decades of investment in brand and image building can be undone overnight (Woodcock, 1994). As it is the responsibility of the communication executive to manage the corporate reputation, it is the task of the communicator to prevent further damage being done to that reputation.

The strategy for coping with the crisis must already be in place. Its essential theme must be effective and powerful communications with the organization's most important audiences. Sometimes the most important message is saying what critical constituents *expect* you to say. The practitioner may well be coping with the organization's weaknesses and attempting to recover loss of faith in the organization. Thus it is essential to have a good spokesperson in a crisis.

What the communicator says needs to be shaped in such a way that it reflects in the most favourable possible way on the organization. Common sense is one of the rarest commodities available to most executives in a serious crisis (O'Rourke, 1997). A well-developed crisis communication programme – and one well rehearsed by the organization – can prevent a crisis turning into a full-scale disaster.

## Appearance of control

> One of the things that Exxon found enormously frustrating with the early hours of the *Valdez* disaster was the escalating flow of events.

> Exxon complained that before their own communications command centre was operational, several government and environmental groups were on the scene. They had already held press conferences and they had defined a complete agenda for what they would consider to be an adequate response to this disaster. This all happened before the people at Exxon had even arrived on site and before they had been able to make their own evaluation about how much oil was on the water and what action the company would need to take.
>
> adapted from O'Rourke (1997)

An organization cannot afford to give the impression that it has lost control of any situation which is perceived to be a crisis. So when a crisis develops it is essential to give every appearance of being in control. The organization must be able to communicate fast, accurately and skilfully with a whole range of important audiences. This will reduce the likelihood of the situation escalating out of hand. If the organization fails to communicate information requested by key stakeholders, this deficiency could very well result in wild rumours, much speculation and the impression that the organization was not prepared in the first place.

The first object of the plan should be to ensure that the problem is identified precisely. These are the questions:

1 What happened?.
2 Why did it happen?
3 What must be done to ensure a swift return to normal operations?
4 What needs to be done to ensure that no one suffers any further disaster?
5 What needs to be done to make restitution to those who have suffered harm or loss?

## Gaining control

The object is to help get the situation under control as soon as possible, so the next question may be is there reliable information? The crisis may be taking place whilst the organization is far from certain about the nature or full extent of the disaster.

The plan should identify the potential impact of the crisis and this needs to be done very early on. The intent will be to restore the confidence and goodwill of external constituencies. The plan needs to cope with the problem in a way which takes into account corporate obligations and the importance of retaining the goodwill of vital constituencies.

## Messages of reassurance

In virtually every crisis an important task for the communication department is to deliver reassuring messages. A crisis can impact seriously on a company's trading position, on its share price and indeed on the long-term viability of the organization. The successful implementation of an emergency communication plan can assist powerfully in the restoration of confidence in an organization suffering a crisis. When the crisis erupts it is essential to judge accurately when to react; and when not to do so. Mike Regester, a crisis management specialist (quoted by Bond, 1994c) says that it is very important to paint a picture of professional, competent people ready to swing into action very fast.

Kaufmann et al. (1994), in asking what communications strategy executives should follow in a crisis, suggests that the first thing that the executive should do is to address these questions:

- Could non-disclosure be fatal or lead to further injury?
- Is the organization the culprit or the victim?
- Are the fictions surrounding the crisis worse than the facts?
- Can the organization afford to respond after the crisis?
- Can the organization afford not to respond?

Goodman (1994) suggests that the communication component of the crisis management programme must give:

- instructing information – telling audiences how they should behave
- adjusting information – enabling an audience to cope with the emotional aspects of the crisis
- internalizing information – forming the basis on which audiences will make long-term judgements about the organization's image.

## Send the right messages

Communication executives have a critical role to play in ensuring that whatever problems exist they are put into perspective and communicators need to ensure that they do not send the wrong messages. The information given must be credible as well as truthful. The facts that are released must be up to date and they should plan for the worst case.

The communication department will maintain control over the information flow; assisting in the development of strategies which will help to influence and shape the perceptions of important audiences. By issuing accurate information about the crisis, and by the way that it is being handled (and by doing it at the right time and in the right place), the organization increases the likelihood that its constituencies will perceive that it has control of the crisis.

Winner (1993) relates that one communication director favours speedy, honest, accurate handling of any problem as soon as it emerges. It is necessary to maintain the organization's credibility in the eyes of key constituencies. The communication strategy must be to tackle the problem head-on and to give as much of the right sort of information as one possibly can.

# If a delay in communicating is unavoidable

## The case for full disclosure: what you don't say can hurt you

A policy of full disclosure means conveying information that is complete and timely. In the event of a chemical leak at a plant, for instance, a full disclosure policy advocates describing the events that led to the crisis, the crisis itself, and the firm's response. For crises that are developing over an extended period, such as a hostage situation at a company's headquarters, a full disclosure policy might involve ongoing communications that continually update all affected parties about the events surrounding the crisis. Unless, of course, others' well-being would be jeopardized by further disclosure. Questions must be answered completely and without delay. When an accurate response cannot be given immediately the organization must begin investigations and issue a response as fast as it possibly can do so. Full disclosure implies by definition that information about the crisis is neither withheld nor delayed, but is issued as completely, accurately and quickly as possible.

adapted from Kaufmann, Kesner and Hazen (1994)

When, for whatever reason, the communication department is not able to respond to the crisis immediately – perhaps until necessary investigations have begun or until preliminary results been obtained – it should issue initial communications as soon as possible. When it does this the information given must be helpful and not misleading.

In order to prevent rumours some organizations release partial information about crises. This in turn can cause problems. To start with it can result in misleading conclusions – because information is taken out of context. A really sad example emerged in the wake of problems surrounding the Dow Corning breast implant.

As a result of misleading information released about the implants, in at least two instances women performed surgery on themselves in order to remove their implants. Experts familiar with these incidents have said that a 'wave of confusion and emotionalism has swept over many women whose lives have been affected by the implants.' A surgeon who operated on one of the victims after her self-mutilation stated 'this is a situation where misinformation and sensationalism by the media have created this hysteria'.

adapted from Kaufmann, Kesner and Hazen (1994)

If an organization has to issue holding statements – as an interim measure with the aim of offering the media reassurance until the time when more detailed information is available – that is permissible. But the communication offered must be well designed. Such action will demonstrate that the organization is doing all that it can to work with the media (a critical audience at such a time) to ascertain the parameters, scale and nature of the problem. As the communication executive at B.A.T. Industries commented, 'when the unexpected comes you form the policy and do it fast. If the crisis is totally unexpected it's perfectly credible to hold people off for half a day. You cannot be ready for everything. The art is doing what comes naturally.'

The communication executive should define and draw up emergency plans and responses in a crisis plan developed to deal with any foreseeable events. These plans involve the formation of crisis management teams. These teams will need to include senior executives from critical management disciplines, marketing, finance, the legal people and communications. A specialist in the technical side of communications should be a part of a crisis action team (Nudell and Antokol, 1988). Good organizations bring in the communication people at the beginning not at the end, for professional communicators have skills and training that facilitate their making a vital contribution to all stages of a crisis (Jackson, 1995). The key to successful crisis management is to have executives who are trained to deal with reporters and other publics under crisis conditions (Heath, 1994). The executives selected, whatever their management discipline, must be men and women capable of working under conditions of extreme pressure and stress. The crisis management team will need to be given freedom of movement and decision-making capacity.

In a desperate crisis the organization's communication department may not have enough personnel to cope with all eventualities so it may be necessary for some non-communication executives to speak for the organization. This is a special responsibility. Senior executives from other management disciplines need to be prepared for this eventuality and they need to be equal to the challenge. If a manager is inexperienced in dealing with the media one more unwanted headache may be created for the communication executive and, in the worst scenario, one problem can lead to another.

According to Chris Woodcock, Deputy MD of Countrywide Communications (quoted by Bond, 1994c), communication executives are remarkably blasé about corporate reputation, yet for many organizations if a problem occurs there may be little time to think. It is essential, therefore, that the communication department details and trains delegated employees on how to deal with media audiences in a crisis. Heath (1994) notes that the central focus has to be the creation of a single Voice, which needs, he says, to speak for a corporate culture that exudes openness, candour and honesty and sets the tone.

As already noted, Guth (1995) is concerned about the perceived lack of planning for crises. Kaufmann et al. (1994) relate an incident that proves how important it is for someone somewhere to communicate – and fast and accurately – in a crisis. A recent incident involved a tanker driver in North

Carolina. The truck driver was given instructions that in the event of an incident he was to call company headquarters and to say nothing about the incident himself. When he was involved in an accident which caused a spillage on the highway he refused to comment. As a result, those at the scene were unaware of what his truck contained. So, emergency teams were forced to handle the spill as though it involved toxic chemicals. The local media was on the scene and warned other motorists to avoid the area. Rumours spread and frightened nearby residents. When a company spokesman was finally reached many hours later he advised that the tanker contained only cooking oil.

Among 24 organizations visited by the author only one revealed no plans for dealing with a crisis. With the exception only of Yorkshire Tyne-Tees Television (who said 'we have not gone down that road') each organization had plans for managing crises.

Most plans are written out, some in manuals. The then Director of Corporate Affairs at Storehouse takes a rational approach, 'having not plans, but mechanisms'. He went on to say 'my responsibility is to see that plans exist in the companies (Storehouse is the holding company for Bhs and Mothercare) and that I am included in the crisis management loop'. He continued, 'in as much as any crisis requires handling, they would consult me about it and decide at what level to handle it'. The Director of Group Public Relations at Vaux Brewery Group took the same approach, saying that 'the brewery has a practical plan rather than something written down'.

The then Director of Public Affairs at British Airways (suffering a non-fatal crisis during the summer of 1997 due to major staff disruptions) commented that BA has an overall corporate plan (based at Heathrow Airport) in which the communications department – together with the Operations Director – plays a central role. The Public Relations Manager at the Avon and Somerset Constabulary commented that 'our plans are very much in existence. One thing is being able to react. If there was a crisis involving any utilities we would act in a co-ordinating role. We practice with the nuclear people.'

The then Acting Director of Corporate Affairs at W.H. Smith reported that his company has a central crisis manual (dealing with three levels of crisis). Lloyds/TSB referred to similar arrangements which it adapts as necessary. Supermarket chain J. Sainsbury has similar arrangements in collaboration with security; likewise GlaxoWellcome, which has specific plans for articles and products. It could well be the case that the existence of fixed plans in a manual might impose a degree of rigidity of movement at a time of crisis. In such a situation flexibility could well prove to be of great advantage.

The then Communication Manager at Tennent Caledonian Breweries referred to plans which, as his company is the Scottish subsidiary of Bass plc, are part of the wider plan drawn up by the Bass group. Tennents said that their plan would be put into place in collaboration with their group headquarters. He referred to a problem suffered by TCB in early 1996 with plastic fragments in bottled beer. He noted that in such a situation it was preferable to 'damage the brand, but not the company'.

# The importance of fast reactions

Sainsbury's found itself coping with a crisis last year. After the BSE problem arose, CEO Dino Adriano, informed staff (and most importantly butchers) about the situation. He stressed that employees should be kept informed. The supermarket also ran a specially produced report on health and safety issues related to packaged meat. In addition, Sainsbury held phone-ins for its staff to make sure that they all knew the correct way in which to proceed.

adapted from *PR Week* (1971)

# A pivotal role for communications

In the TWA Flight 800 disaster in the summer of 1996, it was 16 hours before the Chairman and CEO were able to be on site at the Long Island TWA command centre and until they were there nobody was speaking effectively from a position of leadership. That was the main source of the criticism that TWA faced afterwards. Something in the TWA plan should have provided for the real possibility that their principal spokesperson might not be able to be at the scene for two thirds of a day.

adapted from O'Rourke (1997)

# The best way to handle communications in a crisis

It is quite acceptable to shape communication releases in such a way that they focus on a story which is given in the most favourable way possible for the organization. It does help if the spokesperson expresses real concern and if the sympathy being expressed is genuine.

# The legal side versus the communication people

The then Director of Corporate Communication at British Airways referred to the *debate between the legal people and corporate communication* and spoke of the problem of *liability versus corporate image*

in conversation with the author

Common wisdom holds that communication practitioners and attorneys do not always see eye to eye with each other on what to say to the media in a crisis

(Fitzpatrick and Rubin, 1995). She adds that both the risk of legal liability and the need to protect corporate reputation *must* be considered.

> In 1993 General Motors challenged MBC over its Dateline program's depiction of the exploding pick-up truck petrol tank. Communication strategy and legal posturing became inexorably intertwined. General Motor's major player was also its legal counsel, Harry Pierce. He was rewarded with a very senior position and also maintains control over corporate public relations. In terms of reputation management, one must wonder whether these two functions are best combined in one office.
>
> adapted from Schenkler (1997)

> Bad advice often results from going to non-communication people; or it can come about after a showdown between the communications people and the legal people. The legal side worries about litigation; the communications side, whilst aware of the legalities, also has to think in terms of the image of the corporation and its reputation once the situation has been resolved.
>
> adapted from Flanagan (1995)

Many lawyers advise an organization to avoid public statements altogether. On the other hand, most experienced communication practitioners feel an obligation to give the public the facts; and to present them to their audiences in non-emotive terms. Many academics and professionals suggest that full disclosure (disclose everything and disclose it fast) is a better course of action (Kaufmann et al., 1994). Human nature being what it is, the full truth will probably emerge in any case and, in addition, the more straightforward an organization is the more likely it is that it will be forgiven by key audiences.

> In many crises the firm's potential liability may be trivial compared with the risk of alienating customers, employees, or regulators. Pagan (1985) points out that corporate lawyers tend to believe that openness brings with it the risk of even greater legal exposure. Yet, he says, this is the single greatest obstacle to businesses learning to function well politically during times of crisis. It is hardly surprising, then, to hear advocates of full disclosure advise firms to cage their lawyers. The argument goes that corporate counsel are not able to see the forest from the trees. Company lawyers may not see the long range effects of crises because they focus too sharply upon the short term threat of litigation.
>
> adapted from Kaufmann, Kesner and Hazen (1994)

There has long been a debate concerning which of these two positions is the best to adopt. If it is better to say nothing, for how long can the organization afford to say nothing? The answer may well be that it is better to be open; to tell a relevant factual story; and to make full and immediate disclosures about the circumstances surrounding the events. The then Director of Public Affairs at British Airways commented that 'in today's climate it is insufficient to do it well; you have to be perceived to have handled it well; otherwise your organization will suffer as a result'. He continued, 'my job is to manage the relations in a crisis and to ensure that everything that we are doing in that role is properly conveyed'.

A fair amount of communication work is concerned with attempting to put right a situation that has gone horribly wrong. The then Director of Public Affairs at British Airways spoke about this. He referred to the 'debate between the legal people and corporate communication' and spoke of the problem of 'liability versus corporate image'. He commented, 'they do not sit well together', and continued that 'unless you communicate you run an unacceptable risk with your reputation'. This is a matter on which Cunard might have had some thoughts after the disastrous re-fit of flagship liner *QE2* several years ago.

> Cunard allowed the QE2 saga to become a mega crisis when it should have cut its losses once it became clear that the ship was not fit to set sail. Cunard totally forgot how to manage its reputation.
>
> The shipping company's attempts to appease QE2 passengers looked like a knee-jerk reaction – a really cardinal PR sin. For a while the reported compensation appeared to increase in value by the day; in fact, almost in direct proportion to the amount of media coverage that the debacle attracted.
>
> As a single event it cost Cunard much more than the expense of cancelling a cruise and paying for additional anchorage – high though that would have been. Viewed in a wider commercial sense the shockwaves could affect the current bid by Cunard's parent, Trafalgar House, for Northern Electric
>
> The QE2 fiasco could weaken its arguments if it is perceived to have had scant regard for the customers of one of its important – and well known – subsidiary companies.
>
> adapted from Bond (1995)

# Communicating during a financial crisis

Crisis communication has much to do with financial audiences. The common picture of a crisis may be that of a train crashing or a commercial terrorist impregnating tins of baby food with poison. In corporate terms, the sudden departure of the CEO (which happened recently to W.H. Smith), or a third profit warning in as many months (as recently emerged from Laura Ashley Holdings), or an unwelcome take-over bid (as happened to hotel chain Forte two years ago), or the discovery of heavy losses in a company with which you are scheduled to merge (as happened to BT as they were proceeding with their proposed merger with American telecoms giant MCI) are all big crises.

In the event of a take-over bid communication can be an important weapon. When Australian Alan Bond attempted to take over industrial conglomerate Lonrho in 1988 he was subjected to a powerful and sustained communication campaign generated by then Lonrho CEO Tiny Rowland, which not only saw off his bid approach but, in addition, took Bond to personal ruin.

> Compare the Exxon approach with that of Shell chairman, Bob Reid, who immediately apologized in public when his company polluted the Mersey. He came over as a credible person and then communicated some other vital messages about the importance of oil and how hard the industry works to control pollution, what they were going to do about it, and so on.
>
> Michael Bland, *writing in Strategic Public Relations*, 1995

Communication with financial audiences is a vital component of crisis management design. It sets out to deal with corporate crises that impact upon financial constituencies and on those resulting from financial problems. Financial communication can make the difference between survival and extinction for the organization. Financial crises can result in loss of confidence in the parent company; they can lead to a run on the share price (as happened to Guinness when several of their directors were arrested), or the disappearance of customers. In the worst scenario it can lead to an organization being extinguished (Barings Bank) or it may become vulnerable to a take-over bid (as happened to the White Star Line after the *Titanic* sank).

## Impact on unfavourable news on company share price

Financial crises give the communication function the critical role of maintaining contact with financial audiences; of restoring lost confidence; and of helping to ensure that the corporation's share price accurately reflects the underlying value of the business.

In the late 1990s the price of shares in B.A.T. Industries has (in the opinion of many analysts), failed for some time to reflect the underlying worth of the corporation's net assets. This situation has arisen due to unfavourable criticism targeted at the company because of its exposure to possible legal claims from the American anti-smoking lobby. Some analysts feel that the company's share price has discounted the balance sheet value of American subsidiary Brown and Williamson to zero. If this is correct – and if Brown and Williamson has a net value in excess of zero – then the share price is failing to reflect the true underlying value of the group.

# Poor crisis communications lead to loss of confidence

> When the unexpected happens, be sure to apply the cardinal rule of crisis communications **'tell it all and tell it fast'**
> Dilenschneider and Hyde quoted in Kaufmann et al,
> *Business Horizons*, (1994)

The failure of an organization to communicate well with the financial audience can lead to a total loss of confidence from analysts and investors alike. This is one of the problems that has plagued Lonrho plc for over half a decade. It adds up to a loss of faith in an organization. If faith is lacking the corporation may end up completely estranged from the media and the City. This underlines the critical importance of good corporate communications. Inspiring confidence is at the heart of corporate communication. If communication conduits can be kept open there is always the possibility that, as underlying problems are brought under control, the confidence lost as a result of a crisis situation will return.

Communication executives need to acknowledge the problem. Financial journalists and City analysts must be given a clear idea of the scale and nature of the problem and how it is being brought under control. When this has been done, internal communications assume critical importance. The complete restoration of lines of communication between senior executives and employees has a very important role to play in the recovery of morale among staff. Restoration of morale will impact greatly on the long-term recovery prospects.

> Last Christmas was not a happy one for Sainsbury's as it trading statement showed that profits had slipped and that, as a result, the share price would fall. David Sainsbury and Dino Adriano did a live broadcast to tell employees the news before it hit the press. Sainsbury's management was able to overcome these crisis issues by communicating quickly, effectively and honestly to employees
> *PR Week* (1997m)

At a time of crisis a developed communication programme is critical to the success and possibly the continued existence of the organization. Research before this book was written among major corporations in no way sustained Guth's finding in 1995 of an alarming absence of crisis planning – in fact the opposite was found. All save one of the organizations visited had developed plans for crisis management in which the communication practitioner plays a pivotal role. The plans of some are quite sophisticated. For example, no organization recognizes the communications implications of any corporate problem with greater clarity than the world's favourite airline.

A crisis concerns the future of an organization as well as its present. When the crisis has passed, key publics will have a revisionist view of the organization. In the case of the White Star Line, owners of an unsinkable ship that sank, the reputation may be ruined; likewise Townsend-Thoresen. In the instance of a company who handles a crisis brilliantly (the British Midland air crash at Kegworth is an excellent example) the opposite is true. Win or lose, corporate communications – or the lack of them – will play a pivotal role.

> After the Zeebrugge ferry disaster Townsend-Thoresen never said
> that it was sorry – the brand collapsed.
>
> Bond (1995c)


## Truth at all costs in a crisis?

> In some crises it is better for the corporation to offer the public full
> disclosure, but in other situations silence is better.
> Kaufmann et al, *Business Horizons*, (1994)

Are questions answered truthfully when a crisis occurs? One question which does concern crisis communications is whether or not the communication team should be wholly truthful. It is a question that has been addressed by few writers. Do seasoned and senior communication executives believe in *truth at all cost*?

> An organization must never lie when caught in a crisis
> Kaufmann et al, *Business Horizons*, (1994)

A number of senior communication executives were asked if they believed in truth at all costs? Their replies are shown here:

| Reply | % response |
|---|---|
| yes | 25 |
| yes or no | 10 |
| no | 20 |
| if you say something it must be true | 20 |
| up to a point | 10 |
| it would be nice to say so | 5 |
| it depends upon the circumstances | 5 |
| refused to answer | 5 |
| | 100 |

Of all the respondents one, and one only – the acting Communication spokeswoman for J. Sainsbury – said 'I prefer not to answer that question.'

The communicators representing British Airways, London Transport, Morrisson's Supermarkets and Wessex Water answered 'yes'. The Director of Corporate Communications at Whitbread answered 'no'. The Communication Spokeswoman at the Avon and Somerset Constabulary responded 'no ... but I do not believe in lying. I have never lied or countenanced a member of my organization lying. You do not have to say everything.' The then Acting Director of Corporate Affairs at W.H. Smith replied 'yes ... but'.

The Director of Group Public Affairs at B.A.T. Industries offered the opinion that 'anything that you say must be true; but there are times when you have to decline to answer. Then the policy is that you do not say anything.' Likewise, the Head of Corporate Communications at Lloyds/TSB made a similar point 'I believe in truth. It is a reputation business. If you have a reputation of misleading people or telling lies you are dead. You must not lie. You may decline to answer.'

> By definition we have no way of knowing when an organization has been successful at withholding information. In reality, the fact that we have not heard about a particular episode may mean that the company has successfully handled its crisis internally and thus has averted a more public incident. So, we do not see companies which have adopted successful non-disclosure strategies.
> adapted from Kaufmann, Kesner and Hazen (1994)

> Often your success is because the story is not written
> The then Director of Corporate Communication, Storehouse plc,
> in conversation with the author

The Director, Corporate Affairs at GlaxoWellcome enlarged upon this point by saying 'tell the truth. Don't tell lies to anyone; but don't volunteer information that you do not wish to give.' The Director of Group Public Relations at Vaux added 'The worst thing that you can do is to flannel.' The spokesman for BT made the same point, commenting 'more or less; the issue is the whole truth'; whilst his opposite number at Storehouse added 'never tell lies'. He went on 'there are certain areas where I believe in secrecy. There are times when you try not to respond and not to mislead. Often your success is because the story is not written.'

The Group Director of Corporate Affairs at Yorkshire Tyne-Tees Television enlarged upon this: 'Some good communication men could fall down over this. Never lie. Just say that you do not want to answer. Admit there are problems. Always count on the benefit of the doubt.' The then Communications Manager at Tennent Caledonian Breweries elaborated this point by remarking, 'truth depends upon the circumstances. It depends upon various audiences at the time. The most important audience is the media – they can shape how events happen. The first two hours are most important. The police say "truth at all costs". I say "truth up to a point".'

> Of course, full disclosure is not without its own long term risks. There are even occasions when organizations which face crises voluntarily reveal information that shocks or horrifies constituents. This information can actually become a separate and more damaging crisis for organizations. The Ford Motor Company in the US is one example. Ford's handling of the Pinto automobile crisis initially involved liability for injuries caused by the design of the petrol tank. This tank was located at the rear of the car and it was surrounded by sharp metal objects and a cosmetic rear bumper. This design made the car susceptible to explosion if hit from the rear. Following the death of three women who were killed in such an explosion, a grand jury in Indiana handed down a criminal indictment against Ford for 'recklessly creating a substantial risk' to the victims. As part of its defence, the management at Ford revealed that it had conducted a cost-benefit analysis that included an approximate for costs of death ($200,000 per person) and serious burn injuries ($67,000 per person) caused by such collisions. Ford was vilified for this seeming disregard for human life. The damage to Ford's image and corporate reputation from this incident is still inestimable.
>                     adapted from Kaufmann, Kesner and Hazen (1994)

Excepting the practitioner at J. Sainsbury, who declined outright to answer the question, a general trend ran through the answers. Whether the respondent said 'yes', 'no' or 'yes and no', each answered in much the same terms. These executives either believe in complete honesty – and then picking up the pieces – or in honesty only if the whole truth can sensibly be revealed. Most feel that if the facts are best not revealed it is better not to give them.

With the one exception mentioned, all organizations expressed (in their own words) the same broad approach to truthfully answering difficult questions. All but the one agreed that there are occasions when a question can be answered truthfully – but with the whole truth being withheld.

Honesty apart, Howard (1992) shows concern that audiences may not be satisfied that the spokesperson is sufficiently part of the policy-making machine to be wholly credible. Few of those interviewed would have concerned Howard at all. However local media often know and trust local management, so a local spokesperson may very well be more believable and may create more confidence than comments made by a spokesperson from group headquarters. Further, operational personnel may understand technical processes and be better able to explain them.

- Be honest, open and straightforward. Tell a factual story. It almost never pays to be sparing with the truth. 'The short sharp shock is always better in the long term' – Raymond Wilson, Norwich Union
- Emphasize the positive. 'Look at Eurotunnel. People have ended up looking for negatives, rather than seeing the whole array of potential positives.' Nick Fitzherbert, Fitzherbert Partnership
- Bury the ego. Arrogance simply never pays. BA suffered when it looked as if it was trying to overwhelm Virgin. But, with more positive marketing initiatives such as cheap flight offers on Virgin routes, consumer interest has been reclaimed.

adapted from Bond (1995)

## Case study

# Boil water before use

Three Valleys Water supplies water to its 2.3 m customers. They live in Hertfordshire, Bedfordshire, North London, plus parts of Essex and Buckingham-shire. Cryptosporidium is a parasite carried by farm and domestic animals. Following 32 cases of diarrhoea caused by Cryptosporidium, TVW found a low level of the organism in a sample of water on 2 March 1997.

TVW had a crisis management plan, which included their communications manager, Frank Fitzpatrick. This swung into action immediately following the discovery. The objectives of the crisis plan were to inform people in the affected areas as quickly as possible, to respond to media requests and to keep key stakeholders informed about new developments. An emergency meeting was called with local authority environmental health officials at the company's offices on Sunday 2 March to examine the evidence and decide what action to take.

A notice advising customers to boil drinking water was hand-delivered to 300,000 homes on the Sunday and Monday. These were delivered by company staff and the Royal Mail. A media response team was set up headed by Mr Fitzpatrick. This included three personnel from their own communication department, two from a PR agency and ten TVW staff who had been trained to act as a first line, handling calls from the media. A press release was put out at 7.30 p.m. on Sunday 2 March.

Fitzpatrick was selected as the organization's spokesman. In the first 24 hours there were more than 20 broadcast interviews and the media response team handled 150 requests from journalists. The company's customer call centre was staffed overnight for the first few days – and included extra staff trained for crisis situations. More than 38,000 calls were handled in-house plus 19,000 by an overflow agency. 24,000 called a recorded message and there were a further 20,000 operational calls.

The crisis got worse on Wednesday 6 March when, following eight reported cases of the infection in the Luton area, another 25,000 homes were advised to boil water. TVW worked around the clock to overcome the problem. They reportedly spent £40,000 a day on increased sampling. The water company also supplied bottled water to local schools and hospitals.

Finally on Tuesday 18 March TVW announced that the parasite had been eradicated. It lifted the water notice. It then announced it would pay £10 compensation to each affected customer.

'The media was obviously keen to get as much information as possible and while they appreciated that TVW reacted quickly and made themselves accessible, the length of the crisis meant that they had to discover new angles and it was very difficult to find new information to pass on', Fitzpatrick remarked.

Inevitably the media reported problems and expressed criticism. One result of this was that the customer call centre broke down under the sheer volume of the calls. There were also some complaints about the level of compensation.

'I think that in some cases the reporting was not as fair as we would have hoped, but overall coverage was much as we would have expected', said Fitzpatrick. He acknowledged that getting across messages that water was safe to drink if it was boiled – and that the company was working flat out to identify the source of the problem – was difficult .

This was a crisis on a very large scale for the company; and certainly TVW benefited from having a crisis management plan already in place. In addition, the company acted quickly informing customers and allocating resources to handle inevitable interest from its major stakeholders.

The source of the infection has still not been identified. Thus, one of the problems that the company faced was that although it was not necessarily responsible for the infection and despite the fact that it had acted responsibly, by taking ownership of the problem and seeking to solve it, it is still being blamed by many observers.

The crisis has already cost TVW £5m and inevitably it has damaged its reputation in the eyes of some. It is now faces a period of rebuilding.

adapted from Purdon (1997)

## Case study

# Cleaning up oil with a slick operation

On the evening of Thursday 15 February 1996 *Sea Empress* ran aground and spilled 120,000 tonnes of oil over the south west Wales coastline. This could have signalled disaster for the tourist industry. The national media showed images of beaches and wildlife blackened and damaged by oil. The Pembrokeshire telephones – which at that time of the year were usually buzzing with bookings – stopped ringing.

The Wales Tourist Board had to act quickly before the incident became too deeply ingrained into the minds of potential holidaymakers. It drew up a strategy in collaboration with Regester and Larkin to launch the WELSH TOURIST FIGHTS BACK campaign – aimed at reassuring would-be visitors.

This campaign was aimed at re-inforcing the message that the beaches would be clean by the summer. A helpline was set up to give basic information to holidaymakers and to monitor their attitudes and perceptions. 'We had to tread a careful line not to make exaggerated promises to the public but to give reassurances on the basis of truth' explained the WTB communications manager.

This campaign was focused on drawing media interest to the cleanup operation and also to areas that had not been harmed by the oil spillage. It also organized a large number of press visits by journalists from home and abroad.

Once the beaches were clean, phase two of the campaign involved a higher profile strategy to persuade visitors and media to come back. The WTB committed £40,000 towards the campaign and it transferred the lead role to regional tourist company Tourism South and West Wales. It hired Golley Slater to do promotional PR for the 1996 and 1997 seasons.

Local media were sympathetic. The *Western Mail* ran a series of positive stories about tourism in the affected areas. By liasing with the environmental group Friends of the Earth, WTB managed to reduce reports of damage to wildlife. They pointing out that it was as interesting to observe devastated areas during the recovery as it was to see them in their normal healthy state.

As a result, business across all sectors last summer was down between 5 per cent and 10 per cent on average. This compared favourably to Cardiff Business school's initial estimate. This had suggested that tourist income would be down almost 13 per cent (£20.64m out of a projected total of £160m).

The communication manager said that the recovery of south west Wales was a very good example of how communications can turn what might well have been a disaster into a relatively good news story; especially when there was not enough money in the budget to do large scale advertising.

adapted from *PR Week* (1997n)

# Key terms

**CRISIS** A momentous event. A situation (usually unexpected and disastrous) characterized by surprise, a high threat to important values and which has a short decision time.

**CRISIS MANAGEMENT LOOP** An expression used to describe a loosely knit group of executives charged with the task of handling a crisis on a rather ad hoc basis.

**CRISIS MANAGEMENT TEAM** A group of executives formed into a team with the purpose of enabling them to deal with a crisis and its aftermath. The communication executive will be an essential member of such a team. Some members may not be experienced communicators and therefore need to have training in the relevant skills.

**CRISIS MANUAL** A book or handy compendium in which developed and prepared plans for dealing with a crisis situation are written down.

**CRISIS PLANNING** Preparations made by an organization to deal with an unexpected and untoward event. There is no such thing as a universal crisis plan. Some plans may be mechanisms rather than plans laid down in a manual.

**INTERIM STATEMENT** Statement issued to the media on an interim basis to describe what is happening in a crisis; with the intent that a fuller and more complete statement will follow later.

**MECHANISMS** Means to handle a situation on a rather ad hoc basis rather than detailed and developed written down plans.

**RUN ON THE SHARE PRICE** A sharp fall in the share price – followed by a series of further sharp falls caused by alarm (in this instance at the crisis that has engulfed the organization) and concern (about its ability to handle the situation and emerge from it with an intact reputation).

# The background of the communication executive

> I do not think that senior people spend nearly enough time telling the outside world what business is trying to achieve. Directors as a profession are not given enough training. There is a tremendous aura of gifted amateurism. Yes, we do need to be trained and taught how to communicate. The only concern that I would have about this is that you can get to the stage where you end up having to cope with training overload. It must not be allowed to interfere with the main task and this is to achieve long term shareholder value'.
>
> adapted from Tim Melville-Ross, Institute of Directors, PR Week (1997o)

> All the best CEOs and chairmen have got an understanding of what corporate communications is about. However, all too often it is instinctive. They pick it up on the job. Some element of formal training is a good idea. I don't believe that communications is some mystical art worthy only of gurus. It is a business discipline. If top people are trained properly it should make the jobs of communication executives much more effective.
>
> adapted from Philip Dewhurst, Railtrack plc, PR Week (1997o)

## Introduction

We now explore the origins and the role of the communication executive, examining the typical educational and management background, noting both the characteristics which practitioners consider essential and where the executive fits into the organizational structure. We enquire into the status of the executive, the importance attached to the position and whether the position holder is a significant part of the policy making machine. We conclude that the communication executive now has a management position on a par with directors of most other disciplines. We analyse the function that the executive directs, wondering if the task is an approach rather than a technique. The communication executive now plays a powerful role in formulating corporate strategy. It is a role which enables the opening of information channels and one which facilitates the communication to key audiences of organizational messages and themes. Yet, we learn that the power of communications is still not fully understood in some organizations. By the end of this chapter we have gained an appreciation of how the communication executive fits into the organizational structure and why different organizations use diverse job titles for what is essentially the same role.

# The origins of the communication executive

Public relations (the management discipline from which some writers consider corporate communications originates) has been around for much of this century. It has often been performed indifferently; either by encroachers (a term for those not qualified or trained to do the job; Lauzen, 1995) or by those lacking the personal attributes which would enable them to perform well. In this chapter we study the communication director. We study his (and increasingly her) origins and qualifications. We then go on to discuss what it is, exactly, that the director does.

First, we focus on the background and training of the communication executive, examining the characteristics noted most frequently in practitioners at the top of their profession. Does the executive typically emerge from the generalist route? If not, might marketing or journalism be the background? Do multinational corporations practise encroachment? White and Mazur (1995) regard this as a possible threat to the future development of communications practice – they consider that executives from other business areas may have a credibility that those from an orthodox public relations background lack. These are questions of fundamental interest to scholars of corporate communications.

In this segment we endeavour to build a complete picture of the director's characteristics and talents. We then go on to consider what the role of the executive involves. In styling communication directors as 'communication executives', Wright (1995), in a seminal piece of research in this field, and referring specifically to the United States of America, said:

> Few . . . studies have focused solely on communication executives. Although there are more than 150,000 . . . managers in the nation there are only about 250 . . . communication executives. These executives are very busy individuals . . . paid very large salaries . . . not noted for filling out . . . questionnaires or otherwise participating in academic research.

## An under-researched management area

Over many years management scholars have studied public relations and, more recently, corporate communications. Referring to empirical research since 1979 into different communication roles, Turk (1989) notes that there has been little examination of the actual behaviours of communication managers.

Commenting on studies which focus attention on paradigms describing the typical ways in which communication is practised, Wright (1995) remarks that there is little research describing the executive who actually does the communicating. Pavlik (1996) confirms that this is an area which is under-researched and the AMA (American Marketing Association) acknowledge that they have published nothing on this subject. Indeed, some scholars feel that there are fundamental differences between theory and practice in regard to communication functions (Nessmann, 1995).

# Is there a typical model for a communication executive?

As noted, little research exists into the character and personality of the communication executive. Is the practitioner one of a type? White and Mazur (1995) think that perhaps the position requires a mix of functional, managerial, organizational and negotiating abilities.

Botan (1992) reports the belief among academics that good writing may be the most fundamental and important skill required by the communication executive. However, he adds that this assumption may be harmful where illiteracy is high and he instances two reasons why this may be so:

- India, where a major slice of the population do not read, and
- Africa, where Pratt (1985) remarks that traditional communication channels are 'the gongman, the town crier, the market square and the chief's court'.

and corporate communication is practised in both countries. B.A.T. Industries are among a number of multinational corporations who engage consultants to act for them in India.

# The personality types suited for corporate communications

Perhaps some personalities are not suited to the demands of corporate communications. White and Mazur (1995) quote Charles Cook, CEO at Grandfield Rork Collins, describing typical in-house practitioners:

> Communication executives are probably in their mid-forties, and are professional communicators. They will have done something else as well. This may have been a spell in line management or it may have been a spell in the financial sector. A combination of the two is even better. The executive is probably not an ex-journalist. This was, of course, the more traditional background.
>
> adapted from White and Mazur (1995)

Many commentators feel that certain types of people have a natural flair for communication work. Perhaps they might require:

- Self confidence and a positive attitude to life.
- The ability to empathize with people.
- High intelligence and good memory abilities.
- An interest in their fellow humans.

# Perfect PR people

The latest data from the youth market tracking study, Right of Admission Reserved, has identified those three personality groups which are most likely to seek jobs in corporate communications. A sample of 1018 15–24 year olds reveals that New Modernists (23 per cent ), Cool Britannias (14 per cent ) and Corporate Clubbers (12 per cent ) are the groups best suited to a communications career.

Fashionable, creative and bright New Modernists are good director potential for larger agencies. They would instil confidence in clients and bring a touch of individualism to their work. Whilst likely to resent corporate interference they may ultimately work better directing an autonomous in-house team

Corporate Clubbers are predominately female and highly ambitious night animals and are best suited to agencies with clients who have a relaxed culture

Cool Britannias are sharp, sussed and make good executives. They are most likely to switch jobs and will not be troubled by a rigid corporate culture.

> The MD of Twelve Consultancy believes that these results provide employers with fascinating insights. It is clear that different personality profiles are better suited to certain types of communication careers and obviously oung people seeking a job in this sector need to be bright, ambitious and creative.
>
> adapted from *PR Week* (1997p)

# The qualities needed to be a successful communication executive

White and Mazur (1995) suggest that academics who have studied communication practitioners expect them to have:

- Analytical skills.
- Excellent and well developed communications skills.
- An appreciation of culture/cultural differences.
- Business management and political skills.
- Diplomacy and the ability to get on with people.

Certainly excellent communication skills, as the then Director of Public Affairs at British Airways remarked, are much stressed by most organizations. The Group Director of Corporate Affairs at Yorkshire Tyne-Tees Television, then an independent company, emphasized the need to communicate. The Director of Group Public Relations at Vaux Brewery Group went on to speak of the 'need to communicate with people right across organizations . . . so that your publics understand what you want to say'. She continued: 'communicate a message that you wish people to understand, and to react to, in such a way that they will understand'.

Newsom and Scott (1976) quote the head of a US public relations agency who suggests that the following qualities are required:

- an ability to express oneself fluently
- the ability to listen
- to be observant
- the possession of courage and integrity
- self discipline
- intellectual maturity
- sound judgement
- creativity
- to be a quick thinker in a crisis
- to write well

- to possess a sound knowledge of the business
- to be able to prioritize.

> Without trust the message is not likely to be to have the desired
> impact or much positive impact at all for that matter.
>
> Goodman (1994)

A number of senior professional communicators were asked what qualities they considered a successful corporate communicator most needed. This is a summary of their responses:

---

| 1 | Good communication skills |
| 2 | Judgement |
| 3 | Listening skills |
| 4 | Common sense |
| 5 | Integrity |
| 6 | Sociable, gregarious person. |

---

The Director of Group Public Affairs at B.A.T. Industries spoke about the quality of judgement. He referred to this as 'the top quality'. He went on to say that 'if the organization is thinking of doing something, you have to know what your target audience may think about it'. He concluded 'one of the things about judgement is – don't cry wolf.'

The Acting Director of Corporate Communications at J. Sainsbury suggested that 'good listening skills are very important' adding that they are required in order that one may 'understand what the media are asking'. Of course, listening is a major part of the process of communicating. The Director, Corporate Affairs at GlaxoWellcome underlined this, commenting that 'if you're not a listener – forget it! Listening is of equal importance to talking.'

Integrity is referred to as a critical trait. Harrison (1995) comments that if a reporter knows that the communicator is trustworthy and can be relied upon it makes the job of reporting easier. This characteristic was described as 'vital' by the Public Relations Manager at the Northumbria Ambulance Service. This point was reinforced by the Communications Manager at Tennent Caledonian Breweries who emphasized the need for the director to be trusted by his audiences. The Group Director of Corporate Affairs at Yorkshire Tyne-Tees Television advised 'never lie', while his counterpart at Storehouse remarked that 'integrity is enormously high on the list of priorities'. The Public Relations Manager at the Avon and Somerset Constabulary echoed this and the then Acting Director of Corporate Affairs at W.H. Smith remarked that the press 'never forgive you for a "bum story".'

Perhaps a successful communicator should be good with people? London Transport's media spokeswomen commented that the executive needed to be a gregarious person – a people person. The then Communications Manager at Tennent Caledonian Breweries expressed the point well in saying that the communicator needed to be 'a social beast – one comfortable with people and situations.' The Director of Group Public Affairs at B.A.T. Industries referred to the need to 'like your fellow men' another director underlined 'the importance of social skills both inside and outside the organization'.

Most practitioners have clear ideas of the necessary characteristics. A Public Relations Manager of a west country organization summarized it neatly: 'You have to be credible. Would you believe Max Clifford (the internationally famous British publicist who specializes in publicizing notorious stories)'. Many other senior executives produce similar prognoses. Some put different emphases on different strengths. The then Director of Corporate Affairs at Storehouse commented presciently that the qualities demanded 'depended very much upon what the individual company required of their official'.

The Group Publicity Manager at Avon Rubber observed that it was necessary to be 'a believer'. A remark hinting, perhaps, at those management executives (even in large multinational organizations) who remain unconvinced of the strategic power that corporate communications is able to unleash.

## Technical competencies are just the entry point

The Director of Group Public Relations at Vaux Group remarked that 'you either have a gut feeling for it or you don't'. The Director of Corporate Communications at brewery and leisure group Whitbread noted that 'like almost any other senior job in an organization, technical competencies are just the entry point. It is the other qualities that make for good communication directors.'

## Oral and written skills

In a study of management skills Turk (1989) found that 93 per cent of the communication managers who were surveyed ranked both oral and written communication skills as the most important abilities needed by communication executives; certainly an ability to write cogently is a skill which is regarded by most executives as a first essential.

## Ease with senior executives

The ability to feel at ease with executives at the summit of their organizations is considered important; a point illustrated by the then Director of Corporate

Affairs at Storehouse. He writes most of his company's Annual Report. His opposite number at Whitbread writes the Chairman's speeches. Skolnik (1994) quotes a communications director specializing in financial communications – he comments that it is noteworthy that a communication executive has the kind of power which allows him to influence the top officials in his organization when they are crafting speeches. This, he points out, helps *them* to focus their thinking and policy. Accordingly, the communication executive must be able to understand the needs and the beliefs of both the Chairman and the CEO.

## Creativity

The communication executives at both ASDA and Whitbread spoke very strongly of the need for creative imagination and, certainly, creativity is an unusual and remarkable quality. Jackson (1995) considers that her role at the British Library (where she is Head of Communications) is part creative. Research might well prove creativity to be a more important quality for a successful corporate communicator than has, perhaps, previously been recognized. The Director of Corporate Communications at Whitbread developed this point. He referred to the need to see through the consequences of corporate actions: to take the wider view; and to see them 'laterally'. 'Line managers', he says, 'see things in straight lines'. 'Without creativity', he suggested, 'no one will succeed as a communication director.' He continued, 'the successful ones have these qualities . . . unsuccessful ones do not'.

ASDA's Director of Corporate Communications referred 'to the particular need for creativity in her role'; not necessarily from her personally, but to 'allow space for it to happen in others and to harness it for the sake of the organization'. She concluded that 'here at ASDA it's all about creativity'.

## The optimum requirement?

> Your CEO is a resource that must be managed. . . . You must have the CEO properly briefed and media-trained so that when you bring opportunities to him, he's prepared. . . . So it's incumbent on public relations to help him to promote the right things to the right people at the right time.
>
> Skolnik (1994)

White and Mazur (1995) refer to the need for a robust personality who may have to stand up to a strong and perhaps irritated chairman. The Director of Corporate Communications at Whitbread also spoke forcefully of the need for moral courage. He said that you 'have enormous influence, but no power base. The CEO or Chairman carry the authority'. He continued to say that communication directors are rarely interested in hierarchical power. 'Sometimes', he says, 'you have to persuade the CEO to do certain things. Occasionally you have to threaten him by assembling cogent arguments supported by data to support your view. You have to persuade the organization as a whole to go along with your ideas'.

> You must insist on what you know is important. You are the expert.
> You must take charge. Leadership will be responded to by any
> corporate officers, because they both understand and respect it.
>
> Goodman (1994)

Referring to the quality of courage, the communication director at UPS is quoted (Skolnik, 1994) as saying that 'Your CEO is a resource and you must have him properly briefed and media trained so that when you bring opportunities to him he will be prepared.' It is incumbent on the communications executive to help the CEO and the Chairman promote the right things to the right people at the right time. British Airways' then communication executive commented that 'if you have to tell them that their performance was poor, that requires political acumen'. In fact, he remarked 'it takes courage'.

> CEOs require highly-skilled communications and issues support.
> They also need candid advice and feedback that tells them what they
> need to know, not what they want to hear.
>
> Osborne (1994)

The then Acting Director of Corporate Affairs at W.H. Smith added that 'if you believe what you are doing is right – push it through. Having a "yes" person in corporate affairs is lethal'. The Director of Corporate Communications at Whitbread gave an example. He recalled that 12 months after he joined the organization he commissioned research into perceptions of his organization to find out what other 'players' in the City thought of Whitbread. 'The CEO might', he commented, 'have felt threatened by that action.'

## Brainpower

Many communication executives are bright people; often in several senses. A senior practitioner referred to the need for brainpower. The Director of Corporate Communications at ASDA, referred to the need for 'mental firepower', reinforcing her point by saying that 'the issues that you have to become knowledgeable about at short notice are often complex'.

Also important is the ability to work fast, a quality emphasized by the Director of Corporate Affairs at Storehouse. He remarked that 'decisions have to be made quickly on things: decisions which might be right or wrong'. Clearly, the communication executive is in a pivotal position. It is a position in which a judgement has to be made about when to react and when not to react; and sometimes that judgement has to be made very fast indeed.

Intrinsically mental power enables an individual to grasp issues 'at a variety of levels and to communicate the key message', as the spokeswoman for Vaux Group said. This was a view endorsed by the executive at British Airways. Their then Director of Public Affairs said how important it was to understand 'the core arguments with a high degree of critical reasoning'. The acting spokesman for W.H. Smith spoke of the need for an ability to keep several balls in the air at once. He illustrated this, speaking of the IRA bomb blast in June 1996 at the Arndale Centre, Manchester: 'You might keep the annual results in the air while you are at the same time dealing with the Manchester store, which has had its back wall blown out.'

## Energy

An ability to work with energy goes hand in hand with the need for mental agility. The Director of Corporate Communications at Whitbread commented on the need for great stamina because 'you are dealing with a huge operation'. 'There is,' he said, 'always something happening which can impact on operations.' He related that he worked throughout Christmas 1995 due to Whitbread's part involvement in the Forte–Granada take-over bid; and that all the secretarial staff worked on Boxing Day. 'I expect people to do this', he said. He commented that he is often at his desk by 7.00 a.m. and works until late at night. The Director, Corporate Affairs at GlaxoWellcome rehearsed this. There must be 'a willingness never to be off duty. Never to switch off. You accept that as part of the job'.

---

Other attributes referred to by senior practitioners included:

- Being someone who is persuasive – especially with the financial people – Tennent Caledonian Breweries/Yorkshire Tyne-Tees Television.
- Having an ability to give and take criticism: to be resilient. As Tennent Caledonian Breweries remarked, 'Communication is like anything; you are not perfect and can overlook something'. W.H. Smith remarked on 'the need to be able to take knocks and disappointments'.
- 'Having the ability to stay in the background. The senior role in the function should be invisible' – GlaxoWellcome.
- 'Being someone who sees things through with deadlines and is professional' – Tennent Caledonian Breweries – 'there are still too many cowboys.'
- 'Enjoying an empathy with one's audience – one presses different buttons to attract the attention of different audiences' – British Airways.
- 'Being one who is good at networking' – Yorkshire Tyne-Tees Television – who stressed the need for good contacts.

---

■ 'Appearing to be someone with an air of confidence. Positive and optimistic' – London Transport.

■ 'Having the ability to stay calm.' – B.A.T. Industries, who added 'If things go badly wrong, you don't want to make the situation worse.'

■ 'Having leadership skills.'

■ 'Being someone who is able to overcome internal politics.' – a point made by three companies. GlaxoWellcome expanded it, remarking that 'It is important to understand the interaction between senior people at Board Level. You have to be very astute.'

## Credibility

It is important that the communicator is perceived to be credible – both inside and outside the organization. Wright (1995) notes that the credibility of communication executives will be open to question unless they are seen to report directly to senior executives officers. The then Director of Corporate Affairs at Storehouse endorsed this. He commented, 'I report to top people.' He went on to say that 'the information given to me depends upon how highly regarded is my competence. Externally interpersonal skills are important too. You are a salesman – but, an honest salesman. You must be regarded as the natural entry point for your organization.'

Finally, the communication executive must be a person who is able to get on with the job however tough. As the Public Relations Manager at the Avon and Somerset Constabulary commented, 'You bite your tongue and gird your loins and out you go.'

So, these are the most important qualities that senior communication professionals suggest might be useful if a communication executive is to be effective; what are the origins?

Existing academic work in this field is limited. It does not suggest the origins or pedigree of the communications executive. Marketing, advertising, or journalism have all been regarded as fairly traditional backgrounds for communication executives; perhaps the executive has come from one of them – or possibly a good general management background would better equip the practitioner for the task?

> The fact that many practitioners are former journalists helps to explain the fact that they cling to a public information model of public relations. But, recent research suggests that there is a need to prepare for a practice of communications that addresses concerns about the role in the fast approaching global market. This approach goes far beyond media relations. It embraces the concerns of myriads of groups that impact upon the success of any organization
>
> adapted from L. A. Grunig (1992)

# The background of a director of corporate communication

Perhaps marketing is a useful background? Many academics have considered in the past that communications is an appendage or tool of marketing (Nessmann, 1995). However, Kitchen and Proctor (1991) note that public relations in its broadest sense is concerned with a wider range of publics than marketing. They do not see corporate public relations and marketing public relations as mutually exclusive.

Winner (1993) found that there are many former marketing executives directing communication functions. This might suggest a link between the two functions – possibly because they are so alike? Kotler (quoted in White and Mazur, 1995, p.21) suggests that communications are seen as part of marketing and thus are viewed mainly as a support activity for it. Perhaps, instead it is simply the case that the personal traits are similar to both disciplines?

Perhaps advertising is more creative and might be a more useful background? Communication is more of a craft than an art and it certainly requires lateral thinking. This might be the key ingredient for ensuring continuing success in the communication field.

> Journalists are bad team workers and their approach to issues is too narrow.
>
> Public Relations and Marketing Manager,
> Northumbria Ambulance Service, in conversation with the author

A view, and it is one not shared by everyone, is that communication is not a task for ex-journalists; although several high flyers arrived by that route (the Directors of Corporate Affairs at Storehouse and Boots among them). But, not all practitioners regard that as the desirable route. The journalist route was described as 'a narrow way' by the Director of Group Public Relations at Vaux Group. Her counterpart at Northumbria Ambulance said that journalists 'are bad team workers and their approach to issues is too narrow'. However, most practitioners do emphasize that the practitioner needs to understand the requirements of journalists.

Amongst those senior communicators who had entered their profession via journalism, one had experience at a very senior level – the Director Of Corporate Affairs at Storehouse had been Industrial and Economics Editor at ITN where Peter Sissons (the nationally respected television presenter) had been his Number Two.

Certainly, although it may be the traditional route, journalism is not an inevitable one. Amongst very senior communication professionals can be found teachers, an Assistant Professor of Chemistry, a former airline steward (formerly at British Airways, now Director of Corporate Communication at BUPA), and a training officer with Miller Construction. Yet another (the

Director of Corporate Communications at Whitbread) had been a Member of Parliament.

In many instances communication executives entered the field by chance. A small number came from a public sector background (the Communication Manager at Northumbria Ambulance not surprisingly having an NHS background). A few had quite simply worked their way up through the ranks. More often than not the current position holder applied for the job.

## Is a good generalist background preferred?

> It depends upon the organization and its objectives. There is no one way progress.
>
> Director of Corporate Affairs, Boots plc
> in conversation with the author

Is it possible that a senior generalist career might better prepare a communication executive for contact with the different range of business disciplines into which the position will come into contact and the differing perspectives that each will require?

Perhaps, progressing through the communication ranks is a better way altogether of reaching the top? There *are* some professionals who consider it important that the executive progresses through the ranks – among them the then Director of Public Affairs at British Airways and, also, his opposite number at London Transport. Their perception is that this experience gives the senior executive a clearer understanding of the culture and history of the organization. This, they believe, better enables the executive to present the personality of the organization to its publics. The then Acting Director of Corporate Communications at J. Sainsbury stressed the opposing view – the importance of the experience of other companies.

Through the ranks or not, the Director, Corporate Affairs at Glaxo-Wellcome commented on the importance of having an intimate knowledge of the organization and its trading environment. However, there are sound theoretical reasons why the generalist approach could be preferred by a majority of practitioners in today's more complex business environment. The practitioner who has generalized may well develop a quicker grasp of the culture and identity of the organization. With wider perspectives and experiences this kind of career development is increasingly common and brings strong skills into the communication area (White and Mazur, 1995).

Boots' Director of Corporate Affairs summarized the general professional view saying 'it depends upon the organization and its objectives. There is no one way progress.'

# The academic background of a successful practitioner

In a recent study it was noted that many senior communication practitioners have university degrees. A small proportion were obvious highflyers. Of those identified as graduates, five had degrees in English and three in History; the others being a smattering of subjects quite unrelated to communications. Two (the communication executives at Lloyds/TSB and at the Northumbria Ambulance Service) graduated as mature students. Only one revealed formal qualifications in communications.

> Public relations practitioners have always needed to be highly educated persons, with a strong sense of history and knowledge of current events, who are taught to think in a certain way and to solve problems in a certain way. However, tomorrow's public relations practitioners will also need to be far more culturally astute and cosmopolitan – that is, particularly sensitive to the multicultural and international nuances of their organizations' diverse publics.
>
> Kruckeberg (1995)

These findings bear comparison with research which Turk (1989) undertook in four South Western states in the US 10 years ago. Of those surveyed, he found that:

59% had a bachelor's degree
24% had a master's degree
5% had an MBA or legal degree
5% held doctorates.

# Headhunting – a typical approach

The Director of Corporate Communications at Whitbread told the author that few jobs at his level are advertised – most are filled through headhunters. He himself had been approached three times in the previous 12 months. One headhunter had offered him a 50 per cent salary increase. B.A.T.'s Director of Group Public Affairs applied for his position after being asked (in his capacity as head of a consultancy) if he would to find suitable applicants for that position. Yorkshire Tyne-Tees Television approached their director after his success in another role. The then Director of Corporate Affairs at Storehouse was headhunted to Imperial Tobacco from Burmah Oil; and then to Storehouse from that position. The same thing had also happened to the Director of

Corporate Affairs at Boots and also to the then Director of Public Affairs at British Airways. The latter was headhunted back to the airline to be its chief press officer prior to privatization – the headhunters were aware that he knew the business and the requirements of a newly privatized company.

## Experience of consultancies

Many communication executives have experience of working for public relations consultancies. The Director of Group Public Relations at Vaux Group had previously set up her own consultancy from scratch. The Director of Corporate Communication at Whitbread had been with Shadwick, from where he was headhunted to Whitbread in 1990. The Director of Group Public Affairs at B.A.T. Industries had run Charles Barker.

While still a young man, the Director, Corporate Affairs at Glaxo (now GlaxoWellcome plc) found himself deputizing for the head of his department – who subsequently died suddenly. He was promoted to his position two years later. The Head of Corporate Communications at Lloyds/TSB learned the trade in the public sector and moved into the private sector after being recruited from the Government Information Services.

## The communication executive – the nature of the role

Many academics are undecided about the nature of the role of the communication executive. They ponder if the role produces conflicts and, if so, what those conflicts may be and what causes them. They also wonder if the real task is to act as a bridge between an organization and its key publics; and, if so, whether the role extends beyond that. Management scholars have also questioned if the role is invidious in any way and whether the communicator has difficulty working with the CEO.

> Involving communications at board level could prevent a raft of PR experts being disbelieved, ignored or over-ruled – when they were right all the time. Communication experts talk about the difficulty of having a real effect on the strategy of their employers. All too often they are presented with a fait accompli. Executives are remarkably blasé about corporate reputation. It is a basic, misplaced nonchalance that underlies many PR debacles. Senior managers tend not to take the advice that we offer.
>
> adapted from Bond (1995c)

Academics need to consider the boundaries of responsibility given to the communicator and also the extent of the powers as well as the rank and status afforded to this management position. A central matter of interest is whether the executive has a position which commands respect and if the role changes between different environments. Is it possible that some executives struggle to attain positions from which they are able to influence those at the decision-making table? It could be that two parameters face a communication director:

- the source of responsibility
- to whom the executive is responsible.

The role of most communication professionals does have boundaries although at Yorkshire Tyne-Tees Television there were none at the time of their take-over. The Group Director of Corporate Affairs there commented that if the CEO wanted to talk to the minister of National Heritage he would arrange it and would attend himself.

If the communication practitioner functions in a subsidiary of a group the role has an added dimension. At Wessex Water, for example, the Director of Corporate Communications works almost entirely for their water services division. At Vaux the Director of Group Public Relations' role is right across the organization as it is at Avon Rubber. At Vaux the role has grown and expanded and the Director of Group Public Relations is now an operational director for the group as a whole. At Tennent Caledonian Breweries in Glasgow (the Scottish division of national brewer, Bass) the practitioner does not handle brand public relations for national products; nor does he deal with brand public relations for Hoopers Hooch – (a brand of alcoholic soft drink).

# A new role

> Public relations practitioners – if they prove worthy of the task –
> will be called upon to be corporate – that is, organizational –
> interpreters and ethicists and social policy-makers, charged with
> guiding organizational behaviour as well as influencing public
> perceptions within a global context.
>
> Kruckeberg (1995)

Corporate communication is now recognized as a resource. Therefore, just like any other corporate resource, it has to be managed properly. Corporate communication is not a new profession but a new way altogether of looking at communications (van Riel, 1995). It has become a major management discipline in its own right. It has gained recognition as an important strategic tool. Here we look at ways in which the role of the communication executive is changing – for during the 1990s it has been redesignated and realigned.

## An uncertain role

As corporate communications has developed as a key management discipline the role of the communications executive itself is still embryonic (White and Mazur, 1995). It is misunderstood in some organizations and it remains less than clear to academics. Yet it is one of the most essential.

'The task is about what is going on; what is going to happen' remarked the communications manager at Northumbria Ambulance. Her counterpart at the Avon and Somerset Constabulary described hers as 'quite a maverick role'. The Director, Corporate Affairs at GlaxoWellcome added 'It is almost unlimited in its potential.'

It may well be that few managerial roles are as undefined as that of the communication executive; for both the role and function can be quite uncertain. 'The profession needs to work out what it is and who does what', commented the then communication manager at Tennent Caledonian Breweries.

Howard (1992) explored the wider aspects of the communicator role. He suggested that the role of senior communication officials in major organizations might well be a mixture of various different characteristics, such as:

- Planner
- Watchdog
- Catalyst
- Communicator
- Savant
- Stimulant
- Adviser
- Confidant.

Academics not only question whether the senior communications role is multi-functional they have also been unable to decide exactly what is expected of the director. Management scholars ask whether the role varies between one organization and another (Brody, 1988; Guth, 1995). Winner (1993) proposes that the role, and the importance attached to it, vary considerably. There are certainly a variety of different descriptions given to what is essentially much the same function; all put emphasis on different aspects of the same role. Howard (1992) likened the process to throwing a dart at a wall and then drawing a target around it. This does suggest uncertainty about what the role entails.

Writing in 1969, Bowman and Ellis proposed that practitioners exist partly to create and foster relations between organizations and their publics. Lauzen (1995) suggests that 'they provide cultural cross-fertilization with their publics and relay organizational values to and from their audiences'. This too might place the practitioner in an invidious position for the communicator acts as a bridge between the organization and its environments.

If the role is at all ambiguous it might very well prove to be unduly stressful (Winner, 1993). Some practitioners consider that *communicating* presents the very least of their problems (Simon, 1986). Jackson (1995) too questions the role. There is different emphasis in the way a communications director perceives the role from one organizational area to another and from one industry to another and, according to Nessmann (1995), between different countries.

Schneider (1985) confirmed that the size and influence of the communication role does vary within an organization – according to its own size and complexity. She published findings concerning the role as she saw it in relation to the nature of the organization itself:

| | |
|---|---|
| Traditional type of organization | rarely advise management low power/authority |
| Mechanical organization | larger/more power |
| Organic organization | less emphasis on holding press conferences small department/little influence |
| Mixed type of organization management | writing speeches/ counselling/contacting media most power and authority. |

Schneider refers to Hage and Hull (1981), who argued that the scale of the organization, taken together with the complexity of the managerial task, are the two variables that decide the importance of the communication role. Perhaps the role may be quite unimportant if the size of the organization is small?

# An imprecise role

The media spokeswoman for London Transport was not able to identify 'a precise role for her job at all'. But there must be a job specification and it must be drawn up in collaboration with the CEO and the Executive Team. The nature of the task ensures that the specifications will have to be flexible, adaptable to change and reviewed constantly.

## Conveying the personality

The Head of Corporate Communications at Lloyds/TSB perceives the role 'as one of advising the CEO and Chairman on the direction of the organization'. The then Director of Public Affairs at British Airways commented that part of the job is to ensure that the personality and position of the organization on particular issues are conveyed 'comprehensively and honestly to all those audiences who have an interest and are in a position to shape an opinion'. He went on to say that 'you do what any good lawyer does – exemplify your virtues and minimize your vices'. His perception of the role is that it exists to ensure 'that the organization's objectives and point of view are properly communicated'.

## Raising the profile/getting the message across

The then Communication Manager at Tennent Caledonian Breweries saw the task as 'raising the profile of TCB . . . the sign of a good communications man is one who raises the profile of others'. As the Group Director of Corporate Affairs at Yorkshire Tyne-Tees Television expressed it, 'the objective is to get the message across'. The Director of Group Public Relations at Vaux brewery added that one part of her job was to make it possible for 'a communication of ideas internally and externally'. The Group Director of Corporate Affairs at Tyne-Tees Television went on to say that 'the message changes all the time'. He added that within the television industry it 'may not be the same for two weeks running' – making the task of practitioners in that particular sector particularly onerous.

## Harmonizing messages

van Riel (1995) highlights the difficulty when a large variety of internal messages lead to fragmented and contradictory external messages. He adds that organizations are only too aware of the dangers of fragmented communications and he makes the point repeatedly in much of his work. In 1990 he discussed the importance of harmonizing internal and external messages. He suggested that ideally an organization will try to overcome this problem by attuning all communication modalities to each other.

> You spend lots of time ensuring the consistency of the message.
> Director, Corporate Affairs, GlaxoWellcome, in conversation with
> the author

The Director, Corporate Affairs at GlaxoWellcome discussed the question of fragmentation. He said that a practitioner spends 'lots of time ensuring the consistency of the message'. He observed that he is responsible for a wide range of audiences; 'so the message needs choreography and orchestrating'. John. D. Graham, CEO of St Louis based Fleishman-Hillard, said that 'there is a growing recognition among corporate executives that the ability to succeed will depend upon a corporation's ability to communicate effectively with employees, customers, and the public at large'. Orchestrating messages for such a wide range of key constituencies is clearly of fundamental importance.

He went on to emphasize the point, saying that part of his responsibility is to ensure that the messages 'all work together internationally ... ensuring a common face to all organizations. Crucially relating the constant message back to the rapidly changing dynamics of business.'

The role played by the communication executive in helping to shape the direction of the organization is not only demonstrated by efforts to overcome message fragmentation. The Acting Director of Corporate Communications at J. Sainsbury commented that corporate communication gives direction to various departments. She emphasized that different management areas deal with different publics and spoke of how corporate communication advises different departments how to communicate with different key audiences on a variety of topics.

> The role of a communication executive is to help the company understand the impact of its activities on various audience segments throughout society. At the same time it needs to help the company understand the outside environment so that it can structure its own business programmes accordingly
>
> adapted from Skolnik (1994)

## Advisory role

Corporate communication also has an advisory role. At GlaxoWellcome the Director, Corporate Affairs takes the CEO's diary for a whole year and looks at it from a public relations point of view. He suggests how the CEO's schedule can be managed better having regard for the public relations implications. He suggests that no decision should be taken purely for public relations reasons; but that it is essential that the PR implications of all corporate decisions are considered. The Public Relations Manager at the Avon and Somerset Constabulary 'advises her senior officers on the PR implication of policy and decisions'.

## Social conscious

Organizations are beginning to understand that with so many social, political and ethical issues influencing their performance, responsible managers have no choice but to incorporate an awareness of public affairs into their daily management decisions. The organization needs to be able to look up to its communication executive as a wise as well as able person. The confidence that should exist between the organization and its communications director must be mutual, for without doubt there will be many occasions when an organization needs to ask the communication executives advice as to how it should handle a sensitive issue (Winner, 1993).

Sometimes communication executives may have to decide whether certain proposed courses of action could be against the public interest; or even, perhaps, might be socially irresponsible. Simon (1986) queries whether, in such a situation, the director serves as the moral guardian of his organization. Without doubt executives do need to consider whether the values, perceptions and culture of their organizations are at odds in any way with the values, beliefs and ethos of various key publics (Lauzen, 1995).

The then Director of Public Affairs at British Airways sees a role in 'ensuring that the various publics are comfortable with the organization'. Their director commented that 'unlike Geoff Potter (Director, Corporate Affairs, Glaxo-Wellcome plc) I am selling direct to the public'. He continued, 'our communication people support corporate and product identity'.

## An increasingly important role

Until quite recently, some senior management regarded the communicator as little more than an information conduit (van Riel, 1995). As a managerial role it was not only one of the most misunderstood, but was also an untapped resource (Finlay, 1994). However, at the summit of industry this is generally no longer the case. Today the communicator is recognized by a majority of organizations as an executive with a role of increasing importance and many communication practitioners have become strategic advisers to their board (Troy, 1993).

> We are often involved as advisers. With our corporate view, we take seriously our role as an adviser. The CEO consults with us regularly on particular issues. CEOs believe that they are better decision makers because of our participation.
>
> adapted from Skolnik (1994)

The scope of the role is widening. The existence of the communication executive is not fully justified unless the role is given the opportunity to play its full part in the formulation and implementation of corporate strategy. At the most senior level practitioners are involved increasingly in relations with government, in industrial relations and with regulators. Good communications with these key publics have taken on increased and strategic importance. In reality communication executives ought to be a central plank in their top management structure – for their role enables them to assist the processes of:

- improving economic performance
- changing attitudes and perceptions
- enhancing corporate reputation
- image creating.

So, communication is becoming an intrinsic part of every management function. In many ways the communication executive might be likened to a pilot on an ocean-going vessel, helping to navigate the organization towards its chosen destination. The executive is aided on this journey by modern communication tools which increase, change and become more sophisticated by the day – all of which facilitate the taking of positions more quickly than ever before.

## Recognition of the role

Senior management who have yet to appreciate the full power – and the potential impact – of corporate communication may be the very ones who do not yet realize that to function effectively the communication director must be aided by high visibility – and status – throughout the organization. IABC (quoted in White and Mazur, 1995) identifies effective practitioners as those who are part of their company's dominant coalition.

John O. Graham says that 'the communication function in the future will be one that is increasingly recognized and absolutely an integral part of the top management'. Researchers Ryan and Martinson (1985) found that communication executives are typically not satisfied with acting as mere management representatives. They do, they reported, want to be involved in the decision-making process. Indeed in some cases, they say, they need to be. They point out that in an emergency the crisis will not be minimized if the person responsible for communications is not a key player in the decision-making process. However, writing of a survey of European financial institutions reported on in 1992, van Riel said that, in general, communication executives do report directly to the top management. He found that there was frequent contact between the communicator and senior executive officers.

Corporate communication has matured into a key discipline of enlightened and progressive management. There can be little debate that corporate reputation is now one of the critical management issues. This is an issue which major corporations can hardly avoid considering – yet amazingly some still do so. The corporate brand has become a key weapon in competitive strategy. Corporate communication needs to be where it belongs – in, or very close, to the board room.

# To whom does the communication executive report?

Reporting relationships play an important part in the effectiveness of communication practice. Reported studies from the European Centre for Public Affairs and the IABC demonstrate the importance of a direct reporting relationship between senior communication

> executives and senior management. The most effective
> communication specialists are those who become close to
> management at chairman and CEO level
>
> adapted from White and Mazur (1995)

Bowman and Ellis (1969) suggested that if the executive does not have the rank of director then he or she should unquestionably report to one, and Simon (1986) suggests that it is a fact that a sure way of confirming the status of the practitioner is to observe to whom he or she reports.

> A company achieves full value for the communication function if, and
> only if, that function reports directly to the CEO. The CEO is the
> single most important – and potentially the most effective –
> communicator that an organization possesses. Stakeholders depend
> heavily upon the CEO. They expect him to have the answers to key
> questions about where the business is going and how their interests
> will be affected.
>
> adapted from Osborne (1994)

There is one way – and one way only – that an organization's communication executive can properly be part of what Wright (1995) calls 'the dominant coalition' and that is by having a place at the decision-making table and reporting directly to the organization's most senior management. Many commentators stress the importance of the communication executive reporting direct to the CEO. The specialized knowledge and skills that the practitioner brings to an organization justifies a place at the decision-making table. If the practitioner does reports at this level it will ensure that the link between the communication function and top management thinking is as close as possible.

The reporting level for the communication executive impacts on the practitioner's effectiveness. Typically the practitioner reports to the CEO with direct access both to the CEO and to the Chairman, whether the latter is executive or non-executive. As the Group Director of Corporate Affairs at Yorkshire Tyne-Tees Television remarked, 'You have to know your CEO pretty well. It is most important to establish a bond with the CEO. You must trust each others' methods of reaching objectives instinctively.'

As noted, van Riel (1992) found that, generally, communication executives do report to senior management. The Director of Group Public Relations at Vaux Group commented that reporting to the top enables her 'to react very quickly over a wide area of management'. Indeed hers is a 'floating role' (likewise at Avon Rubber) positioned below the Executive Committee. At London Transport the role is sufficiently far down that it causes problems 'because messages are received second and third hand at times'. The communication executive there added that her role should report at board level. In fact she reports to her marketing director; evidence perhaps that some organizations still connect the two disciplines together.

Although most directors do report direct to their CEO, some report to another officer for organizational reasons (and in a survey of 260 US corporations conducted in 1996, Post and Griffin (1997) report over a dozen practitioners having a dual reporting relationship). At Northumbria Ambulance, the Public Relations Manager reports to the Director of Corporate Affairs – but she has ready access to the CEO. Similar arrangements exist at the Avon and Somerset Constabulary, their Public Relations Manager reports to the Deputy Chief Constable. At Avon Rubber the Group Publicity Manager reports to the Director of Corporate Planning.

> For the first time, detergent giant Lever Brothers has elevated corporate affairs to the boardroom. It has appointed a new corporate and consumer affairs director.
>
> John Ballington, Lever Brothers sales director, has been appointed. He takes up the post in July. This is a move which signifies the growing importance to Lever of managing corporate responsibilities.
>
> Ballington's current board position as sales director will be absorbed within the newly created customer development director role. This will be filled by Graeme Miller.
>
> Ballington's responsibility will be to manage Lever's relationships with key stakeholders. These include politicians, environmental groups, trade associations, the media, and other key stakeholders. He will also continue to develop consumer advice services.
>
> The new board appointments are part of the company's drive to adopt a more customer-focused approach.
>
> Lever Brother's chairman Aart Weijburg said 'We have regrouped at Board level. This is intended to reflect the changes in our business and the way our customers need to work. At the same time we are accelerating our corporate and consumer affairs activity'.
>
> adapted from Dempsey (1997)

## The fit in the structure of the organization

> if the senior ... man is not involved at the senior executive level ... probably the decision has been made that they wanted a dog to do a dog's job; rather than to do a proper ... job.
>
> Winner (1993)

Academics question where the communication executive fits into the organizational structure and what the status might be. Wright (1995) considers that the communication executive should have as much power and authority as the directors of other corporate functions such as finance and law – a question of the utmost interest to all who study communication theory and practice (Guth, 1995). If practitioners are excluded from the dominant coalition (ergo from the decision-making process) this inevitably reduces the influence and effectiveness of their communication department (Lauzen, 1995), resulting in its relegation to the level of a low category support function.

> Most public relations people play a role in assisting management to articulate strategies, policies, philosophies, and mission and value statements, . . . I would not look for any sort of elevation of this function to a policy-making position.
>
> Skolnik (1994)

The communication executive must be given a core role in the executive structure if the practitioner is to be able to play a major part in the formulation and delivery of corporate strategy – and some European practitioners are still struggling to attain positions of management in many of their organizations (Nessmann, 1995). van Riel (1992) concluded that a typical organizational chart for corporate communications does not exist. This may be true in Continental Europe but in a typical organization in Britain today – especially those which have undergone extensive change – it is found one level below the chief executive's committee.

At the summit there is the board of directors, which will be quite small. It will not manage the organization from day to day – this is left to the executive committee. This committee is one level below the board and is known by a variety of titles, such as:

- Chief Executive's Committee  – at B.A.T. and W.H. Smith
- Corporate Team  – at the Avon and Somerset Constabulary
- Executive Team  – at British Airways
- Management Committee  – at Lloyds/TSB.

these committees/teams vary in size, but not in importance. They manage the organization from day to day and are very powerful.

The top level in industry is still undergoing enormous change (as recently as January 1996 within British Airways) as new CEO are appointed; but this is the structure found most commonly in major corporations. Within this framework the communication executive is commonly positioned at the second or third layer – an indication of the importance that the organization now places on the communications function.

Whilst the communication executive is usually located immediately below the executive committee there are variations. At GlaxoWellcome a group executive committee (EC) runs the group: the Director of Group Public Affairs (now Corporate Affairs) is not on the EC but contributes to it whenever appropriate through the chairman to whom he reports. Operating below the EC there is a group commercial committee (GCC). The Director of Group Public Affairs sits on the GCC. He is one of two colleagues, the other being the

Director of Corporate Strategy, who report direct to the CEO. They both sit on the GCC because 'it is an important way of picking up stuff that comes through which is crucial to corporate communications'.

A similar situation exists at British Airways. There the Director of Public Affairs is one of 14 executives below the executive team. He reports to the Director of Corporate Resources. Until the recent re-organization he was one of 25 people reporting direct to the chairman. This, he said, was 'not a sensible span of control'. As the Director of Group Public Affairs at B.A.T. Industries reflected 'you do not need to be on the executive committee to know what it is thinking'. Their director continued, 'if there is an initiative that I want to propose, I will attend it'. At J. Sainsbury the Director of Corporate Communications is the only departmental director who reports direct to the CEO; this is perceived as 'important because he is dealing with customers and because he is dealing with the City as well'.

The communications manager is certainly not part of the dominant coalition at Tennent Caledonian Breweries (no longer autonomous – it is largely controlled by its parent company, Bass plc from their Burton-On-Trent headquarters) where the communication executive is straightforwardly a member of the local management team and reports to:

- the managing director–sales, in Glasgow, on local matters
- the communications director of Bass plc, at the group's Burton-on-Trent headquarters, on group matters.

A similar situation exists at Yorkshire Tyne-Tees Television where two separate television companies comprise the Group. Their Group Director of Corporate Affairs is a member of the full board of Yorkshire Television, but not of Tyne-Tees Television. He is one of a small number of group executives who report to the group CEO. At Vaux brewery the Director of Group Public Relations is on the divisional board and has very much a 'helicopter role'; enabling her to be involved at every level.

The repositioning of the role within organizational structures recognizes its new importance. The communication executive may be on the way to the board room, but is definitely not yet there.

# The status of the role

> The status lags the change in the perceived importance of this function.
>
> Director, Corporate Affairs, GlaxoWellcome,
> in conversation with the author

The status of the communication executive depends upon the organization's own view of communications (Winner, 1993) and of how other organizations in its sector regard the communication function. But many management scholars consider it essential that the executive carries authority – and in large organizations he must have a great deal of it.

> What matters for your effectiveness is your access and being inside the information flow.
> Director of Group Public Affairs, B.A.T. Industries plc,
> in conversation with the author

If a communicator lacks credibility with the media it could be that this is because key audiences are not convinced that the practitioner is sufficiently part of the dominant coalition. White and Mazur (1995) confirm this noting that the executive must be listened to. Referring to Terence Collis (formerly Director of Public Affairs, Vickers plc) they comment that he was 'one of the few senior communications officials who not only had clout, but was seen to have it'. David Reed at Whitbread and Alastair Eperon at Boots are without question others among many possible examples who quite visibly have clout.

The communication executive must input into the organization's most important policy-making decisions. Wright (1995) argues that if an organization has a communication executive who reports to his CEO then the executive can have an extremely significant impact in helping to direct the organization's internal and external communications and might do much to clarify any overlap of internal communications, HRM and personnel functions.

> We believe that the function is undervalued by British industry.
> Director, Corporate Affairs, GlaxoWellcome
> in conversation with the author

The issue of whether corporate communications should be elevated to board level has become an area of some debate (White and Mazur, 1995). The strategic value of the communications role is now widely appreciated by more sophisticated management. The communication executive at GlaxoWellcome spoke for many senior communication executives when he commented that 'we believe that the function is undervalued by British industry'. Broom and Dozier (1986) argued that the involvement in organizational decision-making is perhaps more important to the communications professional than any other measure of professional growth.

Communications are represented at board level in very few organizations. Rio Tinto Zinc (Lord Richard Home) and British Gas (John Whybrough) are among exceptions. A number of senior communicators *are* on divisional boards. A number in major corporations – those at Boots and Whitbread are examples – are one level below the group board on the executive committee.

It happens that I am on a par with the managing directors of a number of our businesses. It may be that other organizations have a different view. In theory I could be asked to go off and run Boots Opticians or Halfords.

The Director of Corporate Affairs, Boots plc,
in conversation with the author

The question of their status within the organization appears not to bother most professional communicators. Few communication executives show much concern about it. But, the Director of Group Public Affairs at B.A.T. Industries remarked that he would 'rather like it' if he had a seat on the board 'as it would complete the recognition that the role has been growing'. This was echoed by Boots' director, who commented 'it was made clear where the reporting level would be. I would rather be on the group board clearly. If it was further away I would not have taken the job.'

# The management title allocated to the role

Frequently, corporate communication is thought of as the collective name for all communication disciplines. As long as the individual disciplines of corporate communications, corporate identity corporate culture, public relations and so on have not been defined precisely in theoretical terms this can only be seen as an aid — and not a complete solution.

adapted from Nessmann (1995)

Corporate communications has close associations with the management discipline of public relations. As a result, academic literature refers to the two disciplines in largely similar terminology. Accordingly many communication titles originated with public relations and they vary according to the country of origin. Here our concern is with the role and function of what previously was known as the public relations director. In the United Kingdom what has become a rather broad, imprecise communications discipline is referred to variously as:

- Corporate Affairs
- Corporate Communications
- Public Affairs.

Evidently there are different job titles granted to the executive who is responsible for the communications function (White and Mazur, 1995). The original styling public relations director has disappeared at the highest level in some countries – for public relations has become debased; but, this has not occurred in the United States of America.

> Many communication experts have looked at the role and have tried
> to give it a name.
>> Director of Corporate Communications, Wessex Water plc,
>> in conversation with the author

No one term is adopted broadly anywhere. There is a whole plethora of different titles. Many communication experts have examined the role and tried to redesignate it having regard for:

- what the role involves
- the importance attached to it by the organization.

# The director of corporate communications

These issues are of central interest to all academics who study communications. To simplify matters perhaps we should adopt the styling 'Director of Corporate Communications'. It is a helpful term, it covers most eventualities and is used increasingly.

Senior executives, whatever their titles, perform very similar tasks (Jackson, 1995). Occasionally two people with the same job title have quite different roles. Apparently van Riel (1992) finds that the term 'corporate communications' is not much used in financial circles; but no one term is adopted universally. There is a whole range of different titles. Many writers would agree that job/departmental titles can be very unreliable guides to duties (van Riel, 1992).

## Knowledge of the organization

The Head of Corporate Communications at the British Library says that the communication specialist brings key attributes to the organization (Jackson, 1995):

- communications skills – knowing what formats and media to use – when and how best to get a message across – it 'matters greatly if I decide to tell the world about a major matter and tell only the *Sun* newspaper'
- a broad and deep knowledge of the organization – what it feels like, what its tone is, its culture
- what is going to happen next – good antennae and forecasting skills.

Communications have a crucial role to play in the total business system (Winner, 1993). Clearly the communication executive must understand the culture of the organization, its perceptions and its people so that he or she is able to communicate its image, messages and themes to important constituencies. Thus the practitioner must have considerable knowledge of their organization.

Writing in 1986, Simon suggested that every senior communicator should know the organization from top to bottom and Howard (1992) suggested that the director should be strongly aware of the organization's:

- corporate identity
- corporate philosophy
- style
- structure.

# A changing role – a wonderful job!

Some practitioners stipulate that to be really effective the ideas that they put forward *must* lead to changes in action. Management's original perception of the communications role – merely one of publicity – has changed out of all recognition, although there are still executives in some traditional organizations who have not made use of the full potential of communication with key constituents. Practitioners in organizations which have undergone great change stress the importance of giving the communicator a central strategic role. In today's global market place the communication executive assists in the formulation of corporate strategy and in promoting the perceptions of the organization, its messages and themes, to significant publics. The role of the corporate communicator has developed into an approach rather more than a technique (White and Mazur, 1995) and it is now a key part of a multi-faceted management discipline.

The director of corporate communications is responsible for developing a strategic communication process which, when implemented, earns respect and acceptance for company policies from the organization's publics (Sperling, 1983). Thus the executive is the voice of the organization to a whole variety of different audiences in varying ways (Jackson, 1995).

## A wonderful job!

Some senior executives speak of their wonderful job; but go on to say how very tiresome it can be at times. As the Public Relations Manager at the Avon and Somerset Constabulary said (of employees who take actions directly in the face of her expressed advice – and who then leave her to pick up the pieces) 'all you can do is to defend them from the positions that they have created'.

# Case study

What is the full-time communication executive supposed to know that others do not? As a manager at the British Library, Marie Jackson has a budget and a dozen staff. Thus she has personnel and financial responsibilities as well as communication duties to fulfil. She pays the bills, she counsels staff.

The communication specialist brings key skills to her organization. In Jackson's case, two examples of this are:

■ communication skills – how best to get a message across.
  Jackson's title is Head of Corporate Communications. She says that it is increasingly used to describe those who once had a public relations title. She regards it as a helpful term. The great majority of her staff are doing day-to-day corporate communication. They are communicating the British Library to those who need to hear of it and about it. They are producing corporate literature and brochures. They are speaking on behalf of the organization in a number of ways.
■ a broad and deep knowledge of the organization – Jackson considers questions like:
  • What does her organization feel like?
  • What is its tone?
  • How is her organization perceived?
  • What is going to happen next?

## Marie Jackson considers the communication director's role

It is the communication executive's task to know the truth about the character and style of an organization and to position it correctly. It is not her job to decide what business the organization is in or what decisions it should make. It is important that decisions are taken with the public relations implications in mind. Communication has a role to play in helping businesses express themselves. We used communication experts in the Library to help the senior management team define the positioning statement which the Library introduced two years ago.

What tools does the communication specialist have to achieve the best positioning for her organization and to ensure that the right feel and messages are transmitted? Jackson's task is to communicate the British Library to a number of audiences as a single, whole organization; to take responsibility for the Library's communication with the media; and to improve internal communications in the process. She sees her role as part creative and part policing. She tries imaginatively and efficiently to make sure that the British Library is known about by the right people – and understood.

Journalists are the most influential communicators in the world, she says. Good media coverage can help you beyond your wildest dreams. Good media relations pay off when you are communicating a complex organization which is not easily understood.

Jackson believes that of all the audiences with which a communication team is communicating, two are head and shoulders above the rest in importance. They are the media and the staff. adapted from Jackson (1995)

# Profile – the typical communication executive

A communication executive in a British organization is twice as likely to be male as female. In his middle forties, the probability is that he has a bachelor's degree in English, History or a Social Science.

There is a 30 per cent probability that he was a journalist (otherwise he entered communications from another area, quite likely by chance) but he realizes that journalism is not an essential background. He is most unlikely to have formal training in communications and definitely does not belong to any professional communications body.

He is a sensible, honest and trusting man: regarded as having integrity. He demonstrates good judgement (particularly with people) and has a confident air. Energetic and capable of working long hours, he is used to meeting deadlines. He does both regularly.

A creative, courageous person he is much aware of internal politics. A good listener, who empathizes with his fellow men, he shows resilience and can take knocks. He is calm and persistent.

Having risen fast through the ranks he is now near the summit of his organization; probably one level below the executive committee – in turn one layer below board level. He will go no further. He has enormous influence, but little real power. He may earn between £75 000 and £150 000. He is a satisfied, contented and humorous person enjoying a very diverting position giving him considerable autonomy.

He reports direct to the CEO with ready access to his Chairman. He is familiar with the many differing publics (which he will probably call 'audiences') with which his organization desires to have relationships. If needs be, he hires consultants, who may well handle the financial audience for him – this being the one area of management communications that many of his colleagues have transferred to their financial director or have contracted out.

He regards the internal public as his most important. He may even think of them as 'ambassadors' for the organization. He is much aware of 'opinion formers' (a recent addition to the many audiences that he has to take into account): they may well rank in importance after the financial audience. The media (of whose influence he is very conscious), MPs, government and regulators follow them in significance.

He might well regard himself as an 'image creator'. He will be very much aware of the strategic value that corporate communication can add when it is included as part of his organization's decision-making process. He will not regard himself as the 'alter ego' of his organization – rather seeing it as his function to sustain and promote the organization and the CEO.

# Key terms

**ALLIED FUNCTIONS** Other management areas which (in the context of communications) are traditionally associated with the communications function (e.g. marketing, advertising).

**ANNUAL REPORT** Publication issued each year by every limited company reporting on its progress – publishing its profit and loss accounts and its balance sheet.

**BOTTOM LINE** The point at which an organizational activity is profitable or not profitable.

**CHAIRMAN** Senior director who takes the chair at meetings of the Board of Directors. He or she presides over the organization. May be executive or non-executive.

**COMMUNICATION EXECUTIVE** Styling adopted by Wright (1995) to describe those who fill the top 250 communication positions in the USA.

**CORPORATE TEAM, CHIEF EXECUTIVES COMMITTEE, EXECUTIVE TEAM, MANAGEMENT COMMITTEE** Group of top executives headed by the CEO – normally numbering between 12 and 24 personnel – who run a major corporation on a day-to-day basis, under the aegis of the main board of directors.

**CROSS-FERTILIZATION** An American expression suggesting that one result of boundary spanning is that ideas, perceptions and thoughts are exchanged between an organization and its constituencies.

**DECISION-MAKING TABLE** The dominant coalition sit at the decision-making table. An expression used to describe the arena in which important decisions are made.

**DOMINANT COALITION** Description given by American academic Wright to a corporation's policy-making machine – the top management executives who make the important decisions.

**EMPATHETIC QUALITIES** Description used to describe how an individual relates to – and understands – the qualities and characteristics of another person.

**ENCROACHERS** Those not qualified or trained for a communication role (Lauzen, 1995).

**FINANCIAL SECTOR** That audience concerned with financial reporting and analysis.

**GENERALIST** One who has experienced a broadly based management training rather than one who has trained in any specific field.

**HELICOPTER ROLE**   This is the author's expression for a role which allows an executive to hover over many parts of the organization involving him or her in the activities of different areas of management.

**LINE MANAGEMENT**   A process of management in which one manager is responsible to another manager further up the line.

**MORAL COURAGE**   The courage to stand up for – and say to others – what one believes to be right.

**MULTI-FUNCTIONAL**   Involving two or more separate management disciplines at one and the same time.

**NETWORKING**   Forming contacts with other business/professional colleagues.

**NON-EXECUTIVE**   One who is not employed full time by the corporation in a management position – yet occupies a position within it – probably an outsider. One not empowered to make executive decisions.

**POLICY-MAKING MACHINE**   The decision-making table; that senior part of the organization where policy decisions are made.

# Chapter 8

# A bright future for corporate communication

'Hyundai allows overseas markets a fair degree of autonomy. In terms of brand image there is no signed sheet to work from but we do have guidance from Korea on how they see the brand', reports the Communications Manager at Hyundai.' This is from the point of view that we do not have a good or bad image but rather no image at all'.

He continues by remarking that the parent company has both corporate and brand strategies worldwide; but that these are largely matters of interpretation. All the franchises communicate with the parent company on a regular basis – and with each other – about the development of brand and image. 'We are', he went on, 'allowed a great deal of freedom in how we pitch it. But, we are limited to the products available'. He believes that communication between countries do not necessarily lead to co-ordinated campaigns. But he acknowledges that they do learn from each other. He remarked that their campaign over Christmas for Accent was created by them. Korean thinking was not pushed down their throats nor was the campaign intended to be pan-European. The communication executive continued saying that with cars 'there are loads of differences in the marketplaces. In order to build the brand the individual countries invest in research to monitor awareness, feeding the information back into future promotional activity'. He added that this research 'does provide dichotomies'.

What do media people think Hyundai is all about – bargain basement prices, of course. But Hyundai owners do not see themselves as bargain basement buyers. The treatment they receive, the reliability of the car and the image are more important to them than the initial cost. They also see themselves as individuals – as idiosyncratic. This all helps to explain the very real problem with international communications. Countries have different national and cultural characteristics but they are also composed of different consumer segments. To attempt to implement an international communication strategy without giving it local messages and themes is to risk communications suicide.                    adapted from Miles (1995)

# Introduction

Some people debate how well the success of corporate communications may be measured. There are practical difficulties – and measuring the results of communication programmes is not always easy. In this chapter, we consider how evaluation can be carried out. As with assessment techniques, the use of external consultants has also increased. The increased use of financial consultants is given by some as the reason that financial communication has become such an influential speciality. Organizations use consultants for various reasons, perhaps because they provide specialist skills which are not available in-house or because a corporation needs help overseas; or because sometimes external consultants can provide a more objective view. But some practitioners are irritated that consultants are sometimes accorded greater attention by senior management. We noted earlier that organizations face an ever growing number of different audiences. None has become more significant than the international audience for an ever increasing number of corporations trade on a global scale. International communications are rapidly becoming intercultural communications and the international audience is one public which needs to be approached with one, clear 'Voice'. Then again corporate communication is uniquely placed to contribute to decision making. 'Issues management' is both preventive and reactive. Here the communication executive is concerned with boundary scanning (also referred to as 'environmental scanning') which enables an organization better to know, understand and interact with its environment. The ability of the practitioner to carry out all these functions may be affected by the resources provided. The provision of adequate funding might well indicate the importance attached to communications by the organization. Many organizations complain of underfunding – although few major corporations have to do so. We have seen that corporate communications plays a role of ever increasing importance in management today. As this book draws to a close we begin to appreciate that not only have communications become a major strategic force, they have also become an enabling process of considerable significance.

# Evaluating communication performance

> The ones who research and resource PR properly are the ones who are really effective.
> the then Communications Manager, Tennent Caledonian Breweries,
> in conversation with the author

## Challenging the value

Some senior executives never actually question whether or not their communications are effective – and whether they should be assessed – they question the value of communication altogether. But CEOs who challenge the very fact that communication policies do impact favourably on the bottom line need only look at the financial cost borne by organizations who have lost the trust of their audiences. They need then to question their own judgement. In some organizations, Avon Rubber is one example that we noted, there may be little awareness of, let alone effective evaluation of, corporate communications.

The Public Relations Manager at the Avon and Somerset Constabulary referred to the 'great debate in the force about the value of communications', which, she added, were 'reviewed annually by the Deputy Chief Constable'. One of the principal objectives of corporate communication is to win the understanding and goodwill of publics. Sceptics need to remember that in terms of cost effectiveness, as the then Acting Director of Corporate Affairs at W.H. Smith remarked, 'it is cheaper to keep a customer than to get a new one'.

Gregory (1997) notes that if communications' return on investment could be measured, senior management would have the tools in hand to evaluate objectively the company's communications performance. So, if corporate communications are accepted as a valuable investment, can that value be assessed – and, if so, how is this achieved? Communication performance is considered worthwhile if it is judged a success. But by what means are communications judged to be a success or otherwise? Perhaps, the best yardstick might be to consider if opinions and attitudes have changed.

## Effective or ineffective?

Evaluating the effectiveness of corporate communication is a subject much discussed by academics, it is fraught with controversy and it is a subject about which there appears to be little clear agreement.

Goodman (1994) remarks that most communication plans are devised and implemented, but their outcomes are difficult to evaluate and analyse. Harrison (1995) notes that the first thing to remember about evaluation is that it only applies to something that can be measured against a standard.

How effective then are the measurements of any communication processes? Ray Whitley, Brand Manager Vaseline, quoted by Mazur (1994), says that, in the past, public relations has been one of the weakest and most difficult areas to measure. He goes on to say that it is not easy, but that you have to start somewhere and that as you progress you can refine and improve your methodology. White and Mazur (1995) agree that it is not easy; they too make the point that the organization must start somewhere.

Communications were previously thought intangible, but growing research suggests that the effectiveness of communication activity needs to be measured; what would the effects be on an organization's overall performance if communication activities were not performed (Fleisher and Burton 1995)? Modern measurement techniques can be used effectively to measure communications, just as they can be used to measure other management techniques. So, building appropriate evaluation methods into communication programmes will help management to assess the specific results of various communication techniques and thus make the planning of future communication strategies more effective.

## The view of professional communicators

The Director of Group Public Affairs at B.A.T. Industries commented that assessment is 'a necessary evil,' adding, 'it is damned difficult to measure. You know when you are doing well. I am a "measuring sceptic – how much does measurement mean?"' The Head of Media Communication at London Transport remarked that her organization was one 'which could not make up its mind about the value of assessment'. The Director, Corporate Affairs at GlaxoWellcome added that assessment needs to show 'that we are getting our message across'. Professionals certainly do conclude that performance is not up to scratch if the organization fails to get its message across.

> The whole hearted commitment to excellent communication practice is best won in the same way that every other management discipline wins. You present a properly researched case and demonstrate the competitive advantage to be gained from having really vibrant, positive relationships.
>                         Lambert (1992), quoted in White and Mazur (1995)

## Practical difficulty

Communication professionals agree that assessment is a complex matter. The Director of Corporate Communications at Wessex Water confirmed that she certainly believes in assessment 'in theory' but, she noted, 'in practice it is very difficult. You cannot point to sales figures as a yardstick. Research can only show what people are thinking – and when they say what they are thinking they may be influenced by what they have heard on radio or television'. The Director, Corporate Affairs at GlaxoWellcome echoed this, saying 'people are people at all levels. They form opinions in all sorts of irrational ways. It is difficult to evaluate.' The Director of Corporate Communications at Wessex Water added that 'in terms of our public relations achievements at the end of the day you end up with a lot of subjective judgements.'

## Measuring successful communication

> Measuring the success, or otherwise, of brand communications has become critically important. Fewer clients treat brand public rela-

tions as a 'quick-fix'. Not only have communications become more expensive – the need to devise integrated, consistent communication in the most cost-effective way possible is making every element of the mix equally important. This is the view of Ray Whitley, brand development manager, Vaseline intensive care range.

Evaluation ultimately must have a bigger role in all areas of marketing communications. In the past communications have been a difficult area to measure. So recently Vaseline has been measuring the work that it has been doing. Whitley comments that 'it is not easy – but, you do have to start somewhere. Then you can review your progress, refining and improving as you go along. You will never know if something is not working unless you measure it. In fact if you have a system of measurement in place you can review and the take action. You have a greater opportunity to be more innovative and to take more risks'.

Whitley concludes that it is better to be able to do something and to be able to evaluate its effectiveness and then to be able to do it again; rather than do something day in day out without ever having any idea successful it has been.

adapted from Mazur (1994)

It is difficult to evaluate the impact of communications with certainty. It may be almost impossible to measure the direct influence of corporate communications on turnover. But some relatively straightforward evaluation methods can be used – at the very least – to gauge the initial response of media coverage. The success of corporate communications, van Riel (1995) suggests, can be measured through perceived changes in knowledge, attitude and behaviour in the organization's target audiences.

## Purpose of measurement

White and Mazur (1995) quote Gordon Knight, Marketing Director of Paragon PR consultancy who suggests that in his firm's experience the objectives of measurement fall into one or more of these categories:

- Did we do everything we said we would do?
- Did we move things as a result?
- Did the 'phone start ringing from the potential prospects?
- Did we avoid a panning from a hostile media?
- Have we persuaded the investment community of the company's future prospects?
- Did we get the big order or fend off the bid?
- Did we do it all for what we said it would cost?

## Recent use of evaluation

J. E. Grunig (1983) noted that few practitioners actually used assessment techniques. A decade later Cutlip et al. (1994) reported only 48 per cent of those that he interviewed in a survey used evaluation. Miles (1995) reported an Institute of Public Relations (IPR) finding that only 28 per cent of those questioned were convinced that using techniques to assess communications was worthwhile. The same paper quoted an IPR evaluation event where 11 evaluation companies presented the case for assessment. It revealed that the level of sophistication was low, with many different available systems (and no simple method) and a whole array of available tools and little to differentiate between them.

## How to measure?

The debatable issue is how to define and evaluate performance. Heath (1994) queries how the efforts of companies to communicate can be measured. He suggests that the effectiveness of communications is dependent upon how well a company speaks with a coherent 'Voice' and the extent to which the Voice creates positive relationships. The Public Relations Manager at the Avon and Somerset Constabulary assesses the success of her communications programme through newspaper cuttings. She reports that 'I keep newspaper cuttings of what we do and evaluate the tone and volume.'

White and Mazur (1995) discuss the methodology of measurement. They comment that the real difficulty with evaluating corporate communications is that, due to the potentially wide range of audiences, measurement has to be a combination of hard fact and soft judgement. The Head of Corporate Communications at Lloyds/TSB reported that his organization has a model by which they can evaluate their sponsorship programme. 'The objective is to get media recognition of who we are and what we are doing . . . they measure how the press department is doing compared with the other banks.' This he achieves, he went on, 'by using a panel of journalists'.

## Three evaluation methods

In a survey on European Financial Institutions' communications, van Riel (1992) identifies the three most frequently used evaluation methods:

1 Monitoring business volume
2 Surveys of customers' attitudes/opinions
3 Analysing media comments.

## Monitoring business performance
Have communications resulted in increased sales?

■ Did the communication programme result in more customers visiting Madame Tussard's?
■ Do more readers use the British Library as a result of recent publicity?
■ How many of the laity were attracted to the 1998 Lambeth Conference after hearing that they could attend on payment of a £10 fee?
■ Are more travellers using rail services on learning that timetable reliabilty has improved dramatically?

## Surveys of customers' attitudes/opinions
An organization identifies how a key audience felt about an issue before the communication programme and ascertains how perceptions have changed as a result of the programme. For example:

■ If carnivores stopped eating beef and then later resumed eating beef following a promotional campaign from the meat industry – the programme might be judged a success.
■ In financial communications success may be measured by a favourable change in the share price.
■ In government relations evidence of a successful lobbying programme may be the abandonment of a proposed piece of legislation. The Department of Transport had planned to build a new by-pass around the city of Salisbury, a project which – it was suggested – would destroy precious countryside. The proposal was the subject of fierce and bitter lobbying by environmentalists. The project was abandoned. The communications programme was judged a success.
■ Communication programmes aimed at creating a new corporate image can be evaluated by conducting market research and image tracking among key publics at the conclusion of the programme; for example, finding out how consumers reacted to the removal of the Union Flag from the tail of British Airways' planes (the views of one well-known consumer, Lady Thatcher, are renowned!) This type of research is expensive; the more so if a major corporation with many significant constituencies is involved.
■ Do voters change their views as a result of political communications? Were the electorate persuaded to vote for Mr Tony Blair as a result of Labour party communication programmes in the 1997 election?

## Analysing media comments
Sandra Macleod, European MD of CARMA, quoted by Cobb (1994) remarked that 'we track what the media is saying about clients, their competitors, the issues in the market. We look for trends, strengths and weaknesses.' David Phillips, MD of Media Measurement, (also quoted by Cobb, 1994) noted 'good

companies are seeking to evaluate their PR and how they appear competitively and how they can manage their communications more effectively'. British Airways is an example of a major corporation which uses 'annual tracking research – among target audiences, parliamentarians and staff'. Their communication executive noted that he 'also completes a quarterly review of coverage to evaluate whether it has been favourable or unfavourable'.

## A second basic model

Other management scholars suggest a basic model by which effectiveness can be judged:

- What communications programme was used – how great was the media coverage?
- Did the communications programme reach the target audience – did they listen to them and did they understand them?
- Were attitudes, perceptions and beliefs changed by the communications programme?

Walter Lindenmann, Director of Research, Ketchum Public Relations (quoted by Cramp, 1994), remarked that it is very 'important that you know what you are evaluating. That means that you have to set specific objectives against which communication activities can be measured – and those objectives must be achievable.' He added that 'the time to think about evaluation is before the communication program is launched'.

The following must be addressed if the communication's assessment is to be judged a success:

---

- Execute a communications audit.
- Define objectives – what are the desired results? This may involve the use of specific goals for particular communication programmes – targeted at specific short-term objectives – for example overcoming a fear of eating beef in the aftermath of the CJD scare.
- Identify the key publics.
- What messages and themes are you trying to send to key publics? What are the present perceptions of those publics?
- Which communication channels are used already? Which need to be used for the next stage of the communication process?
- How do you desire these key publics to react?
- Measure progress during the programme.
- Establish if the desired results were achieved.

---

To which the key responses must be:

- Did the communication programme reach key publics?
- Measure the response to the communication programme.
- Monitor for shifts in public opinions.
- Evaluate if the opinions and perceptions of key publics have changed as desired.

## Measuring communications in action

The following need to be considered if evaluation of the communications programme is to achieve the desired results:

■ Ask if key publics are aware of the campaign. Many writers agree that establishing the extent of the awareness of audiences to a communications strategy is difficult.
■ Question if key publics understand the organization, its personality and for what it stands.
■ Discover the perceptions and attitudes of important audiences.
■ Discover the attitudes of stakeholders on important issues of the day.
■ Ascertain in what way opinion formers and stakeholders are presently affected by the organization.
■ Evaluate newspaper, radio, television coverage – for:
  - the amount of coverage, and
  - its subjectivity.
■ Commission 'before and after' tracking studies to monitor the success of advertisements.
■ Query whether the communication programme reach the desired audiences.
■ Ask if key constituencies were influenced by the communications strategy in the desired way.

Always remember that many management scholars agree that the extent to which publics are influenced by communication programmes is difficult to measure with accuracy.

## Conclusion

Assessment of communications is a subject that arouses very mixed feelings. Sentiments range from those who believe in evaluation – to those who regard it as theologically unsound (the author's expression). Few espouse it with the enthusiasm demonstrated by British Airways – but they do have a high profile to protect. Some ignore it. Many carry it out with marked reluctance.

But the majority of modern organizations do accept the principle that communications must be assessed; but not all are satisfied that the exercise is worthwhile. However, all do carry out assessment to some extent. One senior practitioner professed himself a sceptic. One has introduced his own performance measurement model. Others have an annual evaluation with their CEO. Yet again others have quarterly/half-yearly surveys performed by consultancies. Smaller organizations analyse their newspaper coverage and judge public reaction by press reports.

> As the business market place becomes ever more competitive, internal communication faces the tough task of proving that it is a management tool that adds to overall competitive advantage.
>
> Anthony Goodman remarked that for years people have been trying to prove how much internal communication impacts on the bottom line, he said 'I think that it's not possible.'
>
> He went on to say that 'one could ask whether improved employee satisfaction statistics are down to internal communication, to HRM or to the business itself. But you can never be 100 per cent certain that it was communications "wot won"'.
>
> B-M's Alaric Mostyn is more sanguine 'you can evaluate effectively', he insists. He continued 'it is no more difficult to evaluate internal communication than it is for other aspects of communication – it is easier, you have a captive audience.'
>
> Helena Memory of Hedron warns that any evaluation must be followed by action as, she believes, a lot of evaluation processes fall down because nothing changes after they have taken place.
>
> Internal communication evaluation is largely based upon quantitative research (such as employee and management surveys) and qualitative research (such as focus groups). Michele Levy suggests that, of course, in addition to those mentioned one can also use tools that are more central to a client's own particular business objectives.
>
> adapted from *PR Week* (1997a)

# The use of consultants

> Dealing with the media has long been thought of as the main purpose for which external consultants are used. It cuts across all specialities – for the organization's reputation comes about through its dealings with key audiences and its media profile. Hence the main reason that so many companies hire consultancies is to advise on media relations (or to act as a sounding board or monitor). But, it must not be forgotten that allowing outside consultancies to take over the organization's relationship with the media is fraught with dangers. Their role is to act as a sounding board.
>
> adapted from White and Mazur (1995)

## Reasons for use

External consultants are engaged by most organizations, but in varying degrees. Harrison (1995) lists the following advantages in not using consultants but in keeping communications in-house:

- full time
- one client
- good communication
- continuity
- specialist knowledge
- on the spot
- access
- response to media
- staff loyalty.

Consultants are mostly engaged for specialist functions (financial communications, for instance) where the consultancy has developed skills that are not available within the organization. van Riel (1995) notes that various communications are handed over increasingly to external specialists. He comments that from a financial point of view it is neither possible nor desirable to employ all necessary expertise within one's own company.

Some organizations use outside consultants only for help with financial public relations. 'This is the only area where we hire outside help,' commented the Group Publicity Manager at Avon Rubber; referring to the City and analysts, his opposite number at Storehouse added that 'very few companies do not use Financial PR people'.

Even corporations with very large communication departments use external consultants when the circumstances require. *Air Transport World* (1996) notes the widespread use of agencies used by British Airways – because they choose to employ local knowledge wherever in the world the local community may be (an approach enabling a multinational corporation to target specific local audiences with greater precision). The then Director of Public Affairs at British Airways, speaking from a position of great corporate strength, commented 'we are blessed with forty eight people. So, we can handle a large number of public relations issues, but we do use fifty consultants in outposts.' He added that they consumed £2 million of his budget.

## Advantages

Some reasons why external consultants are engaged:

- An ability to take a view on issues – in effect a second opinion. The external view may add value by:
  - giving a wider perspective, and
  - counselling management, e.g. with strategic planning.

- A better appreciation of micro and macro governmental affairs (public affairs/lobbying) – W.H. Smith commented that they used consultants for political public relations.
- A more detailed and sophisticated appreciation of:
  - legal procedures
  - financial matters
  - brand and consumer public relations
  - sponsorship.
- Wider contacts in specialist areas.
- An immediate delivery of specialist skills which are:
  - not present in-house, or
  - are present but not sufficiently developed, or
  - are absent in-house due to staff shortages.
- Better performance if skills in one area are weak. The then Director of Corporate Affairs at Storehouse remarked that 'the philosophy of outsourcing is not to do things that you think outside people will do better'.
- An international and inter-cultural perspective (see box below).
- Specialist skills in an area where the nature of the skills required is such that they are rarely called upon, for example, in the area of Crisis Management.

---

## International and inter-cultural

Some organizations (British Airways is one example) have their own communication employees stationed in cities overseas such as Brussels and Washington.

Other organizations prefer to use overseas consultants who have specific local knowledge. The Director of Group Public Affairs at B.A.T. Industries referred to a local problem in June 1996 – 'A spat in India' – and added 'I have retained a consultancy to handle it.' But this approach can prove costly:

1 financially, and
2 in terms of lack of consistency and clarity – both of message content and quality, especially with regard to complex issues.

Some corporations use a single agency to communicate for them in several different countries so that a consistent message and image is conveyed in each; but this consistency may be bought at a price, always assuming that it can be achieved at all.

---

## Objective views from outside

An external consultant inevitably brings a fresh, open mind and a degree of objectivity to an issue; particularly if the problem is proving difficult to resolve.

The Director, Corporate Affairs of GlaxoWellcome commented 'it is important to use them ... I don't think that we have a monopoly of perception and understanding of our audiences all the time. It is important to have a sounding board of people you trust to assess how you do something.' The then Acting Director of Corporate Affairs at W. H. Smith remarked that his company used them 'a lot ... that is the way that corporate affairs is going. You get an objective experience outside; without having to pay lots of staff.'

> External consultants may be regarded as a mixed blessing. The then
> communication manager at Tennent Caledonian Breweries
> considered them too easy an option. He would only use them, he
> remarked, 'if they add value, or if one was not able to cope'.

## Problems

There are some circumstances in which external consultants can be a disadvantage.

### 1 Overseas
Where an organization engages consultants overseas the communication executive has a particular problem. The messages and themes from both home and abroad will need to be both integrated and orchestrated.

### 2 Not speaking for the organization
The external consultant brought in to perform a specialist function should not be permitted to speak on behalf of the organization except in exceptional circumstances. This is an aspect of the role about which practitioners feel strongly. The duty of the external consultant will be to offer counsel and to help put agreed strategies in place. The Director of Group Public Affairs at B.A.T. Industries commented on this: 'it is very important that consultants do not speak for you. Speaking to the audience has got to be done by the company.'

### 3 Variance in the quality of performance
Consultancies can vary greatly, both in terms of their quality and of performance. This can result in a company hiring an external consultant who does not provide the expertise for which he or she was engaged.

### 4 Conflict between external and internal views
Sometimes the expectations of the organization are not matched by the performance of the external consultant and a similar situation might occur in reverse. This can lead to difficulties and in the worst scenario a breakdown in communications.

## 5 Sole use of external consultants

A significant number of major organizations have no in-house communication people of their own and, like Lonrho plc, simply retain outside consultants when they need assistance with communications. Some academics have reservations about this approach to the communication function. By definition those external to the organization cannot be as well informed about what is going on inside the organization as are those who are actually on the inside.

## 6 Listened to with greater attention

Consultants are used when needed – and sometimes at considerable cost – but professionals do have mixed views about them. James Maxwell of Scope Communications, quoted by Bond (1994c), remarked that 'another voice is needed – one that's outside company politics, a dispassionate observer'; but the external practitioner and the internal communications executive must have an easy rapport with each other. If they do not do so the relationship will simply not work. Some express concern that on occasions the outside consultant is listened to with greater attention than the in-house director, to whom this can be an irritant. The in-house director may feel taken for granted. The Director of Group Public Relations at Vaux Group commented wistfully that sometimes a consultant is given greater attention than is the executive inside the organization – who may already have voiced the same suggestion that the external consultant is making.

# International or intercultural communications?

> The Body Shop is working on external communications for the
> global market to promote awareness of such issues as animal testing
> and community trade.
>
> *PR Week* (1997r)

## A public that is increasingly important and growing

L. A. Grunig (1992) examines Pfeffer and Salancik's (1978) theory that the effective organization identifies – and then contends with – the demands of the strategic constituencies within its environment. She points out that critical audiences threaten the survival of an organization. Grunig expresses the belief that this theory seems applicable – and increasingly important – in the context of the international arena.

How a company or brand is perceived around the world has a major impact on its success (Chajet, 1997); thus says Booth (1986) the international practice of communication has become the most exciting action in our business. Others see it as the most recent innovation (White and Mazur, 1995). In 1980, among corporations questioned for a survey in the US, virtually no organizations reported their involvement in international communications activity; sixteen years later 35 per cent of respondents had become involved (Post and Griffin, 1997).

---

'Public relations professionals who help determine relationships with priority international publics', writes L. A. Grunig (1992), 'have both a necessary and exciting job – the consequences of what they do may affect the quality of life worldwide for years to come.'

---

The dilemma of accommodating both the organization and its publics is becoming increasingly important as more and more corporations trade on a global scale (L. A. Grunig, 1992). Grunig adds that the relationship across boundaries is complex. At this time of ever increasing globalization, a growing number of organizations find themselves engaged in international communications. Indeed, Graham (1994) considers that being an internationalist is one of the top five prerequisites for success in modern corporate communications.

Illman (1980) assumed that there were no major differences between motivating and persuading people at home and overseas and saw them as functionally the same everywhere; but other scholars find this a risky assumption. Kinzer and Bohn (1985) cautioned that domestic American communication practices forged in what Galbraith, referring to an over-indulgent and affluent American society, called the 'culture of contentment' are likely to be ineffective – and even risky – in some overseas cultures. Botan is one of a number of academics who perceive the real difficulty of establishing a coherent communication policy across borders. One real problem is that different countries have different national and cultural characteristics – just as they are at different stages of social and economic development.

## Intercultural, not only international

> Virtually everyone is being forced into new relationships within social systems that are becoming both increasingly diverse and divisive.
>
> Kruckeberg (1992)

International communications has become the fast growing communication speciality. It is one which Botan (1992) considers should be thought of as intercultural communications – because the process is characterized in different nations by different mixtures of cultural, political and historical contexts. Kruckeberg (1995) adds that tomorrow's communication specialists will need to be culturally astute and cosmopolitan and sensitive to the multicultural and international nuances of their organizations' diverse publics. L. A. Grunig (1992) lends credence to this argument, quoting the CEO of Burson-Marsteller, who remarks that the challenge facing public relations practitioners in the global world is to keep up with publics increasingly more unfamiliar and hostile with every day that passes. Nessmann (1995) notes that two German theorists have been attempting to discover if there is a Europeanness to public communication and whether it is dependent on specific social conditions.

> Doing business successfully in an international, global or
> transnational environment demands your attention to cultural,
> social, political and religious practices – communications is a key to
> each.
>
> Goodman, 1994

Botan (1992) reports numerous instances of the harm done when practitioners engage in communication campaigns but fail to understand the assumptions of the cultures and subcultures underlying them. He refers to the fact that insensitivity to cultural differences during communication campaigns may be expected to exacerbate hidden tensions between developed and less-developed countries. Lederer and Burdick, writing in 1958, report the failure of numerous attempts at image cultivation when the norms and standards of one culture failed to translate to another culture. Nessmann (1995) comments upon the cultural differences in the practice of public relations (as a key branch of corporate communication) from one country to another; and, referring to a study by Coombs, Holladay, Hasenauer and Signitzer (1994), he notes the enormous influence of cultural aspects on communication practice between countries.

Botan confirms that the international public is a fast growing area of interest to scholars in the communications field. The Group Publicity Manager at Avon Rubber sees international communication as a prime audience and one that grows faster by the day – a majority of Avon Rubber's factories are now overseas, mainly in Mexico, the USA and Continental Europe. Boots plc, perhaps perceived by many as a British high street retailer, is yet another major corporation which regards the international audience as one of ever increasing importance. Executives who have successfully created cross-border communications are in the vanguard of helping their organizations to present coherent and consistent communication strategies for culturally and geographically bound traditional values and belief systems will be challenged and tested on all fronts (Kruckeberg, 1995).

## Strategic importance of international communications

National boundaries are fast disappearing and communication has become more complex as businesses compete more in the global environment (White and Mazur, 1995). L. A. Grunig (1992), echoing Botan, finds that communication practitioners will play a role of increasing strategic importance in the coming years, developing and articulating the positions of their organizations on international issues to a range of ever growing overseas constituencies. She suggests that systematic boundary scanning of strategic external constituencies – those that can affect the success or, perhaps even the survival, of the organization – presents a real challenge to communication practitioners. Grunig believes that this is a process made more complex by the number – and changing nature – of the many diverse publics operating in the international arena; some of which may be hostile to the organization operating in their locale.

> Meticulous preparation, co-ordination and local knowledge are essential weapons for companies thinking of entering the minefield that is pan-European PR.
>
> Dwek (1995)

Corporate communication can prove to be an important strategic weapon in the battle for overall international competitive advantage. An appreciation of the culture, language, customs and traditions of others have a tremendous impact on the development of an appropriate communication strategy (Goodman, 1994). Accordingly communication strategies have to be designed to accommodate the cultural and ethnic environment in which they will be implemented. Inevitably communication specialists will be called upon to be organizational interpreters and ethicists influencing and reconciling public perceptions within a global context (Kruckeberg, 1995).

Perhaps communication strategies should not be imposed from some central point such as a corporate centre (de Segundo, 1997) in a different land thousands of miles away (as in Kinzar and Bohn's ethnocentric model). Chajet (1997) reports that many major corporations are including in their global business plan a component with built-in flexibility to enhance their appeal to local market place preferences; whether it be McDonald's advertising meatless hamburgers in Moslem countries or Disney allowing wine to be sold in their French DisneyWorld. White and Mazur (1995) note that (if a co-ordinated international communications campaign is drawn up allowing local adaptations in different overseas markets) a big issue inevitably becomes who controls the co-ordination. Botan (1992) refers to the approach of Kinzar and Bohn's polycentric model, where the host country exercises a high degree of autonomy and underlines the need for the messages and themes to be co-ordinated.

## One clear Voice

The international public may be the single most important link between the organization and its global interests – and that supposes that there is one international public. There may be many. L. A. Grunig (1992) notes that a differentiation of target publics is especially critical to public relations at a global level. She continues that one must think on a global level while still paying attention to individual publics within the worldwide scope.

L. A. Grunig (1992) proposes that research suggests the following are the three strategic publics most constraining to transnational organizations:

- unions – she refers to Dow Chemical's experience in Chile as a powerful example of a company at risk
- stockholders, and in particular
- pressure groups.

The bigger the global organization – and the more widespread its subsidiaries – the less easy it is to communicate with that clear Voice or to communicate a clear identity. For example, Shell International have an active presence in about 130 countries (de Segundo, 1997). Goodman (1994) reflects echoes of Heath (1994) and notes that communications with various publics are more consistent and effective when they are delivered with a clear Voice. Communicating consistent messages and themes across frontiers is one of the greatest challenges facing the communicator in the 1990s. The need to translate a corporate message into other languages and cultures gives corporate communications a strategic role in trans-national activity (Goodman, 1994).

Multinational corporations doing business across borders increasingly need to take macro-governmental and social environments into account when drawing up their communication strategies. In no area of management is there a greater need for an international and intercultural perspective than there is in the field of communications – for the international message needs to be encoded in a form and language that all recipients will understand.

The Director, Corporate Affairs at GlaxoWellcome believes that a central part of his task is to seek out common languages and to discover ways of forming alliances with publics who share a common purpose – so that the messages and themes 'all work together internationally ... ensuring a common face to all organizations. Crucially relating the constant message back to the rapidly changing dynamics of business.' Those communication professionals who have successfully created a bridge enabling their organizations to communicate across borders are responsible for making a direct contribution to their organization's competitive advantage. Thus L. A. Grunig (1992) refers to the relationships between international organizations and their strategic publics.

# Issues management

## Wider perspective of communication executives

> Issues Management is the term of choice among public affairs practitioners to describe a process of identifying, tracking, analyzing and prioritizing political and social issues that impact the organization or are likely to do so in the future. Issues Management is both a key activity and a critical process through which many companies address their external image and reputation. In the view of some experts and practitioners, Issues Management is the critical business process through which public affairs units accomplish their mission.
>
> Dennis (1995)

Many communication professionals are much involved with issues management – although some academics (Post and Griffin, 1997) propose that a minority of professional communicators in the US manifest some disagreement about the objective of issues management programmes. They see the primary role of the communication executive as managing an organization's critical relationships with stakeholders.

Issues management, as with crisis communications, is a branch of corporate communication concerned with preventive and reactive communications. L. A. Grunig (1992) suggests that large-scale, highly complex organizations in particular – with their vast, dynamic market context – dictate a need for constant environmental scanning and interaction. For example, the Shell corporation became embroiled in two major public issues (*Brent Spar* and Nigeria, in 1995) when it had not sufficiently recognized that the underlying expectations of the society around it had changed (de Segundo, 1997).

Lauzen (1995) suggests that communication practitioners are uniquely placed to contribute to organizational decision making. She notes that while communicators share the values of executives in other management disciplines they have a wider perspective of how those values may jibe or conflict with the values of important external publics. She believes that knowledge of many perspectives increases the value of the communications function in the participation of organization-wide strategic decision making.

> Preventive Communication is also referred to as pro-active communication because it has as its central purpose the promotion of an organization's strengths and achievements.

> Reactive Communication, which Kitchen (1993) notes is sometimes referred to in the United States as Vulnerability Public Relations, is concerned with dealing with the organization's weaknesses. Its purpose is to try to restore the faith of key publics in the organization, to recover its good name and to prevent the erosion of market share and turnover.

## Definition

Issues management is that process which allows organizations to know, understand and more effectively interact with their environments (Hainsworth and Meng, 1988), for there are many issues swirling around a company at any time (Post and Griffin, 1997). Matching the organizational structure to its environment often makes the difference between effective and ineffective operations. Successful organic organizations rely upon integrators to co-ordinate the work of the subsystem (L. A. Grunig, 1992). Boundary spanning is thus an essential task of the communication executive.

Preventive and reactive communication practice attempts to anticipate and identify issues and matters of public concern which, if acted upon by stakeholders with sufficient influence, may well impact on the activities of the organization and could affect it adversely in a number of ways. Lauzen (1994) suggests that limitations on resources prohibit managing all potential emerging issues and that, equally significantly, if unimportant issues are identified issues management may be prevented from providing vital information to the organization.

## Increased resources devoted to issues management

In the course of research, Kitchen (1993), discovered a significant increase over the previous decade in both staffing and budgets allocated to issues management; probably because, Post and Griffin (1997) report, the speed and pace at which issues emerge, evolve and intersect other concerns has greatly accelerated in recent times – not least due to enhanced speed of information technology.

Kitchen discovered that the main reasons for these increases were:

1 Environmental turbulence
2 The proliferation of issues and crisis management scenarios
3 More informed or sophisticated consumers

4 The need for better developed media relations
5 The growth in radicalized and vociferous consumer groups
6 The development of pro-active and reactive PR
7 The strengthening of internal management teams and budgets.

## Environmental scanning not strategic

Lauzen (1994) suggests that environmental scanning (noted earlier in a discussion on the contribution of communications to corporate strategy) is not in itself strategic. She proposes that environmental scanning discovers information; but that this discovery process alone does not help the organization adapt to its environment. Managing the organization's business context requires making the information actionable through integration into strategy (Morris, 1987).

## Issues management converts information into the strategic decision-making process

Lauzen (1995) notes that communication specialists use the information gathered in environmental scanning to facilitate management decision making. They also use it, she reports, to create opportunities for the dominant coalition and its key publics to communicate with each other. Accordingly, she suggests, it is only within the context of issues management that the gathering of information is translated into strategic decision making.

> The decision of Shell Oil to sink a North Sea oil platform named the *Brent Spar* brought about an international incident. It involved environmental activists, technical experts, European governments and the general public. The announcement of the deep sea disposal plan led Greenpeace to occupy the North Sea platform. By doing this they gained the attention of media from around the world. What had begun in the remote and isolated North Sea had become a high profile international incident. The conflict roared on until Shell and the UK government abandoned plans to sink the *Brent Spar*. They did this with very great reluctance, continuing to insist that the best technical solution was not being used.
>
> *Brent Spar* was a formidable learning experience for Shell executives. The chairman of the committee of MDs of the Royal Dutch/Shell Group of Companies remarked that Shell had discovered that they had to place a new emphasis on learning and exchanging views.
>
> adapted from Post and Griffin (1997)

# Lauzen's model of the issues management process

## Issue identification

This is the first and most important step. It sets the parameters for the process that follows. Jones and Chase (1979) note that the primary goal of this step is to prioritize the emerging issues (e.g. environmental issues – Greenpeace, product tampering). Lauzen suggests that the issue identification process is made easier if practitioners have strategic knowledge of the issues that impacted significantly on the organization in the past.

## Issue monitoring

Is accomplished by tapping into internal and or external sources of information associated with the organization's activities. It assumes that important changes do not just occur spontaneously.

## Issue analysis

Here the importance and impact of the information gathered so far is assessed. Issues are ranked according to a set of criteria laid down. Issue analysis forces executives to weigh the impact of one issue against another. This is a process which requires some strategic knowledge. The practitioner must evaluate if the issue is likely to occur.

## Message formation

Messages are constructed to address those issues which have been identified as high priority. The first three steps discussed provide guidelines for the message construction.

## Incorporation of the information into strategic plans

Incorporate information gathered into strategic plans. Strategic planning systems co-ordinate actions and help organizations adapt to environments (Lorange and Vancil, 1977). This step requires an understanding of how the information gathered fits into the organization's long-term strategic plan.

adapted from Lauzen (1994)

# Funding the communication function

There is little reference in management literature concerning the funding of the corporate communications function; yet it is a matter which should be of fundamental interest to management scholars. It is also one of some importance for there is ample reference in academic work to those (perhaps more unsophisticated) executives who question the cost of communication and its impact on their bottom line and who regard it as theologically unsound as a management practice.

## The investment reflects the level of importance

White and Mazur (1995) briefly discuss the question of funding. In doing so they suggest that a commitment on the part of an organization to make funding available – so that it is enabled to achieve its strategic objectives – will communicate the importance of those objectives throughout the organization. Perhaps Avon Rubber's commitment to communications is reflected in a comment from their communications executive. He was able to say only that he is 'abysmally funded'. Otherwise excellently managed organizations such as Vaux Group say that their communications function is 'not well enough funded. There is so much that we could do . . . we are not as strong in this area as we should be.' The Head of Media Communication at London Transport added, simply, 'we could do with more'.

## Funding decides what can be done

> Corporate executives who question the budgets allocated to their communication programs will find this quote interesting:
> 'Greenpeace spent a million dollars in two months in connection with *Brent Spar*'. Annualized that is a $6m corporate communications effort. That compares very well against the budgets that most large corporations spend on their own corporate image or reputation.
>
> O'Rourke (1997)

Certainly, adequate funding ultimately decides what can be done properly. Winner (1993) proposes that communications are typically under-funded. Few communication practitioners speak enthusiastically about funding. Some are depressingly negative. The Public Relations Manager at Northumbria Ambulance spoke of 'not being adequately funded' – and that she has to 'suffer efficiency savings'. Her opposite number at the Avon and Somerset Constabulary referred to having 'no funding and only a small travel budget'. She continued 'I cannot do things that other people do, so most of what I do is through the media. I have a frustrating lack of budget. I have to compete for funding with . . . for example, bullet proof vests. I either go out and raise the money myself or find other means of doing the job. I spend a lot of time being creative and using guerrilla tactics to get around funding problems.' The then Communications Manager at Tennent Caledonian Breweries referred to 'being not properly funded' pointing out that he 'required more money than his counterparts in other divisions of Bass plc because TCB is a unique organization'.

## Impact of recession

Winner (1993) suggests that where there are disagreements over the importance of the role those differences frequently focus on the cost effectiveness of communications. This discussion concerns a management discipline that is still wrongly perceived by some organizations as a luxury; even with suspicion by some. Both constructions constrain corporate spending. The recession of recent years is a factor and White and Mazur (1995) refer to the fact that in-house downsizing has been taking place with practitioners having to do more with less. The Group Director of Corporate Affairs at Yorkshire Tyne-Tees Television, although not complaining about the level of investment, said that he had 'been better funded in other years'. Commenting that 'there have been significant cut backs of 20 per cent in the last year', he went on to say that there 'was enough money to pay essential members of the staff – but not enough for press advertising'. Kitchen (1993) found that what was allocated 'this year was not necessarily a predictor of what would occur in the future'.

> Changes of emphasis and expenditure for its own sake are of interest to an academic but not to us; it's all history; it's all over; what we spend next year has got no relationship to what we did last year; and what determines what's going to happen next year is what we think that we can do with products and what we think the opposition's going to do.
> A PR manager, quoted by Kitchen (1993)

## Fundamental support

Otherwise conservative companies like J. Sainsbury prove to be quite liberal with resource if the project is considered important to corporate strategy. Their Acting Head of Communications remarked 'if something is important enough the funding is there'. However, Sainsbury's acting spokeswoman added that 'the board judge the level of importance'. These comments were made immediately after the new JS Reward Card was launched in June 1996. This was a topical matter and one in which the budget was carefully thought through. It was an example of marketing communications, well promoted and, apparently, regardless of expense.

Most very large corporations suggest that, as the Director, Corporate Affairs of GlaxoWellcome said, 'the regime is fundamentally supported' even if the director has to 'fight hard'. GlaxoWellcome displays clear evidence of some major investments in publications that are a real contribution to (a) public awareness, (b) scientific investigation, or (c) promoting the face of the corporation. The Head of Corporate Communications at Lloyds/TSB also referred to the 'adequacy' of his funding. At the same time, he emphasized that his company is not wasteful, saying 'there is no fat in this organization'.

The then Director of Public Affairs at British Airways referred to the debate that he often had with 'the marketing people'; but acknowledged a £7 million budget of which 28 per cent is taken up with 'deadheading'. This budget compared favourably with the £50 000 total at Avon Rubber, but the comparison is, of course, between organizations of different size and from different sectors. The communication executive at B.A.T. Industries said that his department was 'well funded' and added 'if you can make a good enough case you can get the budget'. While, albeit using different terminology, the then Acting Director of Corporate Affairs at W.H. Smith said the same thing.

It is a sad reflection on the public sector that both organizations referred to here are underfunded; even expenditure itself being questioned. However, major corporations clearly secure the funds that they require for communication – with varying degrees of ease. In the case of a handful they have unlimited budgets if the purposes can be justified.

But the question of funding does arouse much passion. Winner's comments prove most prescient. Few organizations share British Airways' happy position of having a truly enormous budget; most cry out for more funding. On that one extreme Avon Rubber's 'abysmal' cry is echoed only by the Constabulary – who have no funding at all.

# The next frontier for corporate communications

The fundamental success of corporate communication in action is for the communicator to be seen as a strategic planner. The easiest thing to do is to announce. The critical thing to do is to have a good policy to announce in the first place. The role of the communication executive is to help the organization understand the impact of its activities on various key constituencies. At the

same time it needs to help the company understand the outside
environment. By having this external knowledge it can structure
its own business programs accordingly

adapted from Skolnik (1994)

Although it has come a long way down the road towards acceptance,
corporate communications still largely fails to receive the recognition and
status afforded to other management disciples (Moss, 1990). Despite the fact
that communication policies have proved useful and important they are not
practised universally nor are they valued universally. Corporate communication is still regarded by so many as an afterthought, a duty for delegation, or a
luxury that cannot be afforded; yet it takes between 20 per cent and 25 per cent
of each day worked by Richard Branson (Fitzherbert, 1994). As one unknown
management writer commented, 'corporations that do not value communications highly are doomed to wither'.

The fundamental problem may well be that, as noted with Avon Rubber and
Lloyds/TSB, many CEOs know little about (and have little understanding of )
the principles of corporate communication. It is in the nature of things that
CEOs generally feel less positive about what they do not understand; and what
they do not understand they do not know how to use. To the contrary,
organizations who have a Chairman or CEO who are conversant with the full
power that communication as a management tool can unleash can be seen to
make full and effective use of communications as a constituent part of their
corporate strategy.

Yet many academics recognize that communication has become increasingly
important in management. White and Mazur (1995) suggest that communication techniques should be used to support marketing activities, branding,
corporate reputation, market penetration and development. For it involves
both (a) helping organizations fit into social environments and (b) the skilful
management of important relationships with those publics on whose support
the organization depends to bring about social and economic development.
Thus corporate communication is both a strategic and an enabling process.

Communication is a much enhanced management tool. The director of
corporate communication is now a very senior figure; typically located at the
third management layer and it may well be that the executive should be
positioned one layer higher – as is the Director of Corporate Affairs at Boots
plc. If this *is* a misplacement of the role it would go some way towards
confirming the suggestion made by Guth (1995) that misplacement undermines
the organization's ability to achieve its strategic goals. If there is such a
misplacement it can surely only result in reduced competitive advantage.

Corporate communications involves systemic boundary scanning of all an
organization's immediate environments. It then requires the systematic
preparation and delivery of appropriate messages and themes. It is the task of
the communication executive to encode these messages into suitable communications and to see that they are delivered with one Voice (Heath, 1994) so that

the meanings are conveyed to key publics. These messages may both empower and mobilize the internal audience and impact on key external stakeholders and opinion formers. They may powerfully influence both the buying decisions of consumers and the regulatory or governmental decisions by audiences at macro-governmental levels.

In the future corporate communication will be involved in dialogue with an ever growing number of different publics, some of which will impact substantially on corporate performance. We can be sure of two things. First, that the number of different and significant publics will increase and, second, that there will be an increase in the importance attached to a management discipline which has taken on increasing significance as both a strategic function and as an enabling process.

## Case study

## Evaluation is fraught with controversy

New evaluation systems, in what is a highly competitive market, are being developed all the time. Therefore, choosing the right system is something of a challenge for any communication executive. Bass Brewers set up a corporate communications department. It then spent six months critically examining the company with Infopress Communications. Having done this it then identified key, measurable messages that needed to be transmitted. 'We ended up with eight, although the norm is more like six', a Bass spokeswoman said. The key messages identified were that Bass needed to be perceived as:

1 innovators
2 steeped in brewing traditions
3 an efficient organization
4 a good employer
5 well disposed to stakeholders
6 the number one brewer
7 a producer only of top flight brands
8 caring towards both licensees and customers

Media coverage is passed on to InfoPress. They analyse this input by means of their media analysis and evaluation service. Independent evaluators use five measures:

1 volume of coverage
2 corporate/brand visibility
3 message delivery/strength
4 impact
5 target audience readership

The client may choose which of these measures to use. As it was the corporate message that was under consideration, Bass had a particular interest in message delivery. They could have chosen to compare the delivery of one corporate message as against the delivery of *another* corporate message. But, they decided not to do this.

The communication executive at Bass receives quarterly reports. However, she could receive them each month. She feels that the longer timeframe provides her with a better balanced view. Bass are happy with the relationship that they enjoy with Infopress Communications; although the practitioner comments adversely on the sheer volume of paperwork (like press cuttings) which the company receives.

Marketing executives want to see what effect communications have on advertising, promotions and so forth. Here Management Tool for Reputation Analysis (MANTRA) helps. It analyses the content of every relevant print or broadcast item around the world. It also monitors the visibility of the brand or logo at events.

CARMA is an import from the US. It provides custom-tailored reports structured according to the precise research objectives. A client may select anything from briefing documents and management highlights through to in depth analysis and forecasting. The CEO of CARMA Europe is enthusiastic about her product; but acknowledges its limitations. 'Media analysis falls short on providing the total answer', she says, 'as it does not cover the wider communication scopes such as public affairs, investor relations and employee relations'.

In short the choice of which firms (and therefore which generic type) of evaluation to select is difficult. This is the case, not least, because there is no one monitoring the monitors!

adapted from Miles (1995c)

# Key terms

**ASSESSMENT/EVALUATION**    The process by which the success – or otherwise – of corporate policies is measured.

**DEADHEADING**    An American expression for the provision of free tickets and passes to journalists.

**GOVERNMENT RELATIONS**    That branch of communication practice which is concerned with relations with government – this expression usually refers to relations at macro level.

**INTERCULTURAL**    Refers to communications which involve different cultural factors as found in relations between different countries (and, therefore, between different cultures). Could, in an abstract sense, refer to relations between organizations with sharply different cultures (for example Buckingham Palace and Asda plc) – but it is not commonly used in that context.

**ISSUES MANAGEMENT**   That process which enables organizations to know, understand and more effectively interact with their environments. Preventive and Reactive communication practice attempts to anticipate and identify issues and matters of public concern which, if acted upon by stakeholders with sufficient influence, might well impact on the activities of the organization.

**TRACKING**   That part of the market research process which tracks movements and changes in consumer perceptions and reactions. Tracking is used by some communication executives to facilitate the development of their communication policies, thus better ensuring that they accurately match the needs of key publics.

# References

Aaker, D. A. (1996). *Building Strong Brands.* New York: The Free Press.

*Air Transport World* (1995). Airline media public relations award. **February**, 47.

*Air Transport World* (1996). Public relations: British Airways. **February**, 40.

Albert, S. and Whettan, D. (1985). Organisational identity. In *Research in Organizational Behaviour* (L. L. Cummings and B. M. Smith, eds), **7**, 263–295. Greenwich, CT: JAI Press.

Argenti, P. A. (1994). *Corporate Communication.* Burr Ridge, IL: Irwin.

Argenti, P. (1997). Dow Corning's breast implant controversy: Managing reputation in the face of junk science. *Corporate Reputation Review*, **Summer/Fall**, 126–130.

Bailey, J. (1997). Pain to head up corporate affairs at Storehouse. *PR Week*, **8 August**.

Balmer, J. M. T. (1997). Corporate identity: What of it, why the confusion, and what's next? *Corporate Reputation Review*, **Summer/Fall**, 183–188.

Barton, L. (1993). *Crisis in Organizations: Managing and Communicating in the Heat of Chaos.* Cincinnati, OH: South Western Publishing Company.

Bedics, B. C. et al. (1987). Educating the generalist practitioner in the skills of public relations. *Journal of Social Work Education*, **23**, 58–63.

Bevan, S. (1997). PR resumes its seat on Inchcape's board. *PR Week*, **30 May**, p. 2.

Bodensteiner, C. A. (1995). Predicting public and media attention span for social issues. *Public Relations Quarterly*, **Summer**, 14–19.

Bond, C. (1994) Calm amid the storm. *Marketing*, **28 July**, 26.

Bond, C. (1995a). PRCA awards. *Marketing*, **10 August**, p. 35.

Bond, C. (1995b). Emergency services. *Marketing*, **12 October**, p. 35.

Bond, C. (1995c). How to avoid foot in mouth disease. *Marketing*, **16 February**, p. II.

Boorstin, D. (1961). *The Image, or What Happened to the American Dream.* New York, NY: Athenaeum.

Booth, A. L. (1986). Going global. *Public Relations Journal*, **February**, 22–27.

Botan, C. (1992). International public relations: Critique and reformulation. *Public Relations Review,* **Summer,** 149–159.

Bowman, P. and Ellis, N. (1969). *Manual of Public Relations.* London: Heinemann.

Brody, E. W. (1988). *Public Relations Programming and Production.* New York: Praeger.

Broom, G. M. and Dozier, D. M. (1986). Advancement for public relations role models. *Public Relations Review,* **12,** 37–56.

Brown T. (1995). Leverage PR for internal communications: Two pros say it's something leaders should tune into. *Industry Week,* **6 February,** p. 24.

Brown, T. J. and Cox, E. L. (1997). Corporate associations in marketing and consumer research: A review. *Corporate Reputation Review,* **Summer/Fall,** 34–38.

Chajet, C. (1997). Corporate reputation and the bottom line. *Corporate Reputation Review,* **Summer/Fall,** 19–23.

Cheney, G. (1992). *The Corporate Person (Re)Presents Itself, Rhetorical and Critical Approaches to PR* (E. L. Toth and R. L. Heath, eds). Hillsdale, NJ: Lawrence Erlbaum Associates.

Cobb, R. (1994). The evolution of evaluation. *Marketing,* **28 April,** 56.

Coombs W. T., Holladay S., Hasenauer G. and Signitzer, B. (1994). A comparative analysis of international public relations: I dentification and interpretation of similarities and differences between professionalization in Austria, Norway and the United States. *Journal of Public Relations Research,* **6.** 23–39.

Cramp, B. (1994). Ahead of the count. *Marketing,* **28 July,** 28.

Cutlip, S. M. et al. (1994). *Effective Public Relations.* Englewood Cliffs, NJ: Prentice Hall.

D'Aprix, R. (1984). *Employee Communications Experts in Action: Inside Public Relations.* New York: Longman.

Davis, J. (1995). The art of spin. *Management Today,* **March,** 72.

Deephouse, D. L. (1997). The effect of financial and media reputations on performance. *Corporate Reputation Review,* **Summer/Fall,** 68–71.

Dempsey, K. (1997). Corporate affairs given elevated status at Lever. *PR Week,* **16 May,** p. 1.

Dennis, L. (ed. ) (1995). *Practical Public Affairs in an Era of Change.* Lanham, MD: PRSA/University Press of America.

de Segundo, K. (1997). Meeting society's changing expectations. *Corporate Reputation Review,* **Summer/Fall,** 16–19.

Dowman, R. (1997). Increased alcohol volume shows what lobbyists are brewing in Westminster. *PR Week,* **8 August,** p. 28.

Dozier, D. M (1990). The innovation of research in public relations practice. In *Public Relations Research Annual* (J. E. Grunig and L. A. Grunig, eds.). Hillsdale, NJ: Lawrence Erlbaum Associates.

Dutton, J. E. and Dukerich, J. M. (1991). Keeping an eye on the mirror: Image and identity in organizational adaptation. *Academy of Management Journal,*

**34**, 517–554.

Dwek, R. (1995). Different strokes. *Marketing*, **16 February,** p. III.

Elsbach, K. D. and Kramer, R. M. (1996). Members' responses to organizational identity threats: Encountering and countering the *Business Week* rankings. *Administrative Science Quarterly*, **41**, 442–476.

*Executive Traveller* (1997a). New corporate identity is part of £6b investment programme. **July**, 10.

*Executive Traveller* (1997b). Furling the flag. **July**, 5.

Faulstich, W. (1992). *Grundwissen Offentlichkeitsarbeit*. Bardowick: Wissenschaftler Verlag.

Finlay, J. R. (1994). The tasks and responsibilities of public affairs. *Business Quarterly*, **58**, 105–110.

Fiol, C. M. and Kovoor-Misra, S. (1997). Two-way mirroring: Identity and reputation when things go wrong. *Corporate Reputation Review*, **Summer/Fall**, 147–151.

Fitzherbert, N. (1994). Counting the cost of clumsiness. *Marketing*, **24 November,** p. xiii.

Fitzpatrick, K. R. and Rubin, M. S. (1995). Public relations vs. legal strategies in organizational crisis decisions. *Public Relations Review*, **Spring**, 21–31.

Flanagan, P. (1995). Ten public relations pitfalls. *Management Review*, **October**, 45.

Fleiger, H. and Ronneberger, F. (1993). *Public Relations Anfänge in Deutschlander. Festschrift zum loo geburstag von coul Hundhausen*. Wiesbaden: Verlag Für Deutsche Wirtschaftsbiographien.

Fleisher C. S. and Burton S. (1995). Taking stock of corporate benchmarking practices: Panacea or Pandora's box? *Public Relations Review*, **Spring**, 1–19.

Fombrun, C. J. (1996). *Reputation: Realizing Value from Corporate Image*. Boston, MA: Harvard Business School Press.

Fombrun, C. J. and Rindova, V. (1996). *Who's Tops and Who Decides? The Social Construction of Corporate Reputations*. Working paper. Stern School of Business, New York University.

Fombrun, C. J. and van Riel, C. (1997). The reputational landscape. *Corporate Reputation Review*, **Summer/Fall**, 5–12.

Gaines-Ross, L. (1997). Leverage corporate equity. *Corporate Reputation Review*, **Summer/Fall**, 51–56.

Garside, J. (1997). Making Britain's symbols sexier. *PR Week*, **23 May**.

Gatwick Airport (1997). Gatwick enters the fast lane. *The London Gatwick Guide*.

Goodman, M. B. (ed.) (1994). *Corporate Communication Theory and Practice*. Albany, NY: State University of NY Press.

Graham, J. D. (1994). Guarding corporate reputation underlies key challenges facing business. quoting. Paper presented to PRSA 46th National Conference. *Public Relations Journal*, **50**, iv(2).

Gray, B. (1996). Internal communications reaching out to lift staff morale. *PR Week*, **May**.

Gregory, J. R. (1997). Return on investment: Calculating advertising's impact on stock price. *Corporate Reputation Review,* **Summer/Fall**, 56–60.

Grunig, J. E. (1983). Basic research provides knowledge that makes evaluation possible. *Public Relations Quarterly,* **28**, 28–32.

Grunig, L. A. (1992). Strategic public relations constituencies on a global scale. *Public Relations Review,* **18**, 127–136.

Grunig, L. A. and Hunt, T. T. (1984). *Managing Public Relations.* New York: CBS College Publishing.

Guth, D. W. (1995). Organizational crisis experience and public relations roles. *Public Relations Review,* **Summer, 21**, 123–136.

Hage, J. and Hull, F. (1981). *A typology of environmental niches on knowledge technology and scale: The implications for innovation and productivity.* Paper presented to University of Maryland Center for study of Innovations, Entrepreneurship and Organization Strategy.

Hainsworth, B. and Meng, M. (1988). How corporations define issue management. *Public Relations Review,* **4**, 18–30.

Hall, R. (1993). A framework linking intangible resources and capabilities to sustainable competitive advantage. *Strategic Management Journal,* **14**, 607–618.

Halliday, K. K. (1992). Understanding investor relations. *Bank Marketing,* **24**, 22–25.

Hambrick, C. (1981). Specialization of environmental scanning activities among upper level executives. *Journal of Management Studies,* **18**, 299–320.

Harrison, S. (1995). *Public Relations: An Introduction.* London: Routledge.

Hart, N. A. (ed.) (1995). *Strategic Public Relations.* Basingstoke: Macmillan Business.

Heath, R. L. (1994). *Management of Corporate Communication.* Hillsdale, NJ: Lawrence Erlbaum Associates.

Holsti, O. R. (1978). *Limitations of Cognitive Abilities in the Face of Crisis.* Toronto, Canada: Butterworth.

Howard, W. (ed.) (1992). *The Practice of Public Relations.* Oxford: Butterworth-Heinemann.

Illman, P. E. (1980). *Developing Overseas Managers and Managers Overseas.* New York, NY: Amacon.

Ind, N. (1992). *The Corporate Image.* London: Kogan Page.

Jackson, M. (1995). Public relations – getting it right. *Learned Publishing,* **8**, 151–157.

Jackson, P. (1994). Did we lose – or give away – our strategic edge? Remarks to Arthur Page Society, NY, USA. 16 March 1994.

Johnson, B. (1994). Prove public relations affects the bottom line. *Public Relations Journal,* **50**, 40.

Jones, B. L. and Chase, W. H. (1979). Managing public policy issues. *Public Relations Review,* **5**, 3–23.

Kaufmann, J., Kesner, I. F., and Hazen, T. I. (1994). The myth of full disclosure: A look at organizational communications during crises. *Business Horizons,* **July/August**, 29.

Kennedy, S. H. (1977). Nurturing corporate images: Total communication or ego trip? *European Journal of Marketing*, **11**(1), 120–164.

Kinzer, H. J. and Bohn, E. (1985). *Public relations challenges of multinational corporations*. Paper presented to International Communication Association Conference, Honolulu.

Kitchen, P. J. (1993). Public relations: A rationale for its development and usage within UK fast-moving consumer goods firms. *European Journal of Marketing*, **27**, 53–75.

Kitchen, P. and Proctor, R. A. (1991). The increasing importance of public relations in FMCG firms. *Journal of Marketing Management*, **7**, 357–370.

Koten, J. (1984). Corporate communications: All together now. *Business Horizons*.

Kruckeberg, D. (1992). Report from the vice-chair. *Public Relations Innovation, Development and Education*, **Spring** (1).

Kruckeberg, D. (1995). The challenge for public relations in the era of globalization. *Public Relations Quarterly*, **Winter**, 36–39.

Kunczik, M. (1993). *Public Relations: Konzepte and Theorien*. Koln: Bohlau.

Lancaster, G. (1995). Crossing the line. *Marketing*, **16 February**, vi.

Lauzen, M. M. (1994). Public relations practitioner role enactment in issues management. *Journalism Quarterly*, **Summer**, 357–367.

Lauzen, M. M. (1995). Public relations manager involvement in strategic issue diagnosis. *Public Relations Review*, **21**, 287–304.

Lederer, W. and Burdick, E. (1958). *The Ugly American*. London: Norton.

Lee, F. (1997a). Lobbying – TMA's bid to stub out smoking ban. *PR Week*, **8 August**.

Lee, F. (1997b). New Labour, new ways of lobbying. *PR Week*, **9 May**, p. 7.

Leichty, G. and Springston, J. (1993). Reconsidering public relations models. *Public Relations Review*, **Winter**, 327–339.

Lindo, D. (1995). Have you checked out your public relations recently? *Supervision*, **November**, 14–16.

Long, L. W. and Hazleton, V. (1987). Public relations: A theoretical and practical response. *Public Relations Review*, **13**(2), 3–13.

Lorange, P. and Vancil, R. F. (1977). *Strategic Planning Systems*. Englewood Cliffs, NJ: Prentice Hall.

MacManus, T. (1993). *Developments in European public relations research and their value for practitioners*. CERP – Education Newsletter.

MacManus, T. (1994). *A comparative analysis of public relations in Austria and the United Kingdom*. Paper presented to the International Public Relations Research Symposium, Lake Bled, Slovenia, p. 13.

Marshall, C. (1997). Speech delivered to the Hard Commercial Edge Conference, 14 July, London, pp. 1–12.

Marziliano, N. (1997). Organizational images: Between being and appearing. *Corporate Reputation Review*, **Summer/Fall**, 158–164.

Mau, R. R. and Dennis, L. B. (1994). Companies ignore shadow constituencies at their peril. *Public Relations Journal*, **May**, **10**(2).

Mazur, L. (1994). A consuming ambition. *Marketing*, 13 January, p. 23.

Meindl, J. R., Erlich, S. B. and Dukerich, J. M. (1985). The romance of leadership. *Administrative Science Quarterly*, **30**, 78–102.

Miles, L. (1995a). From local roots to far horizons. *Marketing*, **16 February**, p. v.

Miles, L. (1995b). Cure for all ills. *Marketing*, **16 March**, p. 35.

Miles, L. (1995c). Measures for measures. *Marketing*, **22 June**, p. xiii.

Mills, A. (1997). The coming of age of investor relations. *PR Week*, **4 July**.

Mitchell, A. (1994). A subtle approach to PR. *Marketing*, **28 April**, p. 53.

Morris, E. (1987). Vision and strategy: A focus for the future. *Journal of Business Strategy*, **8**, 51–58.

Moss, D. (ed.) (1990). *Public Relations in Practice*. London: Routledge

Nessmann, K. (1995). Public relations in Europe: A comparison with the United States. *Public Relations Review*, **Summer**, 151–160.

Newsom, D. and Scott, A. (1976). *This is PR: The Realities of Public Relations*. Belmont, CA: Wadsworth Publishing Co.

Nicholas, R. (1997) Doing it by the book. *PR Week*, 11 June.

Nudel, M. and Antokol, N. (1988). *The Handbook for Effective Emergency and Crisis Management*. Lexington, MA: A. Heath & Co.

Olins, W. (1989). *Corporate Identity: Making Business Strategy Visible Through Design*. London: Thames & Hudson.

O'Rourke, R. (1997). Managing in times of crisis. *Corporate Reputation Review*, **Summer/Fall**, 120–125.

Osborne, J. (1994). Getting full value from public relations. *Public Relations Journal*, **October/November**, 64.

Pagan, R. (1985). The Nestle boycott: Implications for strategic business planning. *Journal of Business Strategy*, **6**, 32–38.

Pavlik, J. V. (1996). Book review: 'Corporate Public Relations'. *Public Relations Review*, **January**, 58.

Pfeffer, J. and Salancik, G. (1978). *The External Control of Organizations*. New York: Harper & Row.

Pincus, J. D. et al. (1994). *Public Relations Education in MBA Programs: Challenges and Opportunities* (pp. 55–71). California State University.

Poiesz, T. B. C. (1988). *The image concept its place in consumer psychology and its potential for other psychological areas*. Paper presented at the XXIVth International Congress of Psychology, Sydney, Australia.

Post, J. E. and Griffin, J. J. (1997). Corporate reputation and external affairs management. *Corporate Reputation Review*, **Summer/Fall**, 165–171.

*PR Week* (1997a). **Summer**.

*PR Week* (1997b). **Summer**.

*PR Week* (1997c) Employees are losing track of company strategy. **20 June**.

*PR Week* (1997d). What the papers say: Some see BA's new image as flights of fancy. **20 June**, p. 6.

*PR Week* (1997e). Sainsbury's shops for a European lobbyist. **13 June**.

*PR Week* (1997f). Public affairs puts the community in context.

*PR Week* (1997g). Breaking down the border barriers. **16 May**, p. 10

*PR Week* (1997h). Putting together MFI's national campaign. **8 August**, p. 11.

*PR Week* (1997i). Corporate identity is misunderstood by senior managers. **27 June**.

*PR Week* (1997j). Changing faces to attract new business. **27 June**.

*PR Week* (1997k). Image changes that fooled nobody. **27 June**.

*PR Week* (1997l). How to figure big on the festival scene. **8 August**.

*PR Week* (1997m). Conquering the critical time factor. **18 July**.

*PR Week* (1997n). Cleaning up oil with a slick operation. **13 June**.

*PR Week* (1997o). **9 May**.

*PR Week* (1997p). Perfect for people. **8 August**.

*PR Week* (1997q). Trying to prove IC's worth to business.

*PR Week* (1997r). **Summer**.

Pratt, C. (1985). The African context. *Public Relations Journal*, **41**, 11–16.

Purdom, N. (1997). Boil water before use. *PR Week*, **30 May**.

Rao, H. (1997). The rise of investor relations departments in the *Fortune* 500 industrials. *Corporate Reputation Review*, **Summer/Fall**, 172–176.

Ressler, J. (1982). Crisis communications. *Public Relations Quarterly*, **Fall**.

Rice, E. (1991). Champions of communication. *Fortune*, 123, **3 June**, 111–120.

Rindova, V. P. (1997). The image cascade and the formation of corporate reputations. *Corporate Reputation Review*, **Summer/Fall**, 189–194.

Roberts, P. W. and Dowling, G. R (1997). The value of a firm's corporate reputation: How reputation helps attain and sustain superior profitability. *Corporate Reputation Review*, **Summer/Fall**, 72–76.

Ronneberger, F. and Ruhl, M. (1992). *Theorie Der Public Relations. Ein Entwurf.* Opladen: Westdeutscher Verlag.

Ryan, M. and Martinson, D. (1985). Public relations practitioners. *Public Relations Quarterly*, **Spring**, 111–115.

Schenkler, I. (1997). Fanning fires; Mitsubishi Motors and the EEOC. *Corporate Reputation Review*, **Summer/Fall**, 131–134.

Schneider, L. S. (1985). The role of public relations in four organizational types. *Journalism Quarterly*, **62**, 358–366.

Seitel, F. P. (1992). *The Practice of Public Relations*. New York: Macmillan.

Signitzer, B. (1992). Theorie der public relations. In *Kommunikationstheorien* (R. Burkart and W. Homberg, eds.). Wien, Austria: Braumuller.

Simon, R. (1986). *Public Relations Concepts and Practices*. New York: Macmillan.

Simons, L. (1997). Simons named motor neurone head of comms. *PR Week*, **23 May**, p. 1.

Skolnik, R. (1994). Portraits of the most admired companies – how public relations helps build corporate reputations. *Public Relations Journal*, **May**, 15–20.

Smith, W. (1997). Boston invites all to beer party. *PR Week*, 8 August.

Spencer, H. (1997). Enlisting the aid of recruitment in communications. *PR Week*, **16 May**.

Sperling, J. (1983). *Job Descriptions in Marketing Management* (pp. 107–108). NY:

American Management Associates.

Srivastava, R. K., McInish, T. H., Wood, R. A. and Capraro, A. J. (1997). The value of corporate reputation: Evidence from the equity markets. *Corporate Reputation*, **Summer/Fall**, 62–67.

Troy, K. (1993). *Managing Corporate Communications in a Competitive Climate*. New York: Conference Board.

Tucker, K. and Shortridge, R. (1994). Behavioral principles in public relations. *Public Relations Journal*, **October/November**, 56.

Turk, J. V. (1989). Management skills need to be taught in public relations. *Public Relations Review*, **15**, 38–52.

Useem, M. (1993). *Executive Defense*. Cambridge, MA: Harvard University Press.

van Raaij, W. E. (1986). *Impressie management: Het communicatiebeleid van de onderneming tekst uitgesproken tijdens de industriele communicatiedag de bond van adverteerden*. Erasmus Universiteit, Rotterdam.

van Rekom, J. (1993). *Measuring corporate identity – its measurement and use in corporate communications*. Paper presented at European Marketing Academy Conference, pp. 1497–1514.

van Riel, C. B. M. (1992). Corporate communication in European financial institutions. *Public Relations Review*, **Summer**, 161–175.

van Riel, C. B. M. (1995). *Principles of Corporate Communication*. London: Prentice Hall.

Wade, J. B., Porac, J. F. and Pollock, T. G. and Meindl, J. R. (1997). Hitch your wagon to a CEO star? Testing two views about the pay, reputation and performance of top executives. *Corporate Reputation Review*, **Summer/Fall**, 103–109.

White, J. and Mazur, L. (1995). *Strategic Communications Management*. Wokingham: Addison-Wesley.

Wilcox, D. L. et al. (1986). *Public Relations Strategies and Tactics*. New York: Harper & Row.

Windahl, S. and Signitzer, B. (1992). *Using Communication Theory: An Introduction to Planned Communication* (p. 89). London: Sage.

Winner, P. (1993). *Effective Public Relations Management*. London: Kogan Page.

Woodcock, C. (1994). How to face crisis with confidence. *Marketing*, **24 November**, p. viii.

Worcester, R. M. (1997). Tomorrow's company is the company you keep. *Journal of Communication Management*, **February**, 256–261.

Wright, D. K. (1995). The role of corporate public relations executives in the future of employee communications. *Public Relations Review*, **Fall**, 181–198.

# Index

abstention, corporate, 36–7
academic background: of communicators, 158
activists/pressure groups, 11, 28, 185
  Greenpeace, 199, 201
advertising, 12, 13
  corporate, 13–15, 52–3
  as employment background, 156
  in integrated strategy, 63–4, 85
  vs consumer PR, 87, 88
Alter Ego ('the face'), 112–14, 116
American Airlines: and media, 37–8
ASDA, 100, 114, 152
assessment, 180–8, 205–6
audience(s), 19–21, 39, 60
  customers as, 15, 34–5, 86–91
  financial, 15, 30–2, 56, 69, 95
  global, 30
  government/politicians as, 9, 35, 82–3
  identifying, 21–3
  and image, 7–8, 11, 53, 64, 66
    based on expectation, 97, 101
    in crises, 129
  internal, 15, 22–7, 39, 64, 68, 80
  media as, 32–3, 131, 188
  opinion formers as, 33–4, 39
  researching, 67–8, 101–3, 185, 187
  see also stakeholders
Avon and Somerset Constabulary:
  communications, 73, 181
  in crises: plans, 132, 139
  evaluation, 184
  financial, 93
  funding, 201–2, 203
  internal, 26, 64
  management, 113, 164, 168

Avon Rubber: communications:
  and financial consultants: use, 189
  funding, 201, 203
  global public, 30, 194
  internal, 25
  lack, 36–7, 71, 72, 181, 204
    and public unawareness, 37, 56, 109
  with local stakeholders, 29
  management, 114, 160, 167, 168
Ayling, Bob, 110

Balmer, J.M.T., 42–3
Barnardo's (Dr), 49, 109
Bass Brewers:
  communications evaluation, 205–6
  as parent, 48, 132, 160, 170, 202
B.A.T. Industries, 35
  communications, 29, 58, 136
    consultants: use, 147, 190
    director: role/status, 114, 139
      in management structure, 170, 172
    financial: responsibility, 94
    funding, 203
    internal, 26
    and strategic planning, 72, 73
  and sponsorship, 85
Bond, Alan, 136
Boots: communications:
  director: role/status, 114, 171–2, 204
  international, 194
  with investors, 31
  and local stakeholders, 29, 99
bottom line, 104–5, 177, 185
boundary scanning, 7–8, 17, 77, 100
  and strategy, 65–8, 195, 199
BP: and Greenpeace, 100

brainpower: of communicators, 153–4
brand/branding:
    corporate, 86, 104
    PR, 87, 90–1, 115
    and subsidiaries' identity, 48
Branson, Richard, 112, 204
*Brent Spar*, 197, 199, 201
British Airways, 35
    communications, 8, 87, 165
        agencies/consultants: use, 189, 190
        and corporate strategy, 71, 90, 141
        crisis management, 132, 135
        financial: responsibility, 94
        and formation: merger, 43, 106
        funding, 90, 203
        globalisation, 40, 109–10, 185
        management structure, 170
        media operation, 33
        tracking research, 186
British Gas, 36, 111, 118–19, 171
British Library, 152, 175–6
Brown, Cedric, 36, 111, 118–19
Brown and Williamson: valuation, 136
BT: communications:
    director: role, 114, 139
    and image/identity change, 46, 65
    and MCI merger, 106, 107, 135
Bud Ice: promotion, 115
Burson-Marsteller: Wall's campaign, 87
Butler Cornfield Dedman, 111

Carling Black Label Lager, 35, 84, 89
CARMA: and evaluation, 185, 206
CEO, 39
    as corporate brand manager, 86, 100
    failure to understand communication,
        71–2, 104, 204
    as public face: PR role, 112–14, 167
    working with, 63, 69–72, 152–3, 159, 167
change, management of, 15, 105–12
Charlton Associates: identity change, 111
Chrysler: image change, 51, 53
City, *see* financial communications
Cockburn, Bill, 70–1
Cole, Michael, 113, 114
Collis, Terence, 171
commitment: of communicators, 154
communication executives, 177
    background:
        education/training, 145, 158
        employment, 146, 155–7, 158–9
    and corporate strategy, 72–3
    job titles, 10, 172–3

in management structure, 168–70, 171–2
    personal qualities, 147–55, 173–4, 176
    role, 80–1, 159–66, 173–6
    status/recognition, 72, 155, 166, 170–2
Communiqué PR, 89–90
communities, local, *see* local communities
Community Context (consultancy), 85–6
Concert (organization), 107
constituencies, *see* audiences
construed image, 101
consultants/consultancies, 39, 116
    as employment background, 159
    use, 36, 94–5, 188–92
consumers
    PR, 15, 34–5, 86–91, 116
    research, 67–8, 101–3, 185, 187
control: in crises, 127–8
Cool Britannias, 148, 149
Cornhill Insurance: sponsorship, 85
corporate advertising, 13–15, 52–3
corporate affairs, 8, 9, 17, 35
    as lobbying, 9, 18, 35, 81–3
corporate brand, 86, 104
Corporate Clubbers, 148
corporate communications, 4–6, 17, 39
    *see also* audiences; crisis management;
        financial communications; identity;
        strategy
courage: of communicators, 152–3
creativity: of communicators, 152
credibility: of communicators, 155, 171
crises, 120–1, 122, 143
Crisis Index, 122
crisis management, 123–4
    case studies, 117–19, 141–3
    and communicators, 124–5, 127, 133, 166
    and delay, 130–2, 134
    disclosure: policies, 130, 134–5, 138–41
    failure, 117–19, 125, 137–8
    financial, 136–8
    and legal liability, 133–5
    planning, 124–9, 144
cross-border communications, 85, 179
    as intercultural, 90–1, 190, 192–7
    *see also* global organizations
culture, corporate, 64, 77, 106
Cunard: and QE2 crisis, 36, 135
customers, *see* consumers

decoding: of image, 51, 52
departmental strategy, 71
disclosure: in crisis, 130, 134–5, 138–41
Dow Corning, 70, 99, 130

economic effects of communication, 104–5, 185
education/training, 145, 158
employees: as audience, 15, 22–7, 64, 68
  in recruitment, 80
employment background: of communicators,
  146, 155–7, 158–9
encroachers, 146, 177
endorsed identity: of subsidiaries, 48
energy: of communicators, 154
environmental scanning, *see* boundary
  scanning
environmentalists, 28, 185, 199
Eperon, Alastair, 171
evaluation, 180–8, 205–6
Exxon: crisis management, 127–8

'face': of organization, 112–14, 116
FFI: and music festivals, 115
financial communications, 39, 81, 92–7
  and consultants, 94–5, 189
  in crises, 136–7
  and key publics, 15, 30–2, 56, 69, 95
Flynn, Paul: on lobbying, 82
Ford: and Pinto crisis, 140
Freud, Sigmund, 3
funding: of communications, 201–3

Gates, Bill: as Alter Ego, 112
Gatwick: image change, 107
General Motors: PR/legal problems, 134
Gillette: consumer PR, 88
GlaxoWellcome: communications, 73
  and consultants: use, 191
  and crisis management, 132, 139
  executive: advisory role, 164
  financial: responsibility, 94
  publications, 53, 203
  reporting structure, 70, 169–70
  and take-over management, 106
global organizations, 66, 100
  BA as, 40, 109–10, 185
  and Brand PR, 90–1
  and global audience, 30
Goodman, Anthony: on evaluation, 188
Goodman, M.B., 129
government: as audience, 9, 35, 82–3
Graham, John D., 163, 166, 193
Great Universal Stores, 36
Greenpeace, 100, 199, 201
Greenwood Tighe: and MFI, 107–8
Grunig, L.A., 193, 196
Guinness: financial crisis, 136
Guth, D.W.: on crises, 122, 125, 126

Halifax Building Society, 27, 29, 100
'halo' effect, 73, 84
Harrison, S., 4, 13, 87
Hart, N.A., 13
headhunting: of executives, 158–9
Heath, R.L., 100, 101, 102, 105–6
honesty: in crisis, 138–41
house style, 46–7, 60
human resources, *see* employees
Hyundai: image, 30, 179

identity, corporate, 37, 41, 42, 44, 60
  change: management, 40, 49, 107–12
  creation, 43, 49, 50
  importance, 48–9
  revealing, 43–4
  transmitting, 45–7
  types, 47–8
  *vs* image, 11, 41–3, 44, 54–8, 111–12
image, corporate, 17, 42, 50–5, 58, 64
  construed, 101
  creation, 55–6, 57, 58
  studies, 59–60
  *see also under* audience(s)
Inchcape, 62
integration: of messages, 18, 60, 80
  as strategy, 12, 63–4, 85, 87
Intel: crisis management, 98
internal audiences, 15, 22–7, 39, 64, 68, 80
international communications, 85, 179
  as intercultural, 90–1, 190, 192–7
  *see also* global organizations
investors, 31–2, 44, 69, 95–7
  institutional, 92, 96, 97
issues management, 15, 197–200, 207

Jackson, Marie, 52, 152, 175–6
job titles, 10, 172–3
Jones, Peter: on BA media section, 33
journalism: as employment background, 33, 156

Kaufmann, J., 129, 130, 134
Kennedy, John F.: image, 57
key publics, *see* audiences
Kitchen, P., 12, 198–9, 202
Knight, Gordon, 183

Laura Ashley, 69, 92, 135
Lauzen, M.M., 67, 197, 200
legal liability: in crisis, 133–5
Lever Brothers, 168
Lindemann, Walter, 186
Lindo, D., 24–5

Lloyds/TSB: communications, 27, 47, 73
  crisis management plans, 132, 139
  evaluation, 184
  financial: responsibility, 93–4
  funding, 203
  under-recognition, 71, 72, 204
lobbying, 9, 18, 35, 81–3
local communities:
  and PR (MFI campaign), 107–8
  as stakeholders, 29, 99–100
logos, corporate, 46, 60, 107
London Transport, 35, 167, 182, 201
Lonrho, 48, 136, 137
  consultants: use, 36, 192
Luby's: crisis management, 123

McKillips, Gary, 79–80
Macleod, Sandra, 185
MANTRA: use, 206
market research, 67–8, 101–3, 185, 187
marketing:
  (and) communications, 12–13, 18
    integrated approach, 12, 63–4, 85
  as employment background, 156
Marshall, Sir Colin, 8
Mathieson, Mike, 115
Mazur, L., 91, 93, 126–7
MCI: and BT, 106, 107, 135
measurement, performance, 180–8, 205–6
media, 18
  for advertising, 13, 14–15
  as audience, 32–3, 131, 188
    case study (American Airlines), 37–8
  in evaluation, 185–6
mental ability: of communicators, 153–4
mergers: management, 15, 106
MFI: relaunch, 107–8
Microsoft: communication, 11, 112
mirror function, 11, 54, 101
mission statements, 44, 78
Mitchell, A., 87–8
monolithic corporate identity, 47
Morgan (J.P.): communications, 72
Morris (Philip): crisis management, 121
Morrison (Wm.): on customers, 34
Mostyn, Alaric: on evaluation, 188

Nessmann, K., 4, 5
New Modernists, 148
New York: transport crisis, 125
Nicholson, Frank, 70–1, 113
Norman, Archie, 114
Northumbria Ambulance, 113, 168, 201
Norwich Union: crisis management, 123

Olins, W., 47–8
opinion formers, 33–4, 39
overseas, *see* international communications

Pan-Continental approach, 4, 5
PepsiCola: identity, 112
performance, economic, 104–5, 185
Perrier: crisis management, 121
persona, corporate, 18, 53–4
persuasion theory, 3, 18
Phillips, David, 185–6
picture, image as, 50, 51, 52
Political Context (consultancy), 85
politics: and communications, 3, 57
  lobbying, 9, 18, 35, 81–3
pressure groups, *see* activists
preventive communication, 198
public affairs, 8–9, 35
public relations, 3–4, 7, 8–9, 15, 16
  and marketing, 12, 13
  personality types, 148–9
  in US/Europe, 2–3, 16–17
publics, *see* audiences

Quaker (foods): on consumer PR, 86

reactive communication, 198
recession: and funding, 202
Redhouse, Jeremy: on PepsiCola, 112
Redoxon: launch, 90
Reed, David, 171
regulation, 9, 18, 35
relationship marketing, 34
reporting relationships, 166–8, 170, 171
reputation, corporate, 17, 97–101
research:
  into communicators, 147
  consumer, 67–8, 101–3, 185, 187
  tracking, 186, 207
Rio Tinto Zinc, 171
Robins (A.H.): crisis management, 117–18
Romero, Joseph, 89

Sainsbury (J.): communications:
  in crises, 132, 133, 137, 139
  with customers, 34
  and family ethos, 70, 114
  financial: responsibility, 93
  funding, 202–3
  internal, 26, 133, 137
  international, 82
  reporting structure, 170
scanning, *see* boundary scanning

Schneider, L.S., 162
Scope: rebranding, 14
*Sea Empress* incident, 142–3
Seagram International: marketing, 91
Sega: at Phoenix Festival, 115
shadow constituencies, *see* stakeholders
shareholders, *see* investors
share/stock prices, 15, 69, 104
Shell, 136, 196
   issues management, 197, 199
Skolnik, R., 152
Smith (W.H.): communications, 71, 73, 203
   and consultants: use, 190, 191
   and crisis management, 132, 135, 154
   director: role, 49, 114
   internal, 67
Sotheby's: lobbying, 35
sponsorship, 83–6, 89, 116
Stagecoach: market research, 103
stakeholders, 11, 27–9, 39, 64, 65
   as shadow constituencies, 19
stock/share prices, 15, 69, 104
Storehouse: communications, 34, 36
   and crisis management, 132, 139
   executive: role, 70, 152, 155
   financial, 31, 34, 63, 94, 98–9
   internal, 27–34, 94
strategy, communication, 16, 43, 45, 61–4,
      72–5
   case study (West Hatch), 75–7
   and key publics/scanning, 64–9
   working with CEO/executive committee,
      63, 69–72, 167, 169
subsidiaries: corporate identity, 47–8
symbols: and corporate identity, 45–7

Tennent Caledonian Breweries:
      communications:
   and consultants: use, 191
   and crisis management, 132, 139–40
   executive: role/status, 160, 170
   funding, 202
   and identity/face, 48, 114
   internal, 27
   sponsorship, 85
Three Valleys Water, 141–2

3M: identity strategy, 37, 109
TMA: lobbying, 83
Townsend-Thoresen, 58, 138
tracking research, 186, 207
training/education, 145, 158
truthfulness: in crises, 138–41
Turner Broadcasting Systems, 79
TWA: crisis management, 133
Tylenol poisoning crisis, 122

Union Carbide: and Bhopal, 112
Union flag, 112
   and BA, 40, 110, 185

van Riel, C.B.M., 4, 5, 11, 12, 54, 163
Vaux Brewery Group: communications:
   and consultants: use, 95, 192
   and crisis management, 132
   director: role, 113, 160, 167, 170
   financial, 31–2, 95
   internal, 25–6
voice, corporate, 85, 131, 196
vulnerability public relations, 198

Wales Tourist Board, 143
Wall's: brand PR, 87
Watney's: corporate identity, 48
Wessex Water, 73, 96, 113, 160
West Hatch church: appeal, 75–7
Whitbread: communications:
   Boston Beer campaign, 89–90
   director: role, 114, 152, 154
      on strategic committee, 71, 73, 171
   financial, 31
   image: research, 14, 21, 153
   internal, 27
White, J., 93, 126–7
White Star Line, 136, 138
Whitley, Ray: on evaluation, 181, 183
Williams Holdings, 48, 99

Yorkshire Tyne-Tees Television:
      communications:
   director, 93, 113, 160, 170
      on crisis management, 132, 139
   funding, 202